Also by Dana Bash and David Fisher

America's Deadliest Election

THE ELECTIONS THAT CHANGED THE WORLD

THE ELECTIONS THAT CHANGED THE WORLD

Fifteen Pivotal Moments
That Shaped How We Live

DANA BASH
AND DAVID FISHER

HANOVER
SQUARE
PRESS

HANOVER
SQUARE
PRESS™

Recycling programs
for this product may
not exist in your area.

ISBN-13: 978-1-335-00217-4

The Elections That Changed the World

Hanover Square Press
22 Adelaide St. West, 41st Floor
Toronto, Ontario M5H 4E3, Canada
HanoverSqPress.com

HarperCollins Publishers
Macken House, 39/40 Mayor Street Upper,
Dublin 1, D01 C9W8, Ireland
www.HarperCollins.com

Printed in U.S.A.
26 27 28 29 30 LBC 5 4 3 2 1

For my grandfather Frank Weinman,
who taught me since I was a little girl how lucky
I am to live in a democracy like America.

"The right to vote is the right upon
which all other rights depend."

—Thomas Paine

Contents

Introduction

IN SIXTH GRADE, I RAN for student body president of my elementary school and won. It was my first, last, and only time on any ballot.

I don't remember my slogan, my campaign promises, or much of anything about my electoral victory. What I do remember is that when in office, I used my position to push the school principal for the regular students (like me) to have the same rights as the kids in the gifted and talented program. They had a yearbook. We regular students did not. They went on a sixth-grade trip to Colonial Williamsburg. We regular students did not. So I drafted a petition and got enough regular students to sign it that we could not be ignored by the school administration.

The principal was not happy with me. I have a vivid memory of being in her office watching her pull out the curriculum books, trying to explain why we didn't get the perks that the "g & t" kids got. She also scolded me for using my position as school president to stir up trouble. But despite the power and age imbalance between us, I somehow knew she was wrong. We all thought the extras the other kids got were unfair, and I had been the one elected to lead, so I did.

In the end, our sixth-grade class didn't get the yearbook or the school trip, but the subsequent sixth-grade classes did get yearbooks of their own. We made a change. My little elementary school election had consequences.

To be sure—the experience did not set me off on a political path. It wasn't until I went to college in Washington that I even started to get interested in politics and at the same time decided to stop fighting my DNA and seek jobs in journalism. My father, Stuart Schwartz, worked for ABC News for more than forty years. He won fifteen Emmys, four Peabody Awards, two DuPont Awards, and an Overseas Press Club Award. The news was the background music of my childhood. We watched it at night during dinner (I joke that the theme music for *World News Tonight* still makes me hungry). It was always on in the morning as I got ready for school. I also would go to work with him a lot, usually on Friday nights when he was on the original team of *Nightline*, because I didn't get to spend much time with him during the week.

In college, as soon as I started my first internship in TV news, at CBS News in Washington, I was hooked. I tried to avoid it, knowing that my father's hours were unpredictable, but I succumbed.

I was very lucky to get my first real job out of college at CNN in Washington in 1993 and even luckier to have covered elections of all kinds in various capacities since then. The most high profile and consequential are of course the presidential elections, but I have also reported on mayoral races and interviewed candidates for state legislature in addition to the Senate, the House and governors' offices, not to mention the most important characters of all—the voters.

I began my career in television news producing interviews, often with dynamic political figures. The first election I covered as an on-air correspondent, day in and day out, was George W.

Bush's reelection campaign in 2004. Since then, I've reported on numerous campaigns up and down the ballot. I've interviewed many of the leading political figures of our time; surprisingly, even after conducting those countless interviews, I have never lost the excitement for asking an important question or finding a way of bringing interesting and sometimes provocative information to my audience. I take great pride in doing that in a nonpartisan manner. I love it. And I know how fortunate I am. Few events are as exciting or dramatic as an election, a duel of ideas and personalities seeded with both real and sometimes dubious promises.

All elections are meaningful, whether millions of people are voting for the leadership of a nation or just a few people are electing a union representative in a local firehouse. Every election sends a message—it might be a statement of approval, it might reflect a desire for change, it might be an expression of frustration with the status quo or a signal of willingness to take a risk.

An infinite number of elections have been held over thousands of years by countless great civilizations, organizations, and groups. They have been held across vast nations, in historic buildings, and in small rooms.

And yet there is no universally accepted way of conducting an election. It can be as simple as a show of hands or involve complicated ballots. But the goal is always the same: An election expresses the will of the people. It is the heart of democracy, the voice people use to determine how they will be governed.

All of which is why the concept of this book, elections that changed the world, first appealed to me. Elections are commonly promoted as "the most important election in our history." That claim is a proven way of raising interest, leading to campaign contributions and motivating supporters of either side to go out and vote. Not to mention the fact that it's human nature for people to think that their moment in time is the most consequential, because for them, it is. But while all elections make a difference, the reality is that most leave only a limited footprint on history, not resonating beyond their area or era. But the more our research continued, the more we realized how much the history we take for granted had been affected by the decisions of anonymous long-ago voters: the Romans who supported Caesar's campaign for consul, those who helped shape their new country in the very first American presidential elections, the twentieth-century Chinese voters who ushered their nation out of an age of empire.

We do not consider the fifteen stories we tell here to comprise a comprehensive list. Readers may disagree with some of these choices or suggest others that might have been included. Good. We encourage that. We hope to provoke that response. There is no definitive list; there is no right or wrong. We tried to include examples of various types of elections, ranging from traditional American presidential elections to sham elections conducted by totalitarian regimes providing the illusion of credibility; from political elections to institutional elections; massive elections in which people remained in lines for miles to small elections in which only a few people participated; elections in which a popular outcome was virtually assured before the first vote was cast, alongside completely unexpected upsets. We chose not to include any contemporary politicians because history has not rendered judgment.

One suggestion: Before you begin reading, take a moment to make your own list of elections, big and small, that changed the world. Maybe you'll be surprised.

Dana Bash

ONE

63 BC: Julius Caesar Elected Pontifex Maximus and Praetor

THIS IS THE STORY of how we got here.

Conquerors shaped the ancient world. Leaders were chosen by blood—either the royal blood that coursed through their veins, or the rivers of blood lost in battle. The earliest of them known to history was Sargon of Akkad, who created the first great empire by unifying Mesopotamia. According to legend, between 2334–2279 BC the self-described "king of the world" overwhelmed at least thirty-four city-states, commanding history's first professional army and ruling his captured lands with an innovative central government.

Egyptian Pharaoh Thutmose the Great used history's first naval force, along with the rest of his armed forces, in seventeen military campaigns that captured 350 cities. By the time of his death in 1425 BC, he ruled much of the Near East, from the Euphrates River to a vast portion of the Nile Valley.

The First Persian Empire was brought together under the sword of Cyrus the Great in 550 BC. The largest empire of ancient history, it stretched from the Mediterranean to the Indus

River and was ruled by a central, multicultural, and multireligious government led by a monarch who inherited the throne.

The brilliant and brutal Alexander the Great created a massive Hellenistic empire, stretching across continents from Greece to India. The Macedonian king had seized power after the assassination of his father in 336 BC. During his thirteen-year reign, he defeated the great Persian empire, founded more than seventy cities—among them several he named after himself, including Alexandria in Egypt—explored and mapped vast territories, opened trade routes, and spread enlightened cultural and intellectual concepts throughout the settled world. His "policy of infusion" merged Greek advancements in science, architecture, theatre, and education with local practices. He brought worlds together by spreading the Greek language and encouraging the development of philosophical concepts that focused on humanism.

The emperor Ashoka gained control of the Mauryan dynasty in 268 BC by murdering as many as ninety-nine of his own family members, then conquered most of the Indian subcontinent. After converting to Buddhism, he spread his newfound religious beliefs, including dharma (righteous living) and tolerance, throughout Asia.

None of these men, nor the others who ruled large chunks of the world for thousands of years, were chosen by their populace. None of them had to win the approval of the people they ruled. None of them had to explain their goals or defend their actions. Their armies, their weapons, their brutality earned them unlimited power. But at some time during those centuries, the concept of people gathering to select the men who would lead them started to take hold. It began in isolated places. Some early tribal societies elected their leaders, often selecting a council of elders rather than a single ruler. The methods used to express their choice were the most basic: raise your voice or your hand to support your candidate.

By the seventh century BC, an assembly of Spartans comprised of male citizens over thirty years old was responsible for electing both its ruling body, the twenty-eight-man Council of Elders, and five magistrates. According to the Greek historian Plutarch, candidates would appear one by one in front of the assembly, and people would yell or cheer for their choice. Judges, known as *tellers*, listened from a nearby room to determine which of them had received the greatest cheers. While an hereditary Spartan king still ruled, the magistrates wielded enormous power; their authority to bring legal charges against the king helped keep the monarch from exerting dictatorial control over the city-state.

Actual rule by the people, called *demokratia*, or democracy, was implemented in Athens by Cleisthenes, who reformed the Greek constitution in about 508 BC. For the first time, rather than a single leader or even elected representatives making all the significant decisions, free, adult male citizens assembled to vote directly on important issues. In addition to electing officials, Greeks voted on new laws, going to war, selecting generals, and even reaching verdicts in criminal trials. In fact, it was a five-hundred-man jury of fellow Athenians that infamously condemned Socrates to death. Citizens voted by raising their hands, writing a name on a shard of pottery, or by a unique secret ballot: They were given two small stones; one of them with a hole in it. The verdict stone was dropped in the first urn, the discarded stone in a second one, so spectators could not determine how someone had voted.

This was the dawn of *politics*, a word derived from the Greek *politikos* meaning "relating to the citizen or the city."

While direct voting applied to many aspects of Athenian life, to reduce potential corruption and increase civic participation, most public officials, magistrates, and jurors were selected by chance, a process known as lottery, or sortition. In this system, men willing to serve in the five-hundred-man Boule, the decision-making legislature, dropped their personal token in a stone device, a *kleroterion*, from which a random selection was made.

While leading Greek citizens, like the enormously respected statesman and general Pericles, engendered tremendous support, the system had no single ruler. The objective was to ensure that the people retained political power rather than entrust it to one man or a small group; in fact, to prevent that from happening, people voted to ostracize—to exile—public figures who had become too powerful or controversial. If six thousand or more voters scratched a man's name on a small piece of pottery, that person was forced to leave Athens for ten years.

While Athens was at its peak in 500 BC, the Roman Republic had just been founded. The last king of Rome, Tarquin the Proud, had been overthrown, exiled, and replaced with a new form of government in which power was separated to prevent any one man from ever again becoming too powerful. The government consisted of two consuls who shared authority, a senate dominated by the aristocrats, and three assemblies representing the various tribes who had come together to form Rome.

The assemblies voted by acclamation, by voice, for high-ranking officials, including the consuls, for magistrates, and on issues of national importance. Although seemingly designed to allow all Roman citizens to participate in choosing the government, in fact it was set up to ensure that wealthy citizens retained the power to influence events. In addition to prestige and decision-making responsibility, elective office also presented profitable opportunities; the money it cost to run a campaign could easily be recovered—and much more—if a man was clever enough. Financial incentive was built into the democratic system—a fact that would never change.

But even with all its defects, an electoral system that provided a model for future democracies evolved in Rome over the next few centuries—and introduced many of the elements, both positive and negative, that would become embedded in that system.

At first, candidates for many offices were selected by a small group and simply approved by the assemblies. But gradually, the concept of competitive elections developed—elections in which two or more people contested for votes. And with that came political campaigns, election days, and, naturally, political corruption.

Gaius Julius Caesar was born into a moderately wealthy family in July, 100 BC. The family claimed to have descended from the Roman goddess Venus, giving them divine lineage. But there was no reason to anticipate the extraordinary influence Caesar would have on history. No reason to believe William Shakespeare would write perhaps his greatest play about his life, or that thousands of years later people would still marvel at his exploits and study and debate his decisions.

At that time the Roman Republic dominated the Mediterranean world, controlling vast territories beyond the Italian Peninsula, including Spain and Greece, Sicily, and parts of North Africa and Asia. The Romans brought with them to these lands an enlightened culture that laid the foundation for future developments in the law and the arts, individual liberties, and a vibrant, structured political system.

It was a somewhat complex system, consisting of numerous layers created to allow widespread participation for all Rome's free male citizens, while in fact it was designed to favor the rich and already powerful. Laws and regulations had been developed to provide the impression that the people were in charge of their government, a right they exercised by casting their votes for the candidates of their choice. In fact, that was no more accurate than it would be in later centuries. However, it still was a significant advance from earlier government structures in which common people had absolutely no voice.

Elected magistrates controlled the daily operations of the government, including running the judicial system, maintaining public works, and managing the financial and administrative affairs of the state.

The government consisted of three branches. To guard against the rise of a single authoritarian leader it was led by two consuls, who were elected for a one-year term. They commanded the military, directed foreign affairs, and even served as judges. Both men had to agree before a decision was implemented, and both of them held veto power.

The senate consisted of several hundred men appointed for life after holding important magisterial positions—former consuls, for example—or by virtue of being members of a wealthy or powerful family. By law the senate was an advisory body, and while it lacked the authority to actually pass legislation, it exerted a powerful influence over the government, directing foreign and domestic policies by issuing decrees which often had the force of laws.

Assemblies could elect magistrates, pass laws, and deal with judicial and military affairs. They were comprised of free male citizens, about 10 percent of the population. (As many as 40 percent of the people remained enslaved.) They were neither elected nor appointed, instead consisting of men who chose to be involved by simply showing up at the designated place at the designated time. Rather than voting as individuals, people were assigned to voting blocs within these assemblies based on their status; their wealth, where they lived, or family. Each bloc had one vote.

There were four assemblies with different responsibilities. And while on papyrus they provided every citizen with an equal voice in his government, in fact the system was designed so that the Comitia Centuriata, which consisted of the richest men in the Republic, maintained control of the city.

Theoretically any free citizen could become a candidate. But there was a formal path to public office known as *cursus honorum*, the course of honors, that politicians traditionally followed. Ambitious free men began their political careers by running for minor or administrative positions, and after proving themselves in that office became eligible for more important roles. Prior service on a lower level and being of age were the only requirements for the different levels of office.

All adult male citizens had the right to vote—but because the elections took place only in Rome and voters had to be there in person, which for many people required a long, difficult, and expensive journey, in reality most people living outside the city were disenfranchised.

The process began when the presiding magistrate picked a day, traditionally sometime in July, as election day. Candidates who met the requirements then announced their intention to run for a specific office. On election day, the assemblies met. The candidates appeared before them wearing a white toga; in fact, the word *candidate* comes from the Latin for "white robed." There usually were several candidates for each office.

Until 139 BC, voters announced their choice orally, but to reduce coercion and intimidation, a law was passed mandating the secret ballot. Voters began inscribing their choices on small wax tablets, which were collected and counted by election officials who then announced the victors.

There were no political parties. Candidates gained recognition and support by working in the judicial system, sponsoring games and banquets, and gaining endorsements from respected officials and friends. Although they were not allowed to stage rallies, they often spent time in the Forum greeting voters. Campaigns generally were more popularity contests than issue oriented. Candidates rarely made policy proposals or expressed opinions about current issues. Advertising consisted mostly of posters painted on walls by professional sign painters, often simple slogans or endorsements. For example, "The fruit sellers incorporated together with Helvius Vestalis recommend M. Holconius Priscus . . ." was found on the walls of Pompeii.

But even then, elections often were reduced to somewhat civilized brawls. Candidates attacked their opponents with negative advertising, attacking their character, morality, or family; suggesting they had committed crimes; or claiming they were controlled by scorned public figures. On those same walls in Pompeii, for example, one candidate derided his opponent as the candidate of "the drunkards and thieves association." During one campaign, the legendary orator Cicero accused Mark Antony of having a homosexual relationship with another politician, "who carried you off from your public trade, and, as if he had bestowed a matron's robe upon you, settled you in a steady and durable wedlock."

Campaigns could be very expensive. Even in ancient Rome support could be bought; wealthy candidates spent their own fortunes while others, like Julius Caesar, were forced to borrow money and often went deeply into debt to finance their efforts. Some losing candidates who could not repay those loans ended up in prison. In the grand tradition of elective politics, corruption was common. Money was necessary to host lavish banquets or events for supporters, or even bribe voters. So-called "bribery clubs" were formed to coordinate and distribute payments to units. In the scandalous election of 54 BC, two candidates for consul supposedly offered ten million sesterces (estimated very roughly to be the equivalent of several million dollars) to the unit that voted first for their support.

There also was widespread intimidation and rampant violence. Organized gangs threatened voters, sparked riots, and blocked assemblies from gathering, at times turning Rome into a battleground.

Rome's electoral system had developed as a bold attempt to ensure that its government represented the will of the people, that kings, emperors, and conquerors could no longer rule by whim. But that system had gradually been eroded and exploited until the shining shell still existed, but the inside had started to rot. It was the perfect situation for a brilliant, ambitious populist like Gaius Julius Caesar to rise.

Caesar was born into a moderately successful political family. Three members of the Juli Caesare family had previously served as consuls. His father had been elected praetor, but his once promising career faltered before he could run for consul. As a young man, long before any personal achievements, Caesar's only value to the established hierarchy was his family name.

To secure a political alliance with that family, Consul Lucius Cinna appointed teenaged Julius Caesar *flamen Dialis*, a priest of Jupiter, and arranged his marriage to his daughter Cornelia. This was a prestigious, lifelong appointment that would have kept Caesar permanently out of politics, but when General Lucius Sulla defeated Cinna in a civil war and seized power, he forced Caesar to resign his priesthood—allowing him to eventually pursue a political career.

Caesar was a man of prodigious talents; his natural charisma allowed him to move comfortably among both aristocrats and plebians, both the wealthy and powerful and the common people, enabling him to form beneficial alliances on all social levels. Even as a young man, he was respected by the elite and embraced by the general population. He was an imposing figure, described by a contemporary as "tall of stature with a fair complexion, shapely limbs, a somewhat full face and keen black eyes." He grew to be an honored military leader who gained renown by personally leading his men into battle, an orator who was able to sway people with his words, and a legendary politician attuned and responsive to the slightest shift in the popular mood. Combined with an intellectual genius that enabled him to influence and manipulate vast numbers of people, seemingly unlimited energy, extraordinary narcissism, and relentless ambition, he was able to rise above all the historic figures who preceded him and earn a place among the Roman gods—and in history.

The twenty-five-year-old Caesar first rose to public prominence when, while sailing to Rhodes to study oratory, he was captured by pirates and held for ransom. Supposedly, he gained the respect of the pirates and urged them to increase the ransom they were asking for him, claiming the original sum was insultingly low for a man of such quality. After being released, he led a naval expedition back to the pirates' lair where he had been held—the first military command of his life—and took his kidnappers prisoner. Eventually, every one of them was crucified. The tale, which portrayed him as a fearless warrior, became the springboard to a political career.

In 81 BC, nine years after joining the Roman army, and being awarded a Civic Crown of Oak Leaves for saving the life of a citizen, he was elected one of sixteen military tribunes, a high-ranking officer. This put him on the *cursus honorum*, marking the beginning of his political career. As Plutarch would later write in *Parallel Lives*, "Caesar immediately won many men's good wills at Rome, through his eloquence in pleading their causes, and the people loved him marvelously also, because of the courteous manner he had to speak to every man, and to use them gently, being more ceremonious therein than was looked for in one of his years."

Caesar was rising. As he gained recognition and popularity, he began forming mutually beneficial alliances with powerful men, among them the military hero and former consul Pompey as well as Rome's richest man, Marcus Licinius Crassus. While building his reputation as a man of the people, Caesar also had expensive tastes, and due substantially to Crassus's financial support, successfully created an aura of success far greater than what he had actually achieved. With the support of Pompey and Crassus, in 69 BC Caesar was elected quaestor, the next step on the course of honors. That also gave him lifetime membership in the senate, providing even more visibility.

Three years later, he was named curator of the Appian Way, the 150-year-old highway that led from Rome to the ports of Southern Italy, Greece, and the Eastern Mediterranean. To restore that vitally important trade and military route, he borrowed large sums of money, putting him in debt but enabling him to continue shaping his image as a man of the people. Unlike most Romans who borrowed money from moneylenders to pursue a luxurious lifestyle, throughout his career Caesar used enormous loans to purchase loyalty and political support, often spending it on public works projects or bonuses for soldiers.

Two years later he was elected *curule aedile*, a prestigious but very costly post. In that office he staged, at his own expense, spectacularly colorful and widely popular games and festivals, while also maintaining responsibility for the upkeep of buildings and roads.

Despite his popularity, his political career had put him so deeply in debt that he was in danger of being imprisoned or exiled. After the pontifex maximus, the highest priest, died in office, he decided to run for that position, partially to prevent prosecution. The role, guardian of the state's religion, responsible for the vestal virgins and maintaining "peace with the gods," was a powerful, lifetime, and potentially lucrative position, so winning this election would provide the protection from creditors he so desperately needed. His political career, his freedom, and what was to become his place in history were at stake.

It was a bitterly contested election, with all the pomp and promises, the excesses and corruption that had become part of the Roman political system. His two opponents were accomplished politicians, both influential aristocrats and senators. Basically, it was their experience against Caesar's popularity. Bribery played a significant role; Caesar was forced to borrow even larger sums to support his campaign; supposedly Catulus had offered to cover most of his debts to withdraw. He turned down that offer, staking his future on this election.

There would be many other elections in Caesar's future, but arguably none of them were so important; a loss would shatter the illusion of invincibility he was so painstakingly building and perhaps mark the beginning of the end of his political career. He would become forgotten in history, less than an afterthought.

He knew the stakes. The outcome of many elections is easily forecast, but not this one. Each of the three candidates seemed to have roughly equal support. They each spent significant sums on bribes. According to Plutarch, on the morning of the election, his fate about to be decided, Caesar kissed his mother goodbye, telling her, "Mother, to-day thou shalt see thy son either pontifex maximus or an exile."

While for decades the College of Pontiffs had selected their leader, a recent change in the law allowed one of the assemblies, the *comitia tributa*, to elect the new head of the state church. The combination of personal popularity and extensive bribery was too much for Caesar's opponents to overcome, and while there were claims of fraudulent vote counting, he won the election. His political future was secured.

To further consolidate his power and raise additional funds to pay off his debts, several months later Caesar ran for the office of praetor. He also won that election, giving him the political base that he would exploit for the next two decades.

The number of his enemies had grown with each success, and they began actively trying to stop him. Weeks after being elected praetor, Consul Cicero accused one of the opponents he had defeated, Lucius Catilina, of plotting to overthrow the government and seize control. In that election Caesar had supported Catilina, and afterward his longtime rival, Cato the Younger, joined Cicero in suggesting that Caesar had participated in a failed conspiracy. Among the flimsy evidence was the fact that Caesar had argued that the captured traitors be imprisoned for life instead of being executed. Cato himself had convinced the senate to invoke the death penalty. They were strangled.

Rather than the accusations damaging his reputation, Caesar was praised for his stance that no Roman citizen should be executed without receiving a trial in the senate. Other politicians, grasping the will of the citizenry, rallied to support him, further strengthening his power base.

He had become an unstoppable force, moving forward with the strength of the massive Roman ballista, hurling bolts and stones against all enemies and obstacles. In 59 BC, after winning significant battles in Gaul, he ran for consul against two opponents. He was forty years old. His popular support, again accompanied by massive bribes, led to an overwhelming victory. His first act in office was to ensure transparency, publishing the minutes of the senate and the assemblies, making them accountable to the people.

That done, the history that people would be reading for two thousand years began to unfold. Rome's government system was a noble experiment, but the reality of it proved flawed in practice and vulnerable to manipulation. To deal with the emerging problems, to try to ensure the survival of some form of government by the people, he took increasingly controversial steps that gave him great personal power. Perhaps one reason Caesar has remained a pivotal historic figure is that he publicly displayed all the complexities and shades of human nature, the good and the bad of it. Once he gained power, he refused to surrender any of it, believing his decisions enhanced the public good.

Together with Pompey and Crassus, Caesar formed the historic First Triumvirate to stabilize the government, then began enacting the reforms that would eventually lead to the end of the Republic. It was an uneasy alliance between clever, ambitious men, held together by Crassus. Using their combined wealth, influence, experience, and resources, step-by-step, law by law, declaration by declaration, they took authority away from the senate and took it for themselves. They put their most loyal supporters in decision-making positions in Rome and in the provinces and gained effective control of the treasury.

The Triumvirate lasted until Crassus was killed in battle by the Parthians in 53 BC. Caesar and Pompey turned on each other and began battling for power. Caesar had spent most of the decade leading his army to the conquest of Gaul, bringing Roman culture to a vast swath of Europe. The following year, while Caesar's army was winning great victories and expanding the Republic's territory, Pompey was in Rome, being elected the sole consul—in essence the unchecked leader.

In 49 BC the senate, fearing the immensely popular Caesar would return as a conquering hero and gain control of the government, ordered him to disband his army and return to Rome as a private citizen. It put Pompey in command of the army should Caesar refuse. In response, Caesar made his fateful decision: Knowing his refusal to accept the decree would ignite a civil war, he supposedly quoted the Athenian Menander, *alei iacta est*, "the die is cast," and in January led his army across the Rubicon River. He began marching on the city. The magnitude of that decision is reflected by the fact that the phrase "crossing the Rubicon" has come down through the ages to mean making an irrevocable decision.

While neither Caesar nor Pompey wanted this fight, there was no turning back. As Caesar's army moved rapidly toward the city, Pompey and most of the senate were forced to flee. Once again, Caesar was in control of Rome. Under Roman law, in critical situations, including war or revolution, one man could be named dictator and be given power to make all state decisions for as long as six months. Caesar served as dictator for eleven days, until the election that named him consul for 48 BC was held. While the reality was that he already held dictatorial power, he insisted that an election be held to maintain the illusion of a democracy.

Pompey was defeated that year and fled to Alexandria—where he was eventually killed. Caesar followed him there and began his legendary affair with Cleopatra, eventually defeating her enemies and installing her as ruler of Egypt. In the next few years, he was officially appointed dictator four more times, for periods as long as a year, and in 44 BC was appointed dictator for life. While the framework of Rome's democratic system continued to exist, "elected" officials had no power. Caesar's control of every aspect of the government was complete. There was even an attempt to name him king. He ruled from a golden chair in the senate, statues were erected in his image, his birthday was recognized as a public holiday and he became the first living person in Rome to be honored with a coin bearing his image.

Gradually, as he seized more and more power, the people who had once revered him began turning against him. The irony was unassailable; Caesar was destroying the democracy he had once fought so fervently to protect. Graffiti described him as a tyrant and urged that he be removed. A conspiracy against him, including at least sixty senators, led by Senator Marcus Junius Brutus, was formed in 45 BC. On the Ides of March, March 15, 44 BC, they attacked. During a senate session held in the Theatre of Pompey, Caesar was stabbed at least twenty-three times and according to legend died at the base of the statue of Pompey.

The man was dead, but his impact on the world was already resonating throughout history. In his will he named his grandnephew by birth, Gaius Octavius, who was known as Augustus or Octavian, his adopted son and heir, granting him his name, his estate, and the loyalty of his followers. In 31 BC Octavian established his power by defeating Antony and Cleopatra's army in the Battle of Actium. In 27 BC, the senate named him Rome's first emperor, marking the official founding of the Roman Empire, which dominated the world for the next five hundred years. Augustus and the emperors who followed in Caesar's path instituted political, cultural, moral, military, and religious reforms that would later come to play a significant role in Western civilization.

Certain aspects of Caesar's legacy are obvious: In his honor the month of Quintillis was renamed Julius, or July. He changed the calendar itself; working with Egyptian astronomer Sosigenes, they replaced Rome's 355-day lunar calendar, which required continuous revision to maintain seasons and festivals, with the 365-day solar-based Julian calendar in 46 BC—the longest year in history, lasting 445 days in order to make the adjustment.

By placing Augustus in power, he laid the foundation for the transformation of the Republic into the Roman Empire, spreading the concepts of governing and society that he embraced (and in some instances had created) to arguably the entirety of the Western world.

Caesar greatly expanded Rome's influence by granting citizenship to people in captured territories, including all of Gaul. More importantly, he did not impose Rome's culture on conquered peoples, instead allowing them to retain their own local practices, which over decades and centuries became infused with Roman ideals. His written description of his two incursions into Britain basically served to introduce the island to the world and is recognized as the first written history of that land.

His lasting impact even extends to language; the words *czar* and *kaiser*, meaning emperor, are derived from his name. And thanks to Shakespeare, "beware the Ides of March" is a common warning to be wary about the future.

As a military tactician, his revolutionary belief in the value of speed, flexibility, and intense training in battle changed the way armies fought. His emphasis on planning strategy based on intelligence rather than employing brute force is still studied by military leaders.

As a politician he proved the value of populist reform for all those who would come after him: redistributing land, canceling or reducing debt, providing libraries, and making the government more transparent and responsive to public opinion. While holding dictatorial powers, he continued to recognize some structures of a democratic government, meeting with the legislature, generally respecting decisions of the judiciary, and allowing Romans to at least feel they had a voice in their government.

He was an extraordinarily complex figure, fiercely loved and hated.

As Caesar's biographer, Suetonius, wrote of the assassination, "All the conspirators made off, and he lay there lifeless for some time, until finally three common slaves put him on a litter and carried him home, with one arm hanging down."

TWO

1265: Consequences of the Magna Carta

A VOTE WAS ONE of the few powers held by ordinary people. It granted them the right to make a choice. It was a possession, it had value. A vote gave ordinary people a voice in their own future. While the concept of people voting for their leaders was established firmly by Athens and Rome, there also were a number of other societies in which at least some officials were elected. Independent republics on the Indian subcontinent had been voting for representative assemblies since the sixth century BC. Vikings began electing their leaders in the late eighth century. The powerful Republic of Venice also began electing a "doge," the head of state, in the eighth century.

The doge, who was almost exclusively selected from one of the city-state's two most powerful families, was elected for life by a forty-person council of nobles. While commoners could not vote, they actively pressured members of the council with gatherings and banners posted along the canals. Electors voted by dropping balls into an urn. In rare situations when the vote was tied, the doge was then selected by lot.

Outside the realm of government, elections were utilized

as well. The Catholic Church voted to fill its leadership roles; Popes, archbishops, even abbots were chosen in elections governed by canon law. In some of those elections, commoners living in the diocese were allowed to vote. A doctrine issued in 1059 established that the Pope should be elected by cardinal bishops, ordering, "The men of the church shall be the leaders in carrying on the election of a pope, the others merely followers."

Beginning in the eleventh century, merchants and craftsmen began forming economic alliances, guilds, to protect their interests. The forerunners of modern unions, they regularly held elections for leaders in which many members were permitted to vote. Merchant guilds consisted of people involved in both domestic and international commerce and trade; they protected the interests of their members against local rulers, set wages, enforced contracts between members, and at times opened new markets. They used economic penalties like boycotts and expulsion to enforce rules. Craft guilds included the owners and operators of family and small businesses, among them weavers, blacksmiths, cobblers, and bakers. Other guilds offered protection for people in a variety of different professions.

These guilds met several times a year to adopt policies, induct new members, and elect officials. Voting usually was limited to "masters," men who had proved their skills or owned their own business. While the actual method of voting varied, to prevent intimidation and retaliation votes were cast in secret. Voters were given a black ball, which indicated opposition, and proposed new members could be anonymously blackballed or prevented from joining, a term and practice that has existed through centuries.

Even British kings, in rare instances, stood for election. Most often the crown was inherited, based on bloodlines, but when a king died without progeny or multiple relatives claimed the right to succession the matter was sometimes settled by an election rather than fighting. On those rare occasions in medieval England, the monarch was elected by a council consisting of princes, earls and other aristocrats, bishops, and other wealthy or important men known as the witan. The witan, meaning wise men, were first organized in the early seventh century to advise the king on a variety of matters, including foreign policy, taxation, legislation, and land reforms.

The concept of inviting the great men of the kingdom to assemble and provide advice to the leader was common among Germanic tribes and probably was brought to England by their descendants. The first historical mention of the witenagemot, the witan, took place around 600 AD, when the king of Kent assembled trusted advisors to approve new laws. The witan gradually gained power, eventually becoming the only body strong enough to hold a king accountable for his actions and, when deemed necessary, publicly oppose his dictates.

When King Edward the Confessor died in 1066 without naming his successor, the witan convened to elect a new king. England at that time was a loose association of earldoms ruled by powerful nobles—members of the witan—who had pledged allegiance to the throne. Several men claimed the crown, among them Harold Godwinson, the Earl of Wessex, whom Edward on his deathbed had named the protector of the kingdom; the king's cousin William II, Duke of Normandy, who protested he had been promised the throne three years earlier; Harald Hardrada, the king of Norway; and Edgar Aetheling, Edward's great-nephew and the only candidate tied to the crown by blood. In January 1066 the assembly elected Harold, the tested warrior and skilled politician who they believed was best able to defend the realm, as well as their own wealth and status.

The acceptance of a peaceful transition of power decided by voters was still thousands of years in the future. Throughout most of history, what might not be won by the ballot could be won on the battlefield. So while the witan was electing its new leader, the armies of the would-be kings readied for battle regardless. In September, Harold defeated the Viking warrior Harald Hardrada's invaders, but weeks later his army was beaten and he was killed in the Battle of Hastings by William of Normandy, who quickly became known as William the Conqueror. The witan then voted to install Aetheling, but before he could be handed the throne, William took control. After his coronation he abolished the witan, replacing it with the Curia Regis, the King's Court, and seized lands and power from the Anglo-Saxon nobility, which he gave to the loyal Normans.

Kings were conquerors, with an insatiable desire to expand their realm. To accomplish that goal, armies had to be raised and equipped, paid and fed. Conquering was expensive. Kings needed money to pay for their campaigns and had to make deals to get it. Ironically, to maintain power, they were forced to give it up.

At important moments in history, the significance of certain elections was not who won or lost, but rather the election itself. These were events that made a lasting impact on the world.

For example, 1265 AD. Much of the world was in turmoil, great armies were marauding across continents, fighting for land and property—while kings, warlords, and the Church fought for power. The once vast Byzantine Empire, which had recaptured its capital, Constantinople, only a few years earlier, was struggling to regain its great influence, trying and failing to negotiate a treaty with powerful Venice. The bloody two-year-long Hungarian Civil War, in which Duke Stephen defeated his father, King Béla IV, was coming to a conclusion that saw the son seize the crown. The Mamluk Sultanate, a ferocious army built by former slaves from the Caucasus and Central Asia, which had defeated the remnants of the Crusaders to gain control of Egypt in 1250 and beaten the Mongols in battle a decade later, was continuing its relentless drive through North Africa. Civil wars were breaking out in Persia. In Asia, Kublai Khan was battling his brother for control of the Mongol Empire. And in England, the Second Barons' War, a civil war between the army of King Henry III and forces led by the French-born Earl of Leicester, Simon de Montfort, was coming to a bloody end.

In addition to claiming the traditional riches of war, over time the victors began to impose their form of government on captured lands. In most countries or empires this was some form of autocratic rule; common people had few rights and no voice in the decisions that controlled their lives. The ruler, king, emperor, khan, or sultan led by *vis et voluntas*, force and will, simply imposing his decisions on the populace. But in some places, the concept that it was possible for people to pick their leaders had been firmly established.

After King John I succeeded to the throne in 1199 upon the death of his brother Richard (I) the Lionhearted, England was embroiled in a political and military crisis. The nobility was aligned against King John I, who had levied increasingly large taxes on them to finance his futile war against Phillip II of France. The king had lost almost all of the land won by William, fought with the Church and been briefly excommunicated, and was continuing to impose harsh economic policies and demanding more troops from the nobles. Having become convinced that the king was no longer able protect their interests, these land-owning barons demanded that in return for their loyalty, he sign a charter limiting his power and subjecting him to the rule of law. After the barons gained control of London, John realized he had no choice but to agree to it.

This Magna Carta, or "Great Charter," established the rule of law that would become the basis of representative democracies around the world.

The document itself contained sixty-three clauses, written in Latin, that granted new powers to the barons, the Church, and commoners. It included guidance about many of the issues that concerned the aristocracy, among them religion, military service, taxes, government, economics, and the distribution of power. In addition to forcing the monarch to gain their approval for certain actions, it also would eventually establish the foundation of the judicial system. The thirty-ninth clause stated firmly, "No freeman shall be arrested or imprisoned or disseised or outlawed or exiled or in any way ruined, nor will we go against him nor send against him, except by the lawful judgement of his peers or by the law of the land." This would lead eventually to due process, the right to a fair trial, and protection against unjust imprisonment. Perhaps most important to the barons, Clause 61 created a committee of twenty-five barons to ensure the king adhered to the document, allowing them to seize his castles, lands, and possessions if he failed to do so.

The Magna Carta essentially was a peace treaty between the monarch and the barons, loosely based on the Charter of

Liberties, which Henry I had signed in 1100, expanding the rights of nobles. It took weeks to negotiate, and several copies were handwritten on parchment. In June 1215, hundreds of people camped in tents on a lush meadow called Runnymede on the banks of the Thames River in Surrey, working out the final details and preparing it to be signed. On the 15th, King John met with the barons at Runnymede, and his royal seal was affixed to the document.

After negotiating it, agreeing to it, and signing it, the king basically ignored it. While King John is credited in history with reducing the power of the monarchy forever, in fact he went to war against the agreement he had made. In late August, Pope Innocent III wrote that the Magna Carta "would incur the anger of Almighty God" and declared it "null, and void of all validity for ever," because it infringed on the king's rights. The civil war, the First Barons' War, began that November. The following October, John died of dysentery and a fight for the crown resulted in John's son, nine-year-old Henry III, on the throne. At the direction of his regents, who essentially controlled the monarchy, an abbreviated charter was issued. Still another, further modified version was agreed to in 1217, finally ending that war.

No one, absolutely no one, could have imagined the impact this document would have in future centuries or that it would be treasured a thousand years later. The Magna Carta was not intended to establish or grant universal rights. There was no reference to the right to vote, for example. Common working people had little interest in it; it was perceived as a treaty between the king and barons that had almost no effect on their lives. It applied specifically to "free men," men who owned land, representing only a small percentage of the population.

Only gradually did it become clear that some provisions might benefit them.

Initially, it had no impact anywhere else in the world. Many countries, states, confederations, and territories were still ruled by feudal monarchies, often considered divinely appointed, and tempered, if at all, by the powerful, political Catholic Church. If they were even aware of the stirring in England, they completely ignored it. Wealthy, powerful people did not voluntarily give up their wealth or power.

The first practical application of the Magna Carta took place almost fifty years later. By the 1250s, Henry III's failing economic and military policies had put his kingdom in jeopardy. He was considered a weak leader, lacking the ability or support to lead the country through yet another crisis. In 1258 a group of barons, among them Simon de Montfort, the Earl of Leicester, staged a peaceful coup and took control of the government. Faced with arrest and imprisonment, Henry agreed to expand the role of Parliament, placing real power in the hands of a twenty-four-man council, twelve of them selected by the barons and twelve more picked by the king. It was a new form of government, which greatly diminished the king's command.

But just as his father had done, almost immediately Henry began taking steps to restore the crown's authority. In 1264 the Second Barons' War erupted, with de Montfort leading the rebel army. In May, de Montfort captured Henry, who became a figurehead as de Montfort conducted government affairs under his name.

Throughout history, the evolution of political systems has been sparked more frequently by individuals' quests to gain and maintain power than by ideology. De Montfort was in an uneasy situation. Although he held the king captive, he faced considerable opposition. Henry's supporters remained in control of many important castles, other nobles watched de Montfort with envy and planned ways to strengthen their own position, and Henry's loyal queen, Eleanor of Provence, waited anxiously in France for an opportunity to aid her husband.

There was nothing in Simon de Montfort's background that suggested he would champion a radical reform in government. He held no deep philosophical beliefs about human rights. Born and educated in France, he had participated in several Crusades before marrying Henry III's sister and being officially named Earl of Leicester. De Montfort was a clever and ambitious politician; initially, he gained popular support in an anti-Semitic age by expelling the small Jewish community from Leicester, then pursued a self-serving relationship with the king, supporting then opposing him when it was to his benefit. He also was a respected military leader—acceptably brutal when he deemed it necessary—and when the barons rebelled against the king he served at the head of the army, eventually capturing Henry and taking control of the government. In addition, de Montfort captured Henry's son, Prince Edward, using him as a hostage to pressure the king to accept his terms.

After securing Henry's agreement, de Montfort made an extraordinary decision: In 1264 he convened a meeting of advisors, which he referred to as a "parliament"—but for the first time, the group included representatives of commoners. The term *parliament*, derived from the French word meaning to "speak" or discuss, had appeared in official documents issued by Henry in 1236, when he used it to describe members of the royal court who would be meeting to adjudicate a legal situation. Now de Montfort used the term for the radically different assembly he was convening.

It was a remarkable concept: Ordinary men would have a voice in their government. It was also a shrewd strategy. He was proposing a different form of rule, a transfer of significant power from an absolute monarch to an advisory assembly representing the people. It would help him gain the support of the rapidly growing merchant, craft, and landowning classes across the country.

Never before in English history had towns and villages been invited to send representatives to this kind of meeting, this parliament; citizens who would have the same rights as nobles, knights (as nobles who had become soldiers were honored), and clergy. In December 1264, de Montfort, in Henry's name, ordered sheriffs in several counties to send "two of the more law-worthy, honest and prudent knights from each of the counties" to the gathering. Similar writs were sent to free men in several towns, ordering them to elect and send two "prudent, law-worthy and honest fellow citizens or burgesses"—as citizens of a town were known—alongside the knights.

Previously, there had been less formal assemblies in which knights and townspeople were represented, but they had dealt exclusively with tax matters. This marked the first time knights and citizens came together with nobles to discuss, debate, and provide guidance to de Montfort about the great variety of issues facing the government. No instructions were given on how these "burgesses," should be chosen. Some of them were selected by local sheriffs or by a small group of town leaders, but in other places an election was held.

The concept of commoners voting in elections was not especially new in England. During his thirty-five-year reign beginning in 1154 Henry II had granted charters allowing a form of self-government to numerous cities, towns, and councils of boroughs. The methods of choosing town leaders varied, but often a nonelected city council consisting of wealthy or respected citizens, burgesses, elected the mayor.

There were no universal rules or regulations concerning election to de Montfort's parliament. Who was eligible to vote and the methods used to vote differed from town to town. Generally, though, voters included the wealthiest male citizens, property owners, and in some instances guild members. Most men, women, and peasants were excluded. These rudimentary elections were held in public. Voters stood up and declared their choice out loud. Apparently, most elections were not contested; the people generally voted for the most respected members of the town who expressed a desire—and had the money to pay their own expenses—to represent them.

De Montfort's parliament convened on January 20, 1265, and remained in session for almost two months. Among its achievements was affirming support for previously passed legal reforms that clarified land transfer and inheritance rights. The assembly also firmly committed the nation to the Magna Carta, sending a copy of the text to every county, the first time it had been circulated in four decades. At the closing ceremony in Westminster Hall, hundreds of participants sat quietly while documents signed by Henry were read out loud, acknowledging that he would cede some royal power to a council of nobles.

Six months later, de Montfort was dead. Prince Edward had escaped captivity and raised an army; nobles whose power had been reduced by de Montfort refused to support him. After being killed by Edward's soldiers at the Battle of Evesham, his body was dismembered, and various parts were wrapped in cloth and sent to the families of victorious nobles.

Confirming the respect commoners had for de Montfort,

tales quickly spread that these severed body parts had performed miracles. Supposedly, when a priest raised up the Eucharist during mass, de Montfort's hand raised itself and floated in the air above the congregation. A foot was displayed as a relic that believers would visit to pray for healing miracles.

Within a year, King Edward's parliament had nullified the reforms of 1265, restoring his royal powers. But the possibility of participatory government had been planted deep in the political fabric of the nation, and Edward could not ignore it. There was no great clamor from the people for the right to vote; it just wasn't part of the system that had ruled the nation for more than a thousand years. But it was a useful issue that a king could use to expand his popularity—or reduce the power of the nobles. In 1275, Edward convened his first parliament, primarily to approve certain taxes and a body of laws known as the Statute of Westminster, fifty-one clauses codifying the existing laws and turning capricious feudal laws into a structured, predictable legal system. The statute encompassed everything from criminal and civil law to the framework of the legal system and the rights of royals. It also prohibited powerful men from their common practice of using force or intimidation to control elections, proclaiming ". . . the King commandeth upon great Forfeiture, that no Man by force of Arms, nor by Malice, or Menacing, shall disturb any to make free Election." But these safeguards did not expand the right to vote or guarantee representation; the right to vote in these elections was still severely limited—the king decided which social classes would be represented, usually based on which of them he could rely on for support.

That began changing in 1294. Edward desperately needed

to raise money to pay for his wars in France and Scotland and suppress an uprising in Wales. These wars were not going well: The French had sacked Dover, then set it afire. English seamen were fighting the French for control of the English Channel. The Scots had aligned with the French. To pay for all this, the king had arbitrarily imposed harsh taxes on some merchants, demanded larger contributions from the barons, seized church assets, and asked the Church to give half their revenue to the crown. To quell the rising anger, rather than simply imposing new taxes, he convened a parliament to debate them.

Because these proposed taxes would be imposed on merchants, landowners, and tenants in addition to nobles, Edward understood that he would have to gain their approval. Acknowledging that, he invited representatives of the three "estates," or social classes, the nobility, clergy, and commoners, to his parliament. In his summons to them, he justified the inclusive nature of this gathering by explaining that since all people in the kingdom faced this common danger, "the most righteous law of the emperors, that what touches all, by all should be approved."

Once again sheriffs were ordered to "cause two knights . . . to be elected from the aforesaid county, two citizens from each city in the same aforesaid county and two burgesses from each borough, of those who are especially discreet and capable of laboring, to be elected without delay . . ." and travel to Westminster Hall.

About four hundred men participated: nobles, clergy, and commoners. Rather than debating the matters at hand as a single unified body, the three groups sat separately and debated only those issues that directly affected them, each group voting independently of the others.

Six centuries later, British historian William Stubbs would label this the "Model Parliament," the foundation on which British government was built—and exported throughout the empire and beyond. The actual achievements of this parliament were limited; the nobility agreed to pay a subsidy of one-eleventh the value of their "moveable goods," meaning basically anything other than land or items not permanently affixed to that land, including livestock, household goods, farm equipment, and clothing. The clergy voted to pay one-tenth the value, and the commoners agreed to one-seventh. The concept of a progressive tax, in which the tax rate is based on wealth, would not appear in England for more than five hundred years.

More importantly, the independent actions of the estates became the precursor for a bicameral, two-chambered legislature consisting of Lords and Commons. Beginning with the inclusion of knights and elected burgesses—which became known as "the commons"—in 1265, as the jurist and legal scholar Edward Jenks would write, "the thousand diverse interests of shires and boroughs, clergy and laity, magnates and humble folk into one national whole made possible the existence of national legislation."

In reality, this model parliament was no more than a shadow of its future self, what was to become an extraordinary political structure that eventually would provide elected representation to all the citizens of England. When Edward III was crowned in 1327, the right to vote for one's representatives was still limited to a small group of men. The king retained enormous decision-making power. Nobles and the Church had both access and influence in the affairs of the state. Commons had sporadic representation but little real power or influence.

Edward III immediately began modifying the system, resolving that this body of advisors, the Parliament consisting of the three estates, should meet annually. The practice of each group meeting independently, initially begun for convenience since parliament had no designated meeting place beyond wherever the king was, had become more formalized. No one seemed to realize the impact that would have on the structure of government. Eventually, this evolved into the now familiar bicameral legislature; the nobles and clergy forming the House of Lords, the knights and burgesses the House of Commons.

With the beginning of the Hundred Years' War against France, Edward III was forced to make concessions to raise the funds he needed. As a result, he accepted additional limitations on his power, agreeing that he would make no laws or levy new taxes without the consent of the houses of Parliament. Recognizing and accepting the role of Parliament was a monumental concession that would enshrine the concept of shared power between the crown and the people.

The road that had begun in 1265 would be hard, it would be deeply rutted and often dangerous, there would be unexpected twists and sharp turns, but it led eventually to the bicameral government structure in which the common man—and woman—had the power to influence those policies under which they lived.

THREE

November 21, 1620: The Mayflower Compact Brings Self-Government to the New World

THE WINDS OF FATE set the fragile ship *Mayflower* off course and sparked political revolution. Its crew and colonists had been swept into uncharted territory—a place where their laws no longer applied.

In 1620, the seafaring nations of Europe were racing to colonize recently mapped areas of the Americas, rapidly expanding their areas of settlement. Spain had built colonies in Central and South America. France had settlements far to the north, in Canada. The first permanent English settlement, Jamestown, named in honor of the king, had been founded in 1607. The promise of vast riches, just waiting for those brave enough—or foolhardy enough—to make the hazardous journey and endure unknown hardships, lured governments and private companies into launching costly expeditions. The existence of Indigenous people did not deter these adventurers. In fact, at first the Native Americans generally welcomed the settlers, not yet understanding how the clash of fundamentally different cultures would eventually impact their society—and their lives.

Vast amounts of land could be claimed just for the settling. There were abundant natural resources, forests of animals to be trapped and skinned, gold and silver were rumored to be lying in the ground, and crops like tobacco were said to grow to astonishing heights. There were, advertised one company seeking settlers, lands full of treasure "never yet searched." But that promise of wealth was only one of the several reasons people were willing to risk their lives; they also fled Europe for social and religious freedom. This was an opportunity to be a vast ocean away from the rule of kings and princes.

In England, the spirit of the Magna Carta was by now embedded in the government. It was an early form of a constitutional monarchy, ruled by King James I, whose power was still only somewhat limited by the bicameral Parliament. The right to vote in annual elections was mostly restricted to men over twenty-one years old with property, although in some towns that right was extended to other men of some means. But the Church of England retained its power to influence decisions and govern matters of religion. It greatly restricted the religious practices of dissenters—who might also face persecution. Catholics, for example, generally were not allowed to vote.

Among those seeking refuge from religious persecution was a group of Radical Puritans, mostly poor farmers who believed the Church of England was beyond salvation and had voluntarily separated from it. As a result, they were prevented from practicing their religion, harassed, heavily fined, and in some instances even imprisoned. These Separatists, as they were called, fled to Holland where they spent a decade living uneasily, fearful that exposure to local religious practices might taint their children. Living there was difficult; most of them worked in cloth factories and were struggling to survive. They finally decided to sail to America, where they could freely practice their religion—and prevent their church from being weakened by attrition.

A British trading company, the Virginia Company of London, had been granted a charter by King James I to settle a territory near Hudson's River, then part of Virginia. The voyage, supplies, and costs of building a settlement were financed by "merchant investors," a group of men who bought shares in the venture. The actual settlers were promised a single share in the business in return for living and working in America for seven years. After that time, the company would be dissolved and its assets—including the land—distributed to shareholders in England as well as the colonists.

The merchants recruited these Puritans to join the venture, along with an array of other people, among them carpenters, farmers, and tradesmen seeking their fortune in the New World. After several delayed starts, on September 16, 1620, 102 passengers, including about fifty Separatists or "Saints," fifty-two so-called Strangers and indentured servants, an additional twenty to thirty crew members, and two dogs, set sail from Plymouth, England, aboard an overcrowded ship named the *Mayflower.*

These "Strangers" were not Puritans, but the Separatists needed them to satisfy the investors that the proposed colony would be profitable.

The *Mayflower* was a small merchant square-rigger, one hundred feet long and twenty-four feet wide, that had been built to carry as much as 180 tons of cargo between European ports. It had carried wool and furs, wines and brandy, and German silk, but it had never attempted a three-thousand-mile winter voyage across a great ocean carrying passengers and supplies.

Among those passengers were William Bradford and Edward

Winslow, Separatist leaders who quickly gained the respect of the Strangers; Christopher Martin, the company's representative who had purchased supplies for the voyage; twenty-one-year-old crew member John Alden; church deacon John Carver, who had negotiated the arrangement with the company; and military commander Captain Myles Standish.

The two-month-long voyage on the "vast and furious ocean," as Bradford described it, was especially difficult. "The ship would be badly shaken." Too many people were crammed together below decks for far too long. They were hungry and wet, and there was little sanitation. At least two people died at sea. But gradually, a sense of community was forged among the passengers. The Separatists and the Strangers had little in common—until, together, they endured and survived the brutal conditions.

After sixty-six days at sea, the *Mayflower* finally sighted land. But the colonists soon realized that storms had blown the ship far to the north. Rather than reaching Virginia, they were off the coast of Massachusetts. They attempted to sail south, but strong winds made that impossible. On November 21, they finally dropped anchor near Cape Cod. "They were not a little joyful," Bradford wrote. "They fell upon their knees and Blessed the God of heaven who had . . . delivered them from all the perils and miseries."

They were isolated. Alone.

The problem—or the opportunity—they faced was that the Virginia Company's authority did not extend to New England. The company had no rights in Massachusetts. The Puritans seemed content to continue following the dictates of the charter, but the Strangers were firm in their belief that they no longer were legally bound to their agreement. They were free from any restraint; for the first time in their lives they could make their own laws and live the way they chose. It was a daring, and daunting, proposition.

Among those men arguing that their contract no long applied was Stephen Hopkins, who had been a minister's clerk on the *Sea Venture*, which had been sailing to resupply Jamestown in 1609 when it had wrecked. Its 150 passengers and crew had been marooned on the island of Bermuda for nine months, an epic tale of survival that may have inspired Shakespeare to write *The Tempest*. Hopkins then had lived in the Jamestown settlement for several years. Some of those survivors had proposed establishing their own government, but that rebellion was suppressed by Governor Sir Thomas Gates, who imposed draconian rules on the community—even executing one colonist. Hopkins had been tried, convicted, and sentenced to death by Gates for challenging the governor, but his sentence had been commuted. Incredibly, he now found himself in a strikingly similar situation—but in this instance, many others agreed with him.

There was a long and contentious debate. Bradford later remembered "some discontents . . . and mutinous speeches that some of the strangers amongst them had let fall from them." There was a danger the groups would split into factions if an agreement could not be reached, he continued, "for none had power to command them." That was a grave threat; division would make it far more difficult for all of them to survive the coming winter. Unlike Bermuda, with its temperate weather and abundance of naturally growing foods, the New England coast was cold and barren. And the story of the *Sea Venture* survivors, who had been treated harshly by their tyrannical leader, was well-known.

These fears helped them forge a compromise. "Some [were] not well affected to unity and concord," wrote Edward Winslow, "but gave some appearances of faction [and thus] it was thought good . . . that we should combine together in one body, and to submit to such government and governors, as we should by common consent agree to make and choose."

It was a momentous decision: The Plymouth colony would be self-governed. But what form would that government take? How would leaders be chosen? How much power would this new, small government have to impose its decisions?

Long before the *Mayflower* arrived, a rudimentary form of democracy existed in North America. Five Nations of the Iroquois Confederacy had established their own form of representative government more than a century earlier. This political system included a bicameral legislature and a constitution. The oldest woman in each tribal clan, the "Clan Mother," selected the representatives, or *sachems*, to the council. The Grand Council, consisting of about fifty men, debated and determined policy, settled disputes, and negotiated trade with colonists. Representatives from the Seneca and Mohawks met in one longhouse, while sachems from the Oneida and Cayuga met in a different longhouse. Decisions were made by consensus and had to be unanimous. The Onondaga representatives, the Fire Keepers, had the power to resolve disputes and veto decisions. If the Grand Council could not make a unanimous decision, each clan was permitted to act independently.

The Five Nations were united by a written constitution, the Great Law of Peace. Among its 108 laws and principles was number 72, which governed the ownership of land. "The soil of the earth from one end of the land to the other is the property of the people who inhabit it," it read. "By birthright the Ongwehonweh (Original beings) are the owners of the soil which they own and occupy and none other may hold it. The same law has been held from the oldest times." Elsewhere on the continent, the manner in which the English colony at Jamestown would be governed had been determined by the company that chartered and financed it. Within days of its founding in 1607, for example, the leaders of Jamestown opened a sealed box given to them by the Virginia Company that contained the names of seven men acceptable to King James to lead the colony. This council was to select one of them to preside over the colony. As Captain John Smith reported, "The Counsell was sworne, the President elected, which for that yeare was Maister Edw. Maria Wingfield."

This was the first recorded election in an English colony in America. Smith was denied the right to vote because he was suspected of concealing a plan for a mutiny, so only six men voted. In 1612 the first tobacco seeds were planted in the colony, brought there by *Sea Venture* survivors, proving the settlement could be a profitable investment. Other settlements followed quickly; Hampton in 1610, Henricus in 1611, Flowerdew Hundred in 1618. In 1619, a year before the *Mayflower* arrived, the Virginia Company authorized the election of an assembly from all the colonies to meet in Jamestown "to establish one equal and uniform government over all Virginia" whose purpose was to create "just Laws for the happy guiding and governing of the people there inhabiting."

The first elected legislature in America was led by Sir George Yeardley, who had been appointed governor by the company, and consisted of four councilors, and twenty-two burgesses elected by free white males from every town and plantation in Virginia. On July 30, 1619, this representative assembly in America met for the first time, in the new church's choir. Its authority was limited; it was ruled by the appointed governor and any laws it passed had to be approved by the company. The first law passed by this House of Burgesses during its six-day session set the price for tobacco at no less than three shillings per pound. Other legislation regulated morality—no gambling or getting drunk—made church attendance on the Sabbath mandatory, and governed relations with the Powhatan Indians.

As the *Mayflower* lay anchored off Cape Cod, the forty-one adult male passengers—Separatists, Strangers, indentured servants, and crew members—debated how the new colony would be governed. They needed a structure that would ensure cooperation among the different groups, even when they disagreed, while maintaining order and providing for their protection. They were all used to laws and regulations in which they had no say being imposed on them by the crown and its representatives. They had to figure out how to ensure that no single person or entity had the power to make arbitrary decisions for the entire colony—as Governor Gates had done on Bermuda. That power would have to come from the people.

And they had only a very brief period of time to forge this agreement.

While no record of the discussion exists, they set out to create a document that would bind them together by ensuring everyone would have a voice—but they would agree to adhere to the final decisions of the majority. This "Agreement Between the Settlers of New Plymouth" was a commitment to follow the laws they would enact. It was a compact, wrote Bradford and Edward Winslow in *Mourt's Relation*, that the settlers would "submit to such government and governors as we should by common consent agree to make and choose."

This was never intended to be a declaration of independence from the crown. In fact, the document itself begins by pledging allegiance to the king: declaring themselves "loyal Subjects of our dread sovereign Lord King James, by the grace of God of Great Britain, France, and Ireland, King, Defender of the Faith . . ."

But it was different than anything that had ever come before. It was, as Bradford described, ". . . the first foundation of their government in this place." While Bradford was referring specifically to the colony, his words accurately described its eventual impact on the United States. For the first time in the New World, European settlers were establishing an independent government, as flimsy as it was, created with the consent of the people; in return those people would voluntarily cede rights and agree to respect the will of the majority.

No one knows who actually wrote it. Some people have attributed it to Bradford himself. Others to John Carver. Still others suggested that these were the words of William Brewster, who had been educated at university and was known to have written similar agreements for the Saints when they were establishing self-governing churches in England and Holland. All three of those men were respected, educated men, and it is highly likely they collaborated on it.

It isn't known precisely where aboard the *Mayflower* it was signed; historic paintings depict the men in a cabin, but more likely it was somewhere in the cold interior living space below decks. As a sign of the general respect for Carver, he was the first person to sign it. The one-page document, which would become known to history as "The Mayflower Compact," read in part, "in the presence of God and one another, covenant, and combine ourselves together in a civil body politick, for better ordering and preservation and furtherance of the ends aforesaid; and by virtue hereof do enact, constitute, and frame such just and equal laws, Ordinances, acts, constitutions, and offices from time to time, as shall be thought most meet and convenient for the general good of the Colony; unto which we promise all due submission and obedience."

It wasn't necessary to vote to accept it; the document simply put down on paper what had already been agreed to. On November 21, 1620, the forty-one men signed it, acknowledging that the colony would be bound by the decisions of a government they intended to form. Then they had to form it.

The first order of business was electing a leader. Whoever was elected governor would have limited power for a limited period of time. The process was somewhat similar to voting in church elections. Many of the Separatists had previously voted in Europe to elect the minister and other church officers—although there is little evidence that any Strangers or crew members had ever participated in any type of election.

Without question, they all took it seriously; their lives depended on it. They had committed themselves to a unique form of government in which they would pick the person who would lead them into the unknown. Before they had left Europe, John Robinson, the pastor of the Separatist church in Leiden, Holland, which many of them attended, had cautioned them to be careful when choosing their leaders. As they were "not furnished with any persons of special eminency above the rest," he said, meaning that there was no one with sufficient rank or experience in government leadership to be the obvious choice, they should select men who "diligently promote the common good."

There were several candidates. Christopher Martin apparently expected to be put in charge. Martin was a leader of the Strangers, having been hired by the investors to serve as "treasurer agent" in charge of purchasing provisions. In fact, the company had appointed him governor of the *Mayflower* during the voyage. But suspicions about his spending had been raised, especially after he refused to show his records to anyone. During the voyage his arrogance and often overbearing manner had alienated many passengers, and early in the voyage the passengers voted to replace him and selected John Carver as their leader.

The very wealthy Carver had been a deacon of the Church in Holland and a close associate of John Robinson. He had helped negotiate the contract with the Virginia Company, even investing a substantial amount of his own money.

William Brewster was among the most senior and respected Puritans. Having been the church elder in Holland, he had become their religious leader on the voyage, while also earning the respect of the Strangers.

Although mostly self-educated, William Bradford was admired by all the passengers for his range of knowledge—he spoke several languages—his warm nature, and reasonable approach to issues.

As had been done for years in church elections, each of the forty-one men had one vote. The tally was never reported, but John Carver was elected governor of the New Plymouth Colony. By some reports, it was unanimous. No one disputed it. While elections for representatives had taken place in Jamestown, this election was arguably the first democratic election of a government leader in America.

Now Carver's real task began, translating the broad principles of the compact into a viable government structure. Plymouth's government initially consisted of a governor and assistant governor elected annually, but within a few years, that was expanded to include five assistant governors, which became known as the governor's council or, in deference to the monarchy, the "court of assistants." These "magistrates" advised the governor and voted on issues affecting the colony. All the other signers of the compact met as a General Court; this was a rudimentary legislature similar in construction to Jamestown's General Assembly. But the comparison ended there: While Plymouth's governor and his assistants presided over this gathering, the freemen—the citizens—voted on the laws, tried court cases, and advised their leaders. In Jamestown, the governor had been given almost dictatorial powers; he could impose harsh penalties to enforce laws made in England by the company. The settlers in Jamestown had little say in their own government. Conversely, the Plymouth colonists were careful not to allow anyone to have too much power.

Isaac Allerton was elected the first assistant governor, and Myles Standish was elected commander of its militia. As Plymouth was settling, Standish organized its defenses, supervised the construction of fortifications, and eventually led expeditions against local tribes.

Only months after becoming governor, Carver collapsed while working in the fields and died a few days later. Bradford was elected to replace him and served as governor on and off for the next several decades. It was his leadership that would save Plymouth.

Almost half of all the passengers and crew died of malnutrition, disease, or exposure to the elements during the first "sharp and violent [winter]," according to Bradford. It was only with the assistance and guidance of the local Native American tribes that the colony survived. And, against all odds, gradually grew into a prosperous, self-sustaining settlement.

While there were some obvious similarities between Plymouth and Jamestown, which were about 460 miles apart, in reality they were quite different. Jamestown was founded to be a profitable business; Plymouth was created as a religious refuge. The majority of settlers in Jamestown were single men, there to make their fortune, while the *Mayflower* carried twenty-six families, eighteen married women, three of them pregnant, coming there to establish a home and community. Jamestown was governed under a charter by representatives appointed by the Virginia Company, although it began allowing limited participation by the settlers in 1619; Plymouth was self-governed by the compact signed before its residents set foot on land. Jamestown initially was a profit-driven venture, all the property owned by the company; although that changed about 1616 when settlers were given three acres each to grow their own crops. Plymouth was founded with the understanding that after seven years, the colonists would own the land they worked.

The Mayflower Compact made all the difference. It was an agreement made by necessity, drawn up in a few hours; no one could have imagined it would have an historic impact and eventually be considered a significant step in the creation of a democracy. The right to vote, as it had been in most places throughout history, was granted only to free white men over the age of twenty-one. However, holding land or property was not a requirement as it had often been in other societies.

The right to vote was a valuable privilege. When new settlers arrived in 1623, for example, they were permitted to settle there only after consenting to follow the laws of the colony and pay an annual tax—but apparently, they were not granted the right to vote, although they were compelled to attend the annual sessions of the General Court. Anyone not attending was heavily fined. Only after the colony had expanded to distant towns, making the journey difficult, was that requirement dropped.

Within a few years of Plymouth's founding, rumors were spreading in England that some form of democracy had taken hold there. To calm those fears, Governor Bradford actually wrote a reassuring letter stating flatly that those stories were false, because women and children were not allowed to vote in the colony.

The colony had been founded to ensure religious freedom—for Separatists. Catholics were not welcome to live there. Quakers were refused citizenship. Nonbelievers were harassed and on occasion, expelled.

But the essence of the Mayflower Compact survived, and the experiment in self-government was a success. By 1636, the one hundred settlers had grown into a community of almost three thousand people. It was time to codify the laws by which they had been living. These "General Fundamentals" are considered the first written legal code in North America. Essentially a rudimentary bill of rights, it guaranteed the right to vote in free elections, the right to trial by jury, and the right of the government to levy taxes, as well as specifying punishments for an array of crimes.

It began by acknowledging that they were loyal subjects "of the kingdom of England," and retained all the rights of British citizens. But the very first article was a declaration of the colony's right of self-rule, reading "That no act, imposition, law or ordinance be made or imposed upon us at present or to come, but such as has been or shall be enacted by the consent of the body of freemen or associates, or their representatives legally assembled; which is according to the free liberties of the freeborn people of England."

The second article enshrined the right to elect their own leaders, "And for the well Governing this Colony: It is Resolved and Ordered, that there be a free Election annually, of Governour, Deputy Governour and Assistants, by the Vote of the Freemen of this Corporation. Justice to be equally and speedily administered."

These laws permitted the courts to impose the death penalty for a variety of crimes, including murder, treason, arson, and witchcraft. Lesser penalties included a fine or several hours in the stocks—public humiliation—for cursing God or lying in public. These laws also made it a crime for members of the militia to attend church without a loaded musket—for defense against surprise attacks from Native Americans—not to vote in certain elections, or to harbor a Quaker.

The General Court, acting as a quasi-legislature, voted to approve the Fundamental Orders. They were periodically updated, but the government structure and laws that were derived from the Mayflower Compact remained in force until Plymouth merged with the larger Massachusetts Bay Colony in 1691.

Almost a century later, when the Continental Convention was determining how the new country, the United States of America, would be governed, it drew on the fundamental principles embodied in that agreement: The people would have the right of self-government, to make the laws by which they would live. That government existed to carry out the will of the people, rather than impose its will on the people. That government would derive its power from the consent of the people, who would express their desires through regular, fair elections in which the will of the majority ruled. The responsibility for the exercise of that power would be shared, with no single individual, no monarch, having the right to impose his will on the people.

Both the Declaration of Independence and the Constitution

of the United States drew upon those principles to create the new form of government that would become a model for democracies throughout the world. As William Bradford had written more than a century earlier, "Thus out of small beginnings greater things have been produced by His hand . . . as one small candle may light a thousand, so the light here kindled hath shone onto many."

FOUR

1796 and 1800: Adams vs. Jefferson

GIANTS WALKED THE EARTH in 1776. And in their wake, they left history—and a great nation.

The colonists had come to the new land in small boats, sailing by the stars. With little more than courage, determination, and sometimes desperation they had fought nature, they had fought enemies, they had fought an empire—and had survived. Their settlements had grown into cities and pioneers were pushing westward; they had established a thriving economy and created a spirited society; their revolution against a king had become an inspiration for people throughout the rest of the world.

Now came the hard part.

Initially, the thirteen English colonies in America had not sought independence—they wanted respect. But the British government had ignored their pleas; it continued to exercise its control, regulating trade and imposing unreasonable duties—taxes—on a variety of imported goods. Without representation in Parliament, the colonists had no means to fight back. Over time, and out of frustration, a growing mountain of petitions, pamphlets, and speeches were transformed into action. On the night of December 16, 1773, a secret organization called the Sons of Liberty dumped forty-five tons of tea into Boston Harbor.

In an attempt to quell the rising dissent, Parliament passed a series of punitive laws—dubbed by the Americans the Intolerable Acts—which instead further inflamed the situation. The colonists responded by forming the First Continental Congress; delegates from twelve of the thirteen colonies met in Philadelphia in 1774 to try to negotiate a peaceful resolution with the crown—while demonstrating America's own economic power by organizing a boycott of British goods.

Their efforts to reach a compromise failed, and just after dawn on April 19, 1775, the first shots of the Revolutionary War were fired on the village green in Lexington.

The thirteen independent colonies were at war against one of the world's most powerful nations without a functioning central government able to raise the necessary funds, organize the militia, appoint military leaders, and negotiate treaties. Weeks after the fighting began, the Second Continental Congress assembled in Philadelphia to coordinate the war effort—and create that government. Among the delegates appointed or elected by their state legislatures were George Washington, Thomas Jefferson, Benjamin Franklin, John Hancock, and John Adams.

On July 4, 1776, the Continental Congress adopted the Declaration of Independence. The "United Colonies" officially became the United States of America. It was an extraordinarily courageous act. The fifty-six men who signed it put their lives at risk, and then they set out to achieve the seemingly impossible: create a new government structure so enticing that thirteen independent states would voluntarily surrender at least some of their rights to unite in a single national body.

There was no model for it. The vast majority of people in the world were still living under the rule of powerful monarchs. There also were a number of constitutional monarchies, governments in which the ruler's power was tempered by a body of advisors, as well as several smaller republics. The only comparable contemporary nation was Switzerland, a loose confederacy of thirteen independent cantons, each with its own form of government; beginning hundreds of years earlier, the cantons had formed an alliance for their mutual defense, but they had no central government or leadership body.

To loosely bind the states together, the Second Continental Congress had cobbled together bits and pieces of history, philosophy, logic, and common sense to produce the Articles of Confederation, a weak document that established "a firm league of friendship" in which "each state retains its sovereignty, freedom and independence, and every power, jurisdiction, and right which is not by this confederation expressly delegated to the United States."

The central government was given little real power. It consisted of a congress in which each state, no matter how large or small, had one vote. Rather than empowering an executive branch, Congress would appoint a president for a one-year term. This central government was granted the sole authority to declare war, negotiate peace, and conduct some foreign relations, but that power was almost meaningless, as it had no right to levy taxes on the states, regulate commerce, or even enforce the little power it had. It was, as George Washington accurately described, "little more than the shadow without the substance."

The Articles of Confederation proved too weak to unite thirteen states with widely different economies, priorities, and requirements. Although Congress elected a "president of the

United States in Congress Assembled," it was essentially a ceremonial position. Its real value was to demonstrate to the states that they were stronger if they bound themselves together, and that it was possible to do that without giving up all of their sovereignty. The Constitutional Convention that met in 1787, just a few years after the revolution was won, quickly abandoned any attempt to strengthen the existing document and began writing a new constitution.

It took 116 days to draft an acceptable compromise, a constitution that allowed the states to retain sufficient independence while empowering a central government. Numerous different structures were presented and debated. Should the executive be one man or a committee? Should the legislature be one body or two? How should power be apportioned between large and small states to ensure a measure of equal representation? What rights were guaranteed? What checks should be placed on the central government? What laws or regulations could this body impose on individual states? It was an extraordinary balancing act.

The convention worked in secret; members were prohibited from taking notes or speaking with outsiders, which allowed delegates to speak openly and boldly with one another without concern for repercussions or pressure from private interests. As a result, no one knew what compromises had been reached. At the conclusion of the convention a woman confronted Benjamin Franklin and asked what type of government had been formed. His response has resonated through history. "A republic," he responded, then added the warning, "If you can keep it."

This creation was unique. There had never been anything like it. This first written constitution in history created three branches of a central government: an executive; a bicameral legislature, in which one body gave states equal power regardless of size while the other would be responsive to the will of the majority; and an independent judiciary. Each branch had specific powers—but the other branches, and the states, had mechanisms to limit the way those powers were used.

It included a novel quirk: To protect the interests of the smaller states, which feared being trampled by those states with larger populations, rather than the president being elected directly by the people, each state was given a number of electoral votes based on population. Electors, the men who would actually cast these votes, would gather as an "electoral college" and pick the president and vice president. Each elector had two votes, and while supposedly one would be cast for a president, the other for the vice president, both votes had equal weight. There was no provision for determining which vote was for which office. Each state had the authority to decide how to select these electors; some of them were appointed by the state legislature, others were elected by the citizens of that state.

Whatever the manner of selection, there was no question who the first president would be. The enormously popular General George Washington was the unanimous choice. In fact, Washington was so popular that years earlier Colonel Lewis Nicola had suggested that he should become King of the United States. In response, Washington vehemently rejected that idea, writing, "If you have any regard for your Country, concern for yourself or posterity—or respect for me . . . banish these thoughts from your mind." John Adams was elected vice president. There were no political parties and no structured campaign.

In 1792 a somewhat reluctant President Washington was convinced to run for a second term, as the new central government still needed a strong and popular leader to hold it together. But cracks in the system were beginning to appear. While Washington once again was unanimously elected, Vice President Adams was challenged by Thomas Jefferson's Democratic-Republican faction, which represented the growing number of people who believed the central government was growing too strong. Although Adams won, two opposing factions were coalescing around the unsettled question of exactly how power would be shared between the national government and state governments.

That debate became a key issue in 1796, the first contested presidential election in American history. In September, two months before the election, Washington had stunned the young nation by announcing he would not seek a third term. It was an extraordinary commitment to democratic principles, enshrining the peaceful transition of power as a hallmark of American government. Immediately Adams, Jefferson, and several other distinguished men became candidates for the office.

America's first two political parties, the Federalists and the Democratic-Republicans, developed from the debate around the balance of power. In his Farewell Address, Washington had warned against the formation of partisan parties, calling them "potent engines, by which cunning, ambitious and unprincipled men will be enabled to subvert the power of the people and to usurp for themselves the reins of government."

John Adams concurred, having written in 1780, "There is nothing I dread so much, as a Division of the Republick into two great Parties, each arranged under its Leader, and concerting Measures in opposition to each other. This, in my humble Apprehension is to be dreaded as the greatest political Evil, under our Constitution." Those fears made no difference. The Federalist Party had been formed to support a strong central government. Led by Adams and Alexander Hamilton, it supported a manufacturing-based economy and advocated for a national bank, a strong standing army and navy, and the right of the government to levy taxes. Jefferson and James Madison had organized the Democratic-Republican party to oppose some of Washington's policies; the party supported an agricultural-based economy in which the states retained their essential rights against a central government with limited powers. The Federalists favored the educated and wealthy elite and wanted to restrict voting and holding office to landowners, while the Democratic-Republicans wanted all white males to be eligible to vote and serve in office.

The entire 1796 campaign lasted only seven weeks. The Federalists nominated Vice President Adams and Thomas Pinckney. The Democratic-Republicans united behind Washington's former Secretary of State Jefferson and Aaron Burr. Both Adams and Jefferson had been among the leaders in the fight for independence and the creation of the new government. They already had made giant footprints in history.

John Adams had been born on a Massachusetts farm, the son of a church deacon. He and his second cousin, Samuel Adams, had helped spark the revolution with their speeches and writing. John Adams had then spent a decade representing American interests in Europe, helping negotiate the postwar peace treaty with Great Britain and obtaining loans necessary to maintain the government. As a member of the Continental Congress, he worked with Jefferson to draft the Declaration of Independence, and his writing laid the philosophical groundwork for the Constitution. Having served two terms as Washington's vice president, he seemed the natural successor to the presidency.

Thomas Jefferson was the son of a wealthy Virginia plantation owner. His inspiring political pamphlets, among them *A Summary View of the Rights of Man*, were instrumental in building support for the revolution. Jefferson was also acknowledged as the primary author of the Declaration of Independence. During the war, while serving as the acting Governor of Virginia, he barely escaped capture when British forces reached his plantation, Monticello. Afterward, he succeeded Benjamin Franklin as minister to France, then became America's first Secretary of State.

The election of 1796 was the beginning of the effort, now 250 years old and counting, to find an acceptable balance between the power of the federal government and the states. Adams and Jefferson had become close friends while working together to create and draft the Declaration of Independence, but their very different visions for America had driven them apart. It was a short, bitter campaign. The Federalists attacked Jefferson as an immoral atheist. A Federalist newspaper leaked the rumor that the slave-owning Jefferson was having an affair with one of his slaves and claimed that if he was elected, he would free all the slaves and steer the country into another war against England. Conversely, a Democratic-Republican paper described Adams as an aristocrat, a monarchist who intended to have his son follow him as president, calling him a "champion for kings, ranks and titles," in addition to criticizing his weight and dubbing him "His Rotundity."

The Constitution allotted two votes to every elector. At the time and until several years later, the candidate receiving the most votes became president, the person with the next highest total became his vice president. With the then sixteen states participating, Adams received seventy-one electoral votes and was elected the second president of the United States. Jefferson received sixty-eight electoral votes and became the vice president. For the first and only time in American history, the president and vice president represented different parties. "Mr. Adams is President, Mr. Jefferson Vice President," Hamilton wrote. "The Lion and the Lamb are to lie down together."

Adams's Federalist party also won control of Congress, winning fifty-seven House seats compared to forty-nine won by the Democratic-Republicans, and twenty-two Senate seats as opposed to ten members of the opposition.

On March 4, 1797, Adams was inaugurated in Philadelphia's Congress Hall. According to the Congressional Record, to demonstrate his support, George Washington "took a seat as a private citizen," and at the end of the ceremony deliberately walked behind the new president to demonstrate his respect. In Adams's inaugural address, he emphasized his strong support for the Constitution, perhaps in response to the Democratic-Republicans' attacks. "The operation of it has equaled the most sanguine expectations of its friends," he said. "I have acquired an habitual attachment to it and veneration for it.

"What other form of government, indeed, can so well deserve our esteem and love?" There was no other form of government "more pleasing, more noble, majestic or august" than a government "by citizens selected at regular periods, by their neighbors, to make and execute laws for the general good."

Vice President Jefferson also took his oath of office that day and also praised the Constitution—but with a very different emphasis, saying, "I consider the union of these states the first of its blessings."

George Washington's exploits had made him the nation's hero. He'd defeated the mighty British. He'd led the Constitutional Convention. It was almost considered sacrilege to attack him, his policies—or the Constitution. Adams was far more vulnerable; he had no such reservoir of goodwill. During his administration, the Constitution had been tested—and its defects were becoming visible. The debate over the disposition of rights between the federal government and the states—the core issue in creating the new government—remained unsettled. Bitter arguments continued. The election of 1800 was going to define the rights, institutions, and electoral mechanisms embodied in that document. It would become, Jefferson said later, "a revolution in the principles of government . . . as that of 1776 in its form."

Once again, it was Adams facing Jefferson. But this time, the Federalist nominee for vice president was South Carolina diplomat Charles Cotesworth Pinckney, while the Democratic-Republican candidate was once again Revolutionary War hero and New York Senator Aaron Burr.

Perhaps fittingly, it was the First Amendment to the Constitution, which among other rights guaranteed freedom of speech and freedom of the press, that became a focal point of the election. The right to criticize the government and government officials with spoken words or on paper was considered the bedrock of democracy. For centuries, it had been the first right that kings and dictators had restricted.

The Federalists had tested the extent of the First Amendment by passing the Alien and Sedition Acts in 1798. The spirit of this young nation, with its promise of freedom, had attracted tens of thousands of immigrants, a great number of them from Britain, Ireland, and France, looking for economic opportunity or escaping political or religious repression. America needed these people and welcomed them. The Naturalization Act of 1790 required only two years of residency to become a citizen—which then gave them the right to vote.

Unfortunately for the Federalists, these immigrants tended to support the Democratic-Republican party. Fearing their growing influence, and their votes, in 1798 the Federalists passed new naturalization laws which required fourteen years residency before an alien could become a citizen and prohibited people from countries at war with America—or even threatening war, France, for example—from becoming citizens.

Jefferson was furious, declaring these laws were "a most detestable thing . . . worthy of the 8th or 9th century."

A month later the Federalist Congress passed the Sedition Act, which made it a crime to "print, utter, or publish . . . any false, scandalous, and malicious writing" about the government, Congress or the president, giving Adams the power to arrest or deport any alien he claimed was a threat to the country. It was an astonishing piece of legislation that appeared to limit the rights that made this country different from every other nation on earth.

The Federalists defended it by claiming it was necessary to prevent people from undermining the government with lies and propaganda during a vulnerable time as war loomed with France. Democratic-Republicans countered angrily by calling it an unconstitutional and partisan attack on free speech and a dangerous attempt to extend the power of the federal government.

Adams's government also had angered Americans by imposing a federal tax on land, houses, and slaves—fifty cents for each slave between the age of twelve and fifty—to fund the coming war. When farmers in eastern Pennsylvania resisted, Adams dispatched federal troops to quell their uprising. Thirty-one men were arrested—their leader was convicted of treason and sentenced to hanging. While Adams pardoned all of the protestors several months before the election, he still paid a significant political price. The imposition of a federal tax infuriated voters—in addition to people concerned that the federal government was becoming too powerful, members of his own party were furious he had issued any pardons. That was, wrote Hamilton, "the most inexplicable part of Mr. Adams's conduct." The tax had been intended to raise $2 million—but the political damage it caused was incalculable.

The rancorous tone of the 1796 campaign burst fully formed into the 1800 election, which was a roughly equal mix of policy differences and personal attacks. Supporters of both parties firmly believed the election of the opposition would lead to the nation's ruin—and did everything possible to prevent it. The policy issues were broad. Did the people want a powerful federal government or did they favor stronger states' rights? Did they want a central bank to control the nation's finances or agree with Jefferson that that institution would favor the wealthy over agrarian interests? Did they support Adams's pro-British positions or Jefferson's defense of France? Did they believe the First Amendment restrictions of the Alien and Sedition Acts were necessary for the nation's security, or a dangerous abridgement of fundamental Constitutional rights? These were all significant issues that would help determine the future course of America.

But eventually, the campaign got deep into the mud: The campaign was fought primarily through partisan newspapers, which had learned four years earlier that sensationalism sells papers. They battled for readers by flinging wild attacks at the opposition, printing scathing stories and making outrageous claims. Jefferson was described as an "artful, intriguing, industrious and double-faced politician" who could not be trusted, a man who had engaged in an affair with a slave and fathered her child. Should he win, warned one Federalist newspaper, "Murder, robbery, rape, adultery, and incest will be openly taught and practiced, the air will be rent with the cries of the distressed, the soil will be soaked with blood, and the nation black with crimes."

Meanwhile, Adams was described as "a hideous hermaphroditical character," who had "neither the force and firmness of a man, nor the gentleness and sensibility of a woman." Supposedly, it was claimed, he had proposed a marriage between his daughter and King George III's son—and dropped the effort only after Washington threatened him.

Jefferson was an atheist who would destroy Bibles, Adams a religious zealot who would inflict his Bible on the nation. The truth made no difference; demonizing your opponent proved to be a valuable campaign weapon.

States used two forms of voting: The traditional viva voce, simply standing up and declaring one's choice, which was then written down by a clerk. But by 1800, the political parties had also begun printing and handing out ballots listing their candidates or electors. Voters supporting that party would deposit its colorful straight party ticket into a ballot box. There was no secret voting, so voters were still subject to intimidation.

The Constitution permitted states to determine who could vote in their elections. In most states, that was white males over twenty-one. But New Jersey's state constitution granted the right to vote to all property holders regardless of race or gender. As a result, women and people of color participated in the election.

Democratic-Republican Jefferson won the popular vote in a landslide. Although popular votes were not officially recorded, it was estimated Jefferson got about 60 percent of those votes. Officially, he received seventy-three electoral votes, to Federalist Adams's sixty-five. Sixty-five.

The American people had elected their new president. Or so it seemed. The problem was that their votes, in several states, had little more weight than opinion. Under the Constitution, electors from each state, not the people, actually determined who would be president. In ten of the sixteen states, rather than the popular vote, the legislature selected the electors. The man who controlled those states would be the president, and both parties set out to manipulate that selection.

In New York, for example, Hamilton urged Governor John Jay to convene the outgoing Federalist legislature to name the state's electors before the newly elected Democratic-Republican legislature could take their seats. When Jay protested that that was not the will of the people, Hamilton responded his plan was perfectly legal and necessary "to prevent an atheist in religion and a fanatic in politics from getting possession of the helm of state." Jay simply ignored Hamilton's desperate attempt to award New York's electoral votes to Adams.

In several other states, though, the parties were successful in changing the method used to pick their electors. As each elector prepared to cast his two votes, the Democratic-Republican party believed electors from South Carolina and Georgia would cast one vote for Jefferson and their second vote for someone other than Aaron Burr, preventing a tie. For whatever reasons, that did not happen; every Democratic-Republican cast one vote for Jefferson and one vote for Burr.

A major defect in the Constitution had been exposed. The two Democratic-Republican candidates had tied for the presidency with seventy-three electoral votes each. According to Article II, Section 1, Clause 3 of the Constitution, in the event of a tie, the election would be decided by the House of Representatives. Each state would have one vote.

The House was controlled by the Federalists, who now had to choose between Democratic-Republicans Jefferson and Burr. The nation was facing its first constitutional crisis. The strength of the Constitution to hold the union together was questioned.

The House voted and voted and voted, remaining deadlocked for six days through thirty-five ballots. Some Federalists tried without success to make deals with the candidates, trading votes for modifications in their proposed policies. Hamilton, switching tacks, began strongly lobbying for Jefferson, writing "Mr. Jefferson, though too revolutionary in his notions, is yet a lover of liberty . . . Mr. Burr loves nothing but himself—thinks of nothing but his own aggrandizement—and will be content with nothing short of permanent power in his own hands . . .

"By no means, my Dear Sir, let the Federalists be responsible for his elevation—In a choice of evils let them take the least—Jefferson is in every view less dangerous than Burr." Finally, on the thirty-sixth ballot, several Federalists submitted only one vote, enabling Jefferson to become the third president of the United States.

Jefferson was to be inaugurated on March 4, 1801. It was a test of self-government. Throughout history national leaders, kings, and despots had died in office or they had been overthrown by an enemy or a revolution. Many of them had been defeated in battle or chose to abdicate due to age or infirmity, but never before had a leader peacefully handed his power to a member of the opposition and simply stepped away.

There was no hint what actions Adams, Hamilton, or other Federalists might have considered to retain power. Later in American history this handover would become routine, normal, mundane, but at this moment there were serious concerns that it might not happen. The nation was uneasy. The institutions of government were not yet firmly entrenched, and no one knew how they might respond to being challenged. It was a chaotic time; a slave rebellion in Virginia had been put down the previous summer, but there were stirrings of uprisings throughout the country. The existing partisan divisions between North and South, manufacturing and agrarian, had been exacerbated by the campaigns.

The European nations, particularly England and France, watched the proceedings with curiosity and skepticism. Many people believed this experiment in self-government would be short-lived and was doomed to failure. From across the ocean, they saw a country angrily divided by partisan interests; their own histories led them to expect chaos, perhaps leading to a collapse.

But they also viewed this event with some trepidation, especially as the horrors of the bloody French Revolution were still echoing through all the palaces of the Continent. If this new form of government took hold, if the people were able to choose their leaders, how would the impact be felt?

Adams chose not to attend the ceremony—but far more importantly he did not contest it. Very early that morning, he boarded a stagecoach and went home to Massachusetts. In his inaugural address, Jefferson tried to heal the scars left by the bitter campaign, telling his audience "every difference of opinion is not a difference of principle. We have called by different names brethren of the same principle. We are all republicans. We are all federalists."

A precedent had been set. There were no soldiers in the streets, just celebrants. There was no rioting, just calm. Instead of bloodshed, there were handshakes and celebratory fireworks. Cannons were fired in honor of the new president—sixteen rounds of artillery representing the union of sixteen states. The peaceful transfer of power from one party to another that was to become a hallmark of American democracy was done.

In addition to proving the viability of the Constitution, and the commitment to government reflecting the will of the people, the election had consequences that would change the world. The effort to amend the Constitution to preclude a similar crisis in the future began almost immediately. New Yorkers John Jay and DeWitt Clinton supported an amendment requiring electors to cast separate votes for president and vice president. What would become the Twelfth Amendment was proposed in December 1803 and ratified six months later.

The conduct and outcome of the election also solidified the role that two opposing political parties would play in every subsequent American election—as well as the incredible power negative attacks have to motivate voters. It also marked the beginning of the end of the once-powerful Federalist party as a national force, which would basically disappear within two decades.

Jefferson moved into the White House, which was still under construction, two weeks after taking office. After adding an icehouse, a European invention to keep food cool in the summer, he set to work changing the direction of the country. Somewhat ironically, while advocating policies that limited the power of the central government in favor of the states, he also nearly doubled the size of the country and supported exploration of the continent.

In 1803 Jefferson authorized the purchase of more than eight hundred thousand square miles west of the Mississippi River from France for $15 million. The Louisiana Purchase was a questionable expansion of executive power—what Jefferson and his party had campaigned against—as the Constitution did not give the president the right to either acquire territory or significantly increase the national debt. In fact, Jefferson wondered if he might need a Constitutional amendment to complete the deal.

Adams certainly would have proceeded differently, and there is no way of knowing what the outcome would have been. For example, Adams did not share Jefferson's support for the French Revolution. He had been against it, fearing the anarchy it would create, while Jefferson had been a strong supporter. During Adams's administration relations with France had become strained, almost to the point of war, while the US increased trade with England. Officially, America under Adams remained neutral in the French and British conflicts, but Adams's fellow Federalists had tried to push the president into war with France.

Napoleon clearly preferred Jefferson, describing him as a "virtuous enlightened man . . . a friend of liberty and equality," which may well have allowed negotiations to go forward rapidly and smoothly. Eventually, eight new states were carved out of the Louisiana Purchase, while land from the territory became part of seven more states. When the deal was completed,

Tennessee politician Andrew Jackson wrote, "Every face wears a smile, and every heart leaps with joy."

In addition to obvious strategic and economic benefits—and ending the French presence in America—Jefferson's actions supported the concept that the president had implied powers, powers not specifically granted by the Constitution, to make decisions necessary for the security of the country. The doctrine of implied powers greatly increased the power of the office.

Jefferson almost immediately dispatched Meriwether Lewis and William Clark to explore and map the new territory while also searching for a water route across the entire continent. Their much-heralded expedition led to increased trade and ignited national excitement over westward expansion.

The election of 1800 signaled a fundamental change in both American and world politics. It proved the resiliency of a new type of government structure. It demonstrated that government could turn the will of the people into policy. It was, as Jefferson would soon write, "a new chapter in the history of man."

FIVE

1860:
The Election of Abraham Lincoln

AMERICA WAS A NOBLE EXPERIMENT. Nothing like it had ever been tried before. Could people from many different countries of the world, people who spoke different languages, who practiced different religions, who had grown up in different cultures, live together in harmony for the greater good? "The establishment of our new government," wrote George Washington, "seemed to be the last great experiment for promoting human happiness, by reasonable compact, in civil Society."

The country's unique form of government was a challenge to human nature, requiring individuals to voluntarily subvert their own needs, desires, and at times even their economic welfare to the will of the majority. As John Adams warned in an 1814 letter, previous similar efforts had failed: "Democracy has never been and never can be so durable as Aristocracy or Monarchy . . ." he'd written. "Democracy never lasts long. It soon wastes, exhausts and murders itself. There never was a democracy yet that did not commit suicide . . .

"When clear Prospects are opened before vanity, pride, avarice or ambition, for their easy gratification, it is hard for the most considerate phylosophers and the most conscientious Moralists to resist the temptation."

The Roman Empire had collapsed upon itself, a victim of government corruption, economic inequality, internal violence, and civil wars magnified by barbarian attacks. Athens had survived several attempts at political upheaval before being defeated by Philip II of Macedonia. Venice had been conquered by Napoleon.

Democracy might well be, as Plato described it, "a charming form of government." But eventually, he wrote, it would always fail: "Tyranny by its very nature arises from democracy, and the worst form of tyranny and servitude proceeds from the highest and most extreme liberty."

By the 1850s, the American experiment was in grave jeopardy, on the verge of being ripped apart by economic interests competing with moral beliefs. Around the world governments—and people—were watching with great interest, aware that the fate of this effort might well affect them. At that time, most countries were still ruled by a select few who determined what rights their citizens might enjoy. The failure of the American experiment would be a vindication of authoritarian rule.

It was a time for those governments to be cautious. The world around them was changing rapidly; the telegraph had made near-instant communications between different places possible for the first time, and steam-powered printing presses enabled publishers to produce affordable books and circulate newspapers to a mass readership. Railroads had made travel between cities and towns newly practical, while steamships had revolutionized commerce. The invention of the sewing machine, the cotton gin, and powerful looms had led to the creation of a massive textile industry. The Bessemer process made inexpensive steel readily available and sparked construction. People had access to new ideas, new possibilities. And dreams can be dangerous to entrenched institutions.

In America, these innovations had amplified the debate over slavery. Slavery was the foundation of the nation's economy, its leading industry. By 1860 almost four million enslaved people were working on forty-six thousand plantations, their value greater than all the railroads, factories, mills, and banks combined. The two billion pounds of cotton they produced annually accounted for more than half of all exports.

The reality of slavery, treating human beings as property and forcing them to provide labor, often by brutal treatment, was older than recorded history. Babylonian King Hammurabi's code, inscribed in stone about 1750 BC, laid out a set of laws governing the slave trade. For example, "If any one takes a male or female slave of the court, or a male or female slave of a freed man, outside the city gates, he shall be put to death."

In those early societies, someone might become enslaved by being captured in war, sentenced for a crime, or being the child of enslaved people. But by the sixteenth century, slavery had become a profitable business, as European explorers began selling captured Africans. The colonization of the Americas created a demand for slave labor; in 1526 Spain sent the first hundred Africans to a settlement in the South. Within months they escaped and took refuge with Native American tribes. But the slave trade had begun in America.

The English slave trade in the New World began in August 1619, when the *White Lion* traded "Twenty and odd" enslaved people from Africa to the Jamestown colony in exchange for food and supplies. In 1641, Massachusetts recognized slavery as a legal institution. By 1700, it was roughly estimated there were as many as twenty thousand African slaves in the colonies.

But the effort to abolish slavery as morally evil, as a sin, also took root in colonial America. Massachusetts Quakers began protesting treating people as property in 1657, believing it was an affront to the Golden Rule. The 1688 Germantown Quaker Petition Against Slavery was the first written abolitionist protest, although it attracted few supporters.

As slavery grew in Europe and the Americas, so did the abolitionist movements. Spurred by religious leaders and moral philosophers, as well as by increasingly violent slave rebellions and economic problems, Great Britain first declared that slavery had no basis in English law in 1772, although it did not outlaw slavery in its colonies until 1834, when Parliament passed the Slavery Abolition Act. France attempted to abolish slavery in 1794. After Napoleon reinstated it, it was permanently outlawed in all its forms in 1848. Spain began doing away with slavery in 1811, although it took decades before it was finally eradicated.

American abolitionists faced a far more complex reality. There would have been no United States if the Founders had not acknowledged and accepted slavery as part of the nation's fabric. While the Constitution did not specifically address the legality of slavery, it included the three-fifths compromise, in which every five slaves would be counted as three people for purposes of congressional representation and taxation. It also included language requiring escaped slaves to be returned to their owner and prohibiting Congress from outlawing the international slave trade for twenty years. Without these provisions, the Southern states would in all likelihood have rejected the union. Almost a century later, journalist and abolitionist

William Lloyd Garrison declared the Constitution as "an agreement with hell" and burned a copy of it.

For more than seven decades, from the signing of the Constitution to Lincoln's era, Congress had struggled to mollify both sides. It was an extraordinary balancing act, the preservation of the union in exchange for keeping people in chains. Money versus morality. Jefferson, a champion of liberty but also a slave owner, wrote of the contradiction: "Justice is in one scale, and self-preservation in the other."

In 1808 Congress banned the importation of African slaves—but with tens of thousands of children being born into slavery every year, it no longer was necessary. The country handled expansion by admitting one state or territory in which slavery would be permitted with an equal state or territory in which it would be banned. For example, in 1820 Missouri was admitted as a slave state, and Maine as a free state. But as the country continued to grow and transportation and communication brought its people closer together, it became increasingly difficult to forge those compromises.

The 1850 Fugitive Slave Act, which required Northerners to return escaped slaves, had been passed in response to the success of the Underground Railroad and had brought slave catchers into Northern cities. Many people who had willfully ignored the horrors of slavery were confronted by it in 1852 with the publication of Harriet Beecher Stowe's novel, *Uncle Tom's Cabin*, which sold more copies in nineteenth-century America than any book other than the Bible.

When Congress passed the Kansas-Nebraska Act in 1854, which granted settlers in those territories the right to institute slavery, abolitionists in the North responded by founding a new political party, the Republicans. Among the early supporters of that party, which accepted slavery where it existed but adamantly opposed its expansion into the west, was an Illinois lawyer and former one-term congressman named Abraham Lincoln.

The Republicans nominated western explorer John C. Frémont for president in the election of 1856 against Democrat James Buchanan. Republicans promised "Free Speech, Free Press, Free Soil, Free Men," while the Democratic platform supported "popular sovereignty," the right of each state to decide if slavery would be permitted. Buchanan won the election, but Frémont carried eleven Northern states.

The thirteen states that had fought the revolution and ratified the Constitution had now grown into thirty-one states divided by economic interests—the agrarian South versus the industrial North. It was becoming obvious that the string of compromises that had held the country together was no longer possible. In accepting the Republican nomination for the Senate in 1858, Lincoln acknowledged that the time had come for the nation to decide its future—or collapse. "A house divided against itself cannot stand," he warned, quoting the Bible. "I believe this government cannot endure permanently half slave and half free. I do not expect the Union to be dissolved—I do not expect the house to fall—but I do expect it will cease to be divided. It will become all one thing, or all the other."

The presidential election of 1860 promised to be a referendum on the future of the country—and determine if these states would stay united.

The question was debated in 1858 in a remarkable series of seven debates between the candidate Lincoln and incumbent Democratic Senator Stephen Douglas. While in actuality these men were running against each other for the Senate, their verbal conflict also served as a prelude to the 1860 presidential election. President Buchanan had announced he would not seek a second term, and both Lincoln and Douglas were potential candidates for that office. These debates captured national attention. No event in American history had received such extensive coverage from the nation's estimated three thousand newspapers. The telegraph and the use of shorthand enabled papers across the nation to publish complete transcripts literally within a day.

Lincoln and Douglas had known and respected each other for decades. Both men had courted Mary Todd, who supposedly turned down Douglas's marriage proposal in 1842 to marry Lincoln. Four years earlier the two men actually had previously debated the Kansas-Nebraska Act at the Springfield State Fair, and then days later in Peoria. As the *Chicago Tribune* reported about that encounter, "It would be impossible . . . to give an idea of the strength of Mr. Lincoln's argument . . . The effect produced on the listeners was magnetic. No one who was present will ever forget the power and vehemence of the following statement: 'My distinguished friend says it is an insult to the emigrants to Kansas and Nebraska to suppose they are not able to govern themselves . . . I admit that the immigrant to Kansas and Nebraska is competent to govern himself, but—' the speaker rising to his full height '—I deny his right to govern any other person without that person's consent!'"

Lincoln eventually would be acclaimed for ending slavery in America and granting citizenship to former slaves, but initially, at least, that was not his stated intention. During his debates with Douglas, Lincoln proved to be an adept politician, arguing against allowing slavery in new territories while accepting it where it existed, calling for liberty for all without supporting racial equality for slaves. In the town of Quincy, he told twelve thousand listeners, "I am as much as any other man in favor of having the superior position assigned to the white race." He was not in favor of citizenship for enslaved people, he admitted. The Declaration of Independence, he told five thousand people in Alton, was "intended to include all men, but they did not mean to declare all men equal in all respects."

Douglas, conversely, was a firm supporter of states' rights, believing that the slavery decision should be made by the white residents of a state rather than the federal government. Although Lincoln won the popular vote in that senatorial election, Illinois state legislators elected Douglas to a third term in the United States Senate. But the debates transformed Lincoln into a national figure and made it clear the election of 1860 would be contested over slavery in America.

Even having received all that attention, neither Lincoln nor Douglas was assured of their party's nomination for the presidency. Lincoln's political résumé was thin, having been a state representative and a one-term congressman. His political career had begun when he was twenty-three years old, when he ran for the Illinois House of Representatives—and lost. Two years later he ran again and won his first political office.

When Republicans gathered in Chicago to pick their presidential nominee, Senator William Seward was considered the front-runner; Ohio Senator Salmon Chase also came to the convention with considerable support. But many delegates worried the radical anti-slavery views held by both men would doom the party to defeat in the election. Supporters of the more moderate Lincoln positioned him as "everybody's second choice" and the party's most electable candidate.

On the first ballot Seward received the most votes but fell short of the majority needed to win the nomination. Lincoln finished second. Normally that was when dealmaking began. But Lincoln's supporters, who had organized the convention, seated themselves between Seward and Chase voters. After the first ballot, they kept those delegates apart while making their own deals with the Chase supporters. Lincoln won the Republican nomination on the third ballot.

Douglas's path to the Democratic nomination was even more difficult. The party itself was split over slavery; Southern Democrats supported the right of states to govern themselves, while Northern Democrats remained united behind the federal government. It took two conventions and fifty-nine votes before Douglas became the candidate, but disgruntled Southern Democrats walked out and eventually nominated their own pro-slavery candidate, Buchanan's Vice President John Breckinridge.

A coalition of people dissatisfied with all the candidates also formed the Constitutional Union Party, which supported "The Union as it is, and the Constitution as it is." They nominated Tennessee slaveholder John Bell. The Radical Abolitionist Party nominated its own candidate. The upstart People's Party nominated Texas Governor Sam Houston.

The political system was in shambles.

The campaign touched on other issues, among them tariffs, immigration, and the Homestead Act, which offered western settlers free farmland and provided funding for the transcontinental railroad. All of those issues might be debated and resolved. But not the only issue that mattered: slavery.

The country seemed to have run out of ways to put off the problem. The spectacle of Southern states walking out of the Democratic convention was a harbinger of what was coming: The Southern states had been threatening for several years to secede from the union if an abolitionist Republican was elected. America as the world knew it would cease to exist.

The threat of secession had first been raised by South Carolina in 1832, during a dispute over tariffs that Southerners believed threatened not only their economy but the structure of their society. In response Congress passed a bill enabling President Andrew Jackson to send troops to South Carolina to enforce federal laws—in this case, the collection of tariffs.

A compromise had averted that crisis, but it proved that the threat of secession was a powerful weapon—and that if necessary, the North would use the US military to hold the Union together.

Lincoln's nomination was seen as a direct threat to the South. The fact that Lincoln had never said he intended to abolish slavery made little difference. The emotions surrounding slavery were intense—whether a man was for or against it, there was no stronger way of bringing voters to the polls.

Lincoln's own views about slavery had evolved slowly. He had always believed it was immoral, stating during his unsuccessful 1854 Senate campaign, "If slavery is not wrong, nothing is wrong." But he was also a realist and understood and accepted that it was the essential engine of the nation's economy. By 1860, almost 4,000,000 people were enslaved, of a total American population of about 31,400,000. The cotton picked by slaves accounted for 60 percent of the nation's exports and provided jobs for as many as 100,000 people in New England's 700 cotton mills. And he did not believe in racial integration; instead, he publicly favored voluntary deportation and worked to find ways to send willing Black men and women to Central America and Africa.

Throughout his campaign "Honest Abe," as he was known,

tried to convince Southerners—without much success—that he wanted to prevent expansion of slavery, not abolish it where it existed. But as one Tennessee newspaper wrote, "Believe there is the utmost danger to be apprehended from the election of Lincoln."

Following tradition, Lincoln did not personally campaign, instead relying on surrogates and his reputation—while Douglas became the first presidential candidate to hold rallies, during which he made long speeches attacking his rival. The campaign was especially bitter, although it was fought mostly through newspapers. Lincoln's own words were used to raise doubt about his commitment, voters were reminded of his by-then well-known "house divided" speech, and the anti-slavery words of other Republican party leaders were also used against him.

With Northern voters supporting Lincoln while the Southern vote was split between Democratic candidates, Douglas, John Breckinridge, and Constitutional Union candidate John Bell, the outcome was predictable. One Virginia newspaper reported, "We are almost without hope though of averting Lincoln's election, and if that event should overtake us our mind is clear we must revolutionize."

The day before the election, the governor of South Carolina kept the legislature in session. The *New York Daily Herald* reported, "He says he, individually, considers secession the only alternative left, that the indications show the secession of South Carolina would instantly bring about that of the entire South, and that . . . he recommends military reorganization, and that every man in the state . . . should be armed with the most efficient weapons of modern warfare."

An incredible 81.2 percent of eligible voters went to the polls, the highest turnout in American history to that point.

They voted with their voices or by depositing a colorful printed "ticket" in a wooden box or glass bowl. It was called a ticket because it resembled a train ticket; it was handed out by party members or printed in partisan newspapers and listed all of the party's candidates. There was little interest in or ability to keep a choice secret; according to English philosopher John Stuart Mill, "the voter is under an absolute moral obligation to consider the interest of the public, not his private advantage." It was felt that a secret ballot would inevitably lead to people considering their own interest above what was best for society.

There were people who suggested that this impressive number resulted from massive voter fraud, including paying people to vote, "repeaters" voting multiple times under different names, or simply stuffing the ballot box. Electoral fraud has existed as long as elections have been held. Numerous and varied methods have been used, from bribing voters to simply stealing ballot boxes. But there is little evidence it affected the ultimate outcome of this historic race.

Lincoln was not even on the ballot in ten Southern states, as the Republican party couldn't find electors willing to risk their lives by publicly supporting him. In Virginia, no printer would risk their business by creating Republican ballots. But the split in the Democratic party had made his election almost inevitable, and he won with a dismal 39.7 percent of the vote. Lincoln won eighteen free states with 180 electoral votes, but failed to win a single slave state. Douglas was second in the popular vote with 29.5 percent; although he was the only candidate to win both a free state and a slave state he finished fourth in the electoral college with only 12 electoral votes.

When the results were announced two days after the November 6 election, the South responded with fury, referring to Lincoln as "a regional president" who had not received a single electoral vote from the South. On December 20, South Carolina seceded, announcing "the Union now subsisting between South Carolina and other states, under the name of the United States of America, is hereby dissolved." Its state militia began seizing federal military instillations. Within weeks, five other states also seceded. Representatives of those states met in Montgomery, Alabama, in February and formed a new nation, the Confederate States of America. This convention elected Mississippian Jefferson Davis, who had served as both a senator and President Pierce's secretary of war, the Confederacy's provisional president. A popular election was held the following November; he ran for the office unopposed and was elected to a six-year term with 97 percent of the vote.

Efforts were made to prevent the coming war. Douglas made numerous appearances in Northern and Southern states, appealing for unity. Lincoln tried to downplay the looming crisis. It was reported that when asked what he intended to do about the situation, "he flippantly replied, 'he feared it would not last till he got to it.'"

After his election, rumors spread that some unspecified actions would be taken to prevent his inauguration. A Memphis, Tennessee, newspaper reported, "It is beyond a doubt a combination is forming to take forcible possession of the government at Washington." A plot to assassinate Lincoln before he reached the capitol was uncovered; the estimated twenty plotters "justified their acts by the example of Brutus, in ridding his country of a tyrant. One of them was accustomed to recite passages . . . in Shakespeare's play of Julius Caesar."

In his inaugural address, Lincoln tried desperately to assuage Southern fears, telling the nation "I have no purpose, directly or indirectly, to interfere with the institution of slavery in the States where it exists. I believe I have no lawful right to do so, and I have no inclination to do so." He reiterated the Republican party platform, which recognized that each state had the right, "to order and control its own domestic institutions according to its own judgment exclusively."

Douglas attended, overcoming whatever bitterness he might have felt to demonstrate his support for Lincoln—and for a peaceful resolution. During the inauguration ceremony, for example, it was noted by the press that Douglas offered to hold Lincoln's tall silk hat and did so "like an attendant" throughout his entire speech.

But Lincoln's effort to prevent the rebellion failed. "War is inaugurated," *The New York Times* announced, reporting that at four o'clock on the morning of April 12, 1861, "The batteries of Sullivan's Island, Morris Island and other points were opened on Fort Sumter."

"All the political questions that have agitated the country for eighty years must drop out of sight now," Connecticut's *Norwich Bulletin* wrote. "We are either true men or traitors. Forgetting party, we must be simply true or false to our Country."

Lincoln tried to quickly end the war and regain Southern loyalty to the Union, reiterating that he had neither the intention, nor the constitutional power, to end slavery. But events transpired against him. To gain support from Northen Democrats for the Civil War, he had placed a Democratic lawyer and politician turned soldier, General Benjamin Butler, in charge of Ft. Monroe in Virginia. One May night, three escaped slaves arrived there and asked for asylum. The next day a Confederate patrol, under a white flag, demanded their return under the Fugitive Slave Act. Butler refused, reminding them that Virginia had seceded and those laws "did not affect a foreign country."

This complicated matters for Lincoln, who insisted secession was illegal, which meant the Southern states still were entitled to the benefits of the nation's laws. The paradox became a front-page story across the nation. Butler eventually concluded that because the South had put many slaves to work aiding the Confederate army, he legally could declare them "war contraband," making them US government property. Several months later Congress codified Butler's actions as The Confiscation Act of 1861, a bill that applied to slaves who had directly aided, abetted, or promoted the Confederate army, and Lincoln eventually signed it.

That was the beginning of an extraordinary movement in which as many as five hundred thousand slaves escaped from plantations and declared themselves war contraband. In the South, Butler's declaration reinforced their fear that the Union intended to end slavery.

In the weeks following the election there was widespread hope that the rebellion would be brief and limited; Southerners confidently predicted a swift victory, believing they had a better equipped army, the advantage of the war being fought on their territory, and the reality that they were fighting for their economic survival. They also believed England and France, which needed their cotton, would recognize the Confederacy as an independent nation and might provide aid. Northerners, meanwhile, were sure their vast industrial base, network of railroads, and well-trained and equipped army would convince the South to reach a compromise after an initial display of power. In the days following the attack on Fort Sumter Lincoln issued an appeal for seventy-five thousand volunteers—to serve for ninety days.

Instead, the war became a four-year-long bloodbath during which hundreds of thousands of men died.

But through the first years of the war, Lincoln refused to support general emancipation. In September 1862, he tried to scare the South into peace by circulating a preliminary version of the Emancipation Proclamation in which all slaves in the Confederacy "shall be then, thenceforward, and forever free" if the South did not surrender by the beginning of 1863.

On January 1, after the South rejected this peace overture, Lincoln officially issued the Emancipation Proclamation, freeing any slave who could reach Union territory. The document also authorized the Union Army to enlist Black men, a huge boost to its manpower. Eventually 180,000 Black men joined the army and an additional 20,000 enlisted in the Union Navy.

The Proclamation finally shifted the Union's objective from preserving the nation to ending slavery in America. It led directly to the Thirteenth, Fourteenth, and Fifteenth Amendments, introducing the concept—if not the reality—of equal rights for an estimated four million enslaved people.

Even after emancipating the slaves, Lincoln continued to support voluntary colonization. In June 1863, for example, he signed an agreement sending freed slaves to Belize, using funds Congress had already appropriated. It would still be another year before he fully embraced the concept of liberty for all—that "all" including the former slaves.

In November 1863, four and a half months after fifty thousand Union and Confederate troops had been killed or wounded in the Battle of Gettysburg, Lincoln spoke at a ceremony dedicating that battlefield. In words that would resonate through history, he emphasized that while it was generally believed the war was being fought over slavery, in fact it was about the future of democracy. Could a nation "conceived in Liberty, and dedicated to the proposition that all men are created equal . . . long endure?" What was at stake, he concluded, was if "government of the people, by the people, for the people, shall not perish from the earth."

Europe was listening. And watching. The concept of self-government was once again on trial. America remained the only significant democratic government in the world. The war itself, their leaders believed, was evidence that democratic governments were not sustainable, that eventually self-government self-destructed as self-interest triumphed over the general welfare. In their view, investing decision-making power in a strong central leadership—which respected and considered the will of the people—ensured stability.

While England and France remained officially neutral, their economic interests and government sympathies lay with the Confederacy. Queen Victoria had declared England would remain neutral, but her government provided military advisors, warships, and some goods to the Confederacy. French emperor Napoleon III also officially remained neutral, but sold an ironclad warship to the South and took advantage of the situation to invade Mexico, installing Maximilian as its emperor.

Not surprisingly, a vast number of French and British citizens, strongly against slavery, supported the Union.

More than other European nations, Italy, which was in the midst of its own unification effort, identified with the struggle to hold the union together. As many as ten thousand Italian immigrants to America fought for the Union, while a smaller number joined the Confederate army. Early in the war, Lincoln offered Giuseppe Garibaldi, the military commander renowned for fighting to unify the Italian peninsula, the rank of major general and a command in the Union Army. *The New York Times* reported Garibaldi had responded that he would accept—but only if he was made commander in chief of the entire army and the president announced that the ultimate goal of the war was to abolish slavery. Lincoln was constitutionally commander in chief, and he could not accept the second point without alienating several border states. But Garibaldi remained a strong advocate for the Union, writing to the president, "while your tremendous courage astonishes the world, we are sadly reminded how this old Europe, which also can boast a great cause of liberty to fight for, has not found the mind or heart to equal you."

Perhaps the strongest foreign support for the Union came from Russia's Tsar Alexander II. In 1861 the Russian leader had freed that nation's serfs and introduced land reform. The tsar's representatives were quoted in newspapers as saying Russia and the United States enjoyed "a natural community of interests and sympathies." Lincoln may well have seen this emancipation process as a model for what could happen in America and kept informed about Russia's progress and the difficulties in implementing it. Alexander showed his support by sending Imperial Navy squadrons to the Union in both New York and San Francisco.

Any lingering doubt that a Union victory would result in the abolition of slavery throughout America ended during the presidential campaign of 1864. Lincoln ran on a platform of continuing to fight until the South surrendered unconditionally and then transforming the wartime Emancipation Proclamation into a permanent Constitutional amendment. The proposed Thirteenth Amendment to the Constitution read: "Neither slavery nor involuntary servitude . . . shall exist within the United States, or any place subject to their jurisdiction."

To attract Democrats who supported the Union in the war but were reluctant to vote for a Republican, the party temporarily changed its name to the National Union Party and replaced incumbent Vice President Hannibal Hamlin, a Radical Republican, with war-supporting Democrat Andrew Johnson, whom Lincoln had appointed military governor of Tennessee.

Meanwhile, the Democratic Party appealed to those people weary of the war, people who had watched with horror as casualties grew into the tens of thousands. The Democrats' platform called for an immediate ceasefire and a negotiated settlement that allowed slavery to continue in the South. It did not even demand a national reunion. As its presidential candidate, the party nominated the former commander of the Army of the Potomac, General George McClellan, who had been replaced by Lincoln two years earlier for refusing to pursue Robert E. Lee's forces after the 1862 Battle of Antietam.

During his campaign Lincoln told voters that his party had concluded he might not be the greatest or best man in America, but rather concluded, "It is not best to swap horses while crossing the river, and have further concluded that I am not so poor a horse that they might not make a botch of it in trying to swap." McClellan, meanwhile, attempted to modify the Democrats' unpopular promise of peace at any price, even if the price meant dividing the country, instead claiming that he would settle the war only after the South agreed to rejoin the Union—even if that meant slavery would continue.

Lincoln's campaign received a significant boost in September when Union troops captured Atlanta, a vitally important Confederate railroad hub and manufacturing center. That immediately boosted Northern morale, allowing people to finally envision a Union military victory to end the war.

Lincoln was reelected in a landslide. He received 55 percent of the vote, 212 of 234 electoral votes, and won twenty-two of the twenty-five states that participated, ensuring the war would be fought to the bitter, bloody end. His brief Second Inaugural Address began sketching his plans for Reconstruction. He concluded the speech with a promise that, "With malice toward none, with charity for all, with firmness in the right as God gives us to see the right . . ." he would endeavor "to bind up the nation's wounds."

Forty-two days after that second inauguration, and only five days after General Robert E. Lee surrendered the badly outnumbered remnants of his beleaguered army—Lincoln was assassinated by John Wilkes Booth, who shouted as he escaped, "*Sic semper tyrannis!*"—"Thus always to tyrants"—the line attributed to Brutus in Shakespeare's tragedy *Julius Caesar* as well as Virginia's state motto since 1776.

Secretary of War Edwin Stanton spoke for the shattered Union when he said mournfully and memorably, "Now he belongs to the ages." By that point, though, Lincoln had made his lasting imprint on the world. His election in 1860 had sparked a civil war, sending an extremely important message across the world: Democracy—and human rights—are worth fighting for, even worth dying for. The war proved that a republican form of government could survive a clash of ideologies, refuting the once-confident claims of European leaders who predicted its inevitable collapse. In several countries it stirred passions, made people believe change was possible, and caused leaders to reassess their actions.

Similar to the impact of the French Revolution, the Union

victory inspired revolutionary movements and democratic reforms across the globe. Abolitionists gained strength, and within decades, slavery had been drastically reduced. Perhaps most importantly, the United States became an international symbol of hope to oppressed peoples.

It also fundamentally changed the United States by greatly empowering the federal government. While the individual states still retained numerous rights, the central government now had the undisputed power to act for a united nation, allowing it to flex American power internationally. The war also led directly to the passage of the Thirteenth, Fourteenth, and Fifteenth Amendments, which among other things codified the principle of birthright citizenship by granting citizenship to "all persons born or naturalized in the United States," whether or not their parents were citizens, and guaranteed the right to vote to all citizens—men, at that time—regardless of "race, color, or previous condition of servitude."

Not all of the changes were positive. The failure of the Reconstruction effort under Presidents Andrew Johnson, war hero Ulysses S. Grant, and Rutherford Hayes eventually resulted in segregation of the races in the South and the imposition of Jim Crow laws, which essentially subjected former slaves and their descendants to a century of second-class citizenship.

But more than 160 years later, the impact of the 1860 election still echoes through history.

SIX

1911: The Election of Sun Yat-sen as President of China

ALMOST FIVE HUNDRED YEARS—half a millennium—before the United States Constitution was ratified, the Venetian explorer and merchant Marco Polo wrote extensively about China: The city of Kinsay "is beyond dispute the finest and the noblest in the world." The palace of the Great Khan "is the greatest palace that ever was . . . the walls are covered with gold and silver . . . The building is altogether so vast, so rich, so beautiful that no man on earth could design anything superior to it." He described an orderly, innovative culture in which countless millions of people lived in sprawling cities.

Since the beginning of recorded history, China has remained among the largest and most prosperous, mysterious, and intriguing countries in the world. When the foundations of Western civilizations were still being laid, China had already developed the fundamental concepts of an organized society. The fabled Silk Road, the network of trade routes between China and the outside world, flourished for a thousand years, spreading culture, philosophy, religion, and new inventions to developing regions. The Chinese appreciation of the human spirit, advances in rudimentary technology, integration of art and beauty into daily life, and respect for tradition and family helped shape empires and nations.

America's founding fathers took inspiration from China. Benjamin Franklin wrote admiringly, "China was the most ancient, and from long experience, the wisest of nations . . . a stronghold of creativity, knowledge and wealth," and adapted Chinese practices to develop the Franklin stove. Thomas Paine compared the philosopher Confucius to Jesus Christ as "a great moral teacher." George Washington was part of the group that in 1784 dispatched the merchant ship *Empress of China* on the first American trade mission to that country. But while they appreciated the economic success and the stability of the country, they did not take any lessons from its form of government.

From a distance across both time and geography, China was viewed as an advanced, sophisticated nation, but for much of its long history, China existed as an unruly collection of very different regions. Its vast territory and population, which spoke several distinct languages, made it extraordinarily difficult to govern. The history of "The Middle Kingdom," meaning both the "center of the world" and "the country between heaven and earth," can be traced back to 1600 BC, when it was a large monarchy surrounded by independent states with which it frequently was at war. Finally united in 221 BC, it was governed for literally thousands of years by a series of dynasties, ruled by a succession of emperors, each deemed the "Son of Heaven." It was believed that the emperor's power was granted to him by a "Mandate of Heaven," the will of the gods; in turn, the dynasty could maintain its power by governing wisely, honestly, and with respect and concern for the good of the people.

A dynasty often lasted for several hundred years. The title of emperor and the right to rule were subject to hereditary succession, passed along to the eldest son of the empress. If the emperor did not have a son, the empress dowager, either the widow or mother of the deceased emperor, would select the new ruler. Most often that was a male relative. But as with any monarchy, bitter, violent internal struggles often took place inside the Forbidden City for the Dragon Throne.

The Chinese people had no voice in the selection of their ruler.

There were no uniform restrictions on the emperor or checks on his power. Each emperor within each dynasty utilized his "divine power" to rule in any manner he desired. A large, complex bureaucracy was required to enforce the dictates of the ruler. The emperor appointed these civil servants, among them the leaders of provincial governments, all of whom were accountable to the throne. The degree to which the central government could impose its will on distant regions depended on the skill and power of the local administrators.

Each dynasty brought unpredictable and sometimes drastic change to the country. Some of them installed a highly centralized government that ruled directly over the people, while others favored a decentralized government with designated lords ruling the provinces. Some emperors were benevolent, allowing broader individual freedoms and providing opportunities for advancement based on merit, while others were harsh and demanded absolute loyalty to the throne.

A dynasty remained in power as long as it continued to please the gods. But when those gods believed a ruler was dishonest or incompetent, they expressed their anger by allowing wars to occur or creating natural disasters, earthquakes, and famines, or sparking social upheaval. A dynasty could be ended by a powerful warlord or military figure, or the leader of a rebellion—almost always by force—who would then lay claim to the Mandate of Heaven, asserting that his rise to power was evidence of divine approval.

The last imperial dynasty, the Qing dynasty, came to power in 1644 AD, when the Manchu people defeated the Ming dynasty. The Ming dynasty had ruled for 276 years, through sixteen emperors. It was finally overthrown by the Manchus, an ethnic minority from Manchuria with their own history, culture, and language, after the nation was beset by a series of administrative, agricultural, and economic failures that led to famine. The Manchus selected the name Qing after a written character that had a variety of meanings, very broadly implying vitality, clarity, and purity.

The Qing dynasty adopted many of the most successful Ming social, cultural, and political innovations, in particular employing a merit-based system to recruit and reward civil servants. The dynasty prospered in its early years, greatly expanding China's territory and population.

The Chinese government focused on internal affairs, showing little interest in the United States as it was settled and expanding—other than developing a minor trade relationship. When that first American envoy arrived in China in 1784, aboard the *Empress of China*, the Qing government refused to accept his official papers. In fact, it would be another decade before the Chinese finally recognized the first Western representative, English diplomat George Macartney, who arrived in 1793.

Slowly, the ancient Silk Road was replicated by ships sailing across oceans to establish a lucrative trading relationship.

By choice, other than developing trade China remained mostly isolated from the West. The first American missionary settled there in 1830. In 1834, the first known Chinese female immigrant to America, Afong Moy, became a national sensation. As she toured the country, even being invited to meet President Andrew Jackson, curious spectators filled exhibit halls to see the exotic "Chinese Lady" sitting on a throne in a Chinese-looking setting, eating with chopsticks, speaking and singing in Chinese, and displaying her four-inch-long "little feet," the result of foot binding.

China's relationship with the outside world began changing in 1839, when the First Opium War erupted. Facing an epidemic of opium addiction, the Qing government seized and destroyed stocks of British opium imports. Queen Victoria sent the army and navy to protect merchants. The conflict ended in 1842 with the signing of the Treaty of Nanking, which forced the Chinese to increase foreign trade, cede Hong Kong to Britain, and pay significant compensation.

Losing the Opium War to England shattered the strongly held belief in the natural superiority of the Chinese people and weakened the dynasty. It was as if a beautifully fashioned ceramic vase had been cracked—while it might be restored, it would never again be as strong. The early Christian missionaries had also brought with them Western ideas that began seeping into the culture. For three thousand years, the Chinese had known only one form of government. Now the seeds of change had been planted. Chinese scholars and intellectuals began wondering if some of those ideas might be used to strengthen the nation.

China had been smashed open to the West. Over the next

few years major Western nations established spheres of influence in port cities, in which they lived completely free of Chinese control. They made their own laws, enforced by their own police. Many Chinese were humiliated by presence of these foreigners. The inability of the Qing government to prevent the situation further eroded its credibility.

In an effort to counterbalance British influence, in 1844 China and America negotiated the Treaty of Wangxia, the "Treaty of peace, amity, and commerce," which established formal diplomatic relations between the two countries. Five Chinese ports were opened to American ships, and for the first time foreigners and foreign trading companies were allowed to own land in China. Additional provisions allowed Americans to be taught the Chinese language and guaranteed Chinese people the right to emigrate to and travel in the United States.

At its height in the eighteenth century, the Qing empire had spread and prospered across Asia. It had been ruled by a stable government that took great pride in its economic, cultural, and artistic achievements. Its enlightened foreign policy kept other nations at a distance, allowing only limited and beneficial trade. The Manchus were respected—and feared. But while the rest of the world had progressed, China had remained anchored in the traditions of the past. The Manchus had tried to hold on to their power by oppressing opponents rather than changing their policies to deal with new realities.

The Qing dynasty was rapidly losing the support of the Chinese people. Widespread famine led to civil unrest, causing many Chinese to depart to the West, where cheap labor was desperately needed. A trickle that began with the California Gold Rush in 1849 turned into a giant wave of Chinese workers and adventurers coming to the US to work on the Central Pacific Railroad in the 1860s.

Many Chinese also began emigrating to the Kingdom of Hawaii. Chinese merchants had been trading goods for island sandalwood, which was used in furniture making and for incense, for decades and strong ties had developed. Desperate Chinese people fled there to work on the sugar plantations and eventually a significant, vibrant Chinese community developed there.

Among those people who sought economic opportunity in Hawaii was Sun Mei, a peasant from a farming village who had become a wealthy merchant. In 1879, he brought his thirteen-year-old brother, Sun Yat-sen, to Honolulu to pursue his education at a British missionary school. Revolutionary ideas grow slowly, nurtured by time, place, events, education, pressures, and relationships. In Hawaii, Sun learned about the competing political and economic systems of the world and the impact they had on people.

In China, the conservative Qing government was struggling to adjust to its new reality. The Second Opium War, in which the government attempted a final stand against encroaching Western nations, had ended in 1860 in another bitter defeat and the loss of even more credibility. As the *New-York Tribune* would later report, "The Manchus, who until now have intolerably and superciliously run the affairs of the empire and controlled the destinies, even to life and death, of four hundred millions or more of Chinese people to suit themselves, are now frightened."

Young Chinese were beginning to believe change was possible. While studying at the Hong Kong College of Medicine for Chinese in the late 1880s, Sun became part of a group known as the Four Bandits, and began publicly advocating for revolution. "Divine right does not last forever," he wrote, adding, "No longer shall we have reverence for the throne. The Son of Heaven is incompetent. His offices are corrupt. His rule is an abomination. He shall give way to the will of the people."

Rather than continuing his medical career, Dr. Sun joined with other young Chinese to foment revolution. Initially, he attempted to provoke peaceful change; in 1894 he wrote and widely circulated a letter to Viceroy Li Hongzhang, a highly respected statesman and military leader, outlining a plan to modernize China. "The wealth and power of the European nations are the result not only of their having ships and powerful guns . . . but also because their people can fully employ their talents, their land can be fully utilized, their natural resources can be fully tapped and their goods can freely flow. These four elements are the basis of a nation's wealth and strength and the root of good government." He included a series of proposals to implement change along these lines, including universal free education, scientific employment, the abolition of certain taxes, and development of transportation and commerce, quoting American founders like Alexander Hamilton to make his argument.

After Li essentially ignored him, Sun began traveling throughout the world meeting with revolutionary allies, raising funds to support the progressive movement, and spreading the concept of a Chinese republic. If the Chinese did not take action, he warned, their country would be ripped into pieces by the colonial powers. "To save China," he said, "my comrades and I are preparing for a revolution to overthrow the Qing Dynasty."

The government was weakened further in the Sino-Japanese War, when its army was defeated in Korea by Japan. As part of the peace treaty, China paid substantial reparations and ceded the island of Taiwan to the Japanese.

Sun and the Hong Kong–based Revive China Society planned to take advantage of this embarrassing defeat by staging a rebellion. It was to take place in one of Southern China's largest cities, Guangzhou, previously known as Canton, in late October 1895. The revolution was starting! Three thousand armed fighters waited in Hong Kong to board ships to Guangzhou! The success of the uprising there would spread throughout the rest of the country! The dynasty would be overthrown!

But before any of it could happen, informers warned the government; the army prevented the fighters from arriving and several of their leaders were arrested and quickly executed. Sun escaped China to Hong Kong in disguise, eventually taking refuge in Japan. The government offered a bounty of 12.5 pounds of gold—more than $4,000, a fortune at that time—for his capture.

In October 1896, Sun traveled to Britain to raise funds to support his movement. Outside his small group of activists and his enemies in the Chinese government, he was not widely known. But while walking through London to meet a former teacher, he was kidnapped and taken into the Chinese Legation. As he later reported, he was told, "That I should have my mouth gagged and put in a box of some sort and conveyed to China. He told me I should have no chance of escape. I asked him what they would do if they failed to get me off in that way. Then he said they would have me killed here and embalm my body and send it back to China for execution because you know the Chinese punishment extends to the dead . . . That is the order from the Chinese government."

Knowing his life was at stake, he tried desperately to escape.

On a scrap of newspaper he wrote, "I shall be smuggled out of England and into China for execution," and threw it out a window, hoping the wind might carry it to someone who would help him. When that failed, he convinced the legation housekeeper to smuggle a plea for help to his former teacher. That teacher contacted British government officials, law enforcement, and the media. Newspapers reported that Sun was being held captive. Crowds gathered outside the legation. After twelve days he was finally released—and by that time he had become famous, the brave young man who had challenged the emperor. The massive—and sympathetic—publicity had transformed him into a revolutionary leader with real power. He began traveling internationally, gaining supporters and raising funds to finance his revolution.

Revolutionaries are dreamers; they imagine a future that realists often believe is impossible. China had the largest population in the world. It had been ruled by powerful dynasties for three thousand years. The concept that a small group of committed people could overthrow that government was easily dismissed. Many Chinese referred to Sun Yat-sen as "Sun the Big Cannon" for making great promises but producing no results, believing the government would easily swat him away.

Sun Yat-sen was influenced by America's revolution and its Civil War. Among those traits he shared with the founding fathers and Abraham Lincoln were an unshakable belief that change was possible, a strong sense of justice, the faith that others would follow the path that he lit, and a willingness to personally sacrifice and, if necessary, die in pursuit of his values. Sun often quoted Lincoln, citing his commitment to democracy and individual rights.

While the country was officially ruled by Emperor Guangxu, for most of his reign the real power was held by his aunt, the empress dowager Cixi. But in an attempt to quell dissent Guangxu introduced a sweeping series of radical changes, known as the Hundred Days Reform, intended to integrate Western ideas into the government and society. The deeply entrenched bureaucracy resisted; the empress dowager, supported by officials, put Guangxu under house arrest and reversed his reforms.

Beginning in 1897, a "scramble for concessions" had begun as powerful European nations asserted economic control over different regions of China. Germany, for example, claimed the rights to mining and railway interests in the massive Shandong province. Britain exerted its influence in the entire Yangtze Valley. In an attempt to counter that, in 1899 the United States announced the "Open Door Policy," an effort to protect American commercial interests by ensuring that all nations had equal access to Chinese markets. The Chinese people were forced to watch as foreign nations divided their national territory while Christian missionaries attempted to impose their values on them.

The Chinese peasants fought back. Beginning in 1899, "boxers," the name given to men proficient in martial arts, began attacking foreign property and murdering Chinese Christians and missionaries. Their movement gained military support and eventually besieged Beijing, chanting "Support the Qing government and exterminate the foreigners."

An eight-nation coalition, including the United States, initially sent twenty-two thousand soldiers to put down the rebellion, although that number eventually grew to more than fifty thousand troops. After fifty-five days, the siege of the capital city was ended. The government was forced to sign a harsh surrender document in which it agreed to execute officials who had supported the uprising, allow foreign troops to be stationed in Beijing, accept spheres of economic influence, and pay a massive indemnity.

In almost every respect, the door to China was now wide open to the world; the dynasty had finally accepted the fact that to survive, it had to embrace reform. Empress Dowager "Cixi's New Policies" went even further than previous efforts, modernizing the military, introducing educational opportunities, promising massive improvements in infrastructure, changing the legal system to expand freedoms, and even banning traditional modes of punishments and practices like foot-binding.

Major changes in the structure of the government were introduced. In 1905 Cixi accepted the possibility of a constitutional government with a separation of powers and sent ministers around the world to study various political systems. The result was an agreement that within a few years China would become a quasi-constitutional monarchy.

Those reforms might have saved the government but fate, and tradition, interceded. In 1908, Guangxu died and Cixi appointed his nephew, almost three-year-old Puyi, the new emperor. The actual decision-making power was given to his father, whom Cixi controlled, but by tradition could not be named emperor. Incredibly, a day later Cixi died, leaving the government in the inexperienced hands of Guangxu's widow, the new empress dowager.

Throughout the period of turmoil, Sun Yat-sen relentlessly continued building support. He traveled incessantly, spreading his ideas for a new China, advocating for "expelling the Manchus [rulers] and establishing a republic." In 1905 he introduced his political philosophy, which he called the Three Principles of the People: nationalism, democracy, and the people's livelihood. As he explained in speeches throughout Asia and even America, those very general principles included the right of the people to elect their leaders, approve laws, and have guaranteed civil rights.

His revolutionary dreams were becoming reality. As the *Milwaukee Journal* later reported, "The country is vast, without modern transportation, without even a common spoken language. There are none of the conditions that make political unity. Yet Sun Yat-sen . . . set out to tear the nation from the roots of a thousand years and to change it overnight into a liberal government." Beginning soon after the turn of the new century, Sun planned and supported a series of uprisings in cities throughout the country.

The Qing government tried desperately to survive. In 1909 it held the first Western-style elections in China's history, electing delegates to local assemblies, which eventually led to the creation of a national assembly, the Advisory Council, which met for the first time in 1910. Many Chinese did not understand the process. Or care. A Chinese newspaper wrote in despair, "Those influenced by campaigning are like blind men riding sightless horses. Out of a hundred of them, not even a single person understands what sort of thing an election is, or what it means to vote or be elected."

Elections were held in twenty-one of the nation's twenty-two provinces. Voting was restricted to a small group of mostly wealthy and educated men. In most provinces, there was only a single place to vote, requiring voters to travel long distances. There were claims that votes were bought or sold, or that unqualified people were permitted to vote. In several villages, fighting broke out to determine the winner.

Regardless, within days, several of the new assemblies were meeting. In the city of Mukden, "Viceroy Shih congratulated the members on taking part in the inception of a constitutional government and urged them not to fritter away their strength in factional disputes . . . 'If,' he said, 'China was despised by other powers it was mainly because her people were wanting in self-respect.'"

Sun Yat-sen dismissed the elections, refusing to be deterred. In fact, he was in Denver, Colorado, in October 1911 when the revolution began. It had been ignited the previous August, as a response to the government announcing its intention to nationalize railroad development projects in several provinces, guaranteeing massive profits to foreign banks—and insuring Western support for the regime. Tens of thousands of people rallied against the proposal. Strikes, boycotts, and finally riots erupted into open rebellion. In early October, a bomb apparently being made in the Russian Consulate in Hankow exploded prematurely, alerting officials to a planned uprising. In Wuchang, the capital city of the province, thirty-two revolutionaries were quickly arrested—and within hours, four of them were beheaded in the street in front of the viceroy's office.

Rather than extinguishing the flames of change, this response added fuel to the rebellion. Troops the government had sent to the city mutinied. Other soldiers joined them. The spirit of revolution was alive in the streets. Fires were set in other areas of the city. Soldiers that remained loyal to the emperor were overpowered, the viceroy fled the city, and the military commander reportedly was assassinated.

In city after city, government troops joined the revolution. Seventeen provinces eventually declared their independence. Rebels in Shanghai declared to the world, "A republic has been proclaimed at Wuchang." A series of major battles were fought. The loyalist government forces, armed with modern weapons, killed thousands of people, but eventually they were overwhelmed by the massive number of rebels. Eventually, an estimated twenty thousand Manchus were killed. The empress dowager was helpless. In an attempt to save the dynasty, she appointed the greatly respected General Yuan Shikai the country's first prime minister.

After sixteen years in exile, Sun Yat-sen returned triumphantly to China. On December 29, 1911, while the civil war was raging, representatives of the newly independent provinces met in Nanjing to decide "what form of government shall prevail under the new regime" and elect a provisional president. There were three candidates. On the first ballot Sun received sixteen of the seventeen votes. Two thousand years of imperial rule had ended. In response to his election, Sun said, "My single aim is to ensure the peace and contentment of the millions of my fellow countrymen."

On January 1, 1912, Sun arrived in Nanjing for his inauguration. Massive cheering crowds lined the streets as he proceeded from the railway station to Government House. Warships in the river and nearby forts saluted with gunfire. But the situation had changed so quickly that no one knew what to expect from Sun's new administration. A San Francisco newspaper reported that Sun intended to rule for six months, after which national elections would be held.

Instead, Sun promised that he would resign from office when

the Manchus had officially abdicated and peace was restored. He also reassured foreign nations that he intended to honor treaties and that their citizens would not be harmed. He pledged to install a political system modeled on America and England, consisting of a national parliament elected by the people, while the provinces would select their own governors who would be autonomous with regard to local affairs.

As his first official act as provisional president of the Republic of China, he changed time, bringing China into the modern world by abandoning the traditional custom of reckoning time by the beginning of each new dynasty and instead adopting the same Gregorian calendar followed by "the Christian nations."

As the *New-York Tribune* wrote:

> Within the short space of less than a month this ancient Empire of China has undergone a tremendous political change, astounding in its rapidity, marvelous in its completeness and sensational in its execution. Almost overnight the timeworn regime of absolutism such as has been seen in few places in the world has been turned into a constitutional monarchy, with the new found rights of the Chinese people demanded, recognized and granted.

In reality, the Qing dynasty was not done. The empress dowager fought desperately to survive, giving General Yuan eighty thousand ounces of gold bars—the equivalent of $50 million today—to continue fighting.

Sun was fully aware that the government had been surprised by the spontaneous uprising and had been slow to react. He also knew that Yuan commanded a large, well-armed and -provisioned army; while that army might not be strong enough to defeat the rebel forces that had gained control of the South, it still was too powerful to be defeated on the battlefield. If the war continued, tens of thousands more Chinese would die. In November, Sun and Yuan agreed to a temporary truce as they tried to negotiate a settlement—and take the opportunity to reinforce their soldiers. Eventually, more than one hundred thousand men joined Sun's army.

In Paris, international bankers, facing the possibility that "the struggle in the north and the south is apt to continue indefinitely," began discussing the possibility of recognizing two Chinas, the dynastic monarchy in the North and the new republic in the South.

In the United States Congress, a resolution was introduced extending sympathy "to the patriotic people of China on the success which has thus far attended their efforts to construct a republic."

Finally, Sun agreed that in return for the boy emperor abdicating the throne and Yuan pledging to support a representative government, he would resign the presidency of the new government and Yuan would replace him. It seemed like the best path to create a new Chinese republic. In exchange for "good treatment for the imperial family," a substantial annual payment, and a protected residence in the Forbidden City, the dowager empress and the emperor agreed to abdicate.

A statement was issued on February 13. "The majority of the people is in favor of a republic," it read. "From the preference of the people's hearts the will of heaven is discernible. How could we oppose the desires of millions for the glory of one family?

"Therefore, we, the dowager empress and the emperor, hereby vest the sovereignty of the Chinese empire in the people."

Two days later, President Sun Yat-sen took the extraordinary step of resigning from office. The National Assembly paid tribute to him, resolving, "Such an example of purity of purpose and self-sacrifice is unparalleled in history."

He was lauded around the world. American newspapers ran long stories about the events in China. "For fifteen years," wrote the Associated Press, "Sun Yet Sen, a fugitive with a price of half a million dollars on his head, has plotted and planned the overthrow of the Manchu dynasty . . . A little man, with a body of steel and alert brain, this 'George Washington of China' accomplished by intrigue and the pulling of underground wires what 'the father of his country' did in the open by the force of arms and dauntless determination."

Sun's election had also ended centuries of Chinese government stability. For thousands of years, more than four hundred emperors had maintained autocratic rule. A strong central government had managed, somehow, to keep the vast country united; the trade-off of relinquishing individual freedoms in exchange for national security had held the diverse provinces together. Now that was over, replaced by . . . no one knew, precisely. Ambitious men began maneuvering for position—and power. The revolution unleashed decades of chaos.

The first months were promising. At the end of the year, the government held the first nationwide elections for the National Assembly of the Republic of China, electing a legislature with a 274-member Senate and 596 representatives. The right to vote was limited to men over twenty-one years old who were educated or owned property and paid taxes. About forty million people, about 10 percent of the entire population, registered to vote. To ensure national unity, Sun Yat-sen chose not to run for office, instead accepting the post of director of the nation's railway system. But his Kuomintang party (KMT) won a plurality, and its leader, Song Jiaoren, was named premier. Within weeks Song was shot to death; it was speculated Yuan had ordered his assassination.

The embryonic democracy was crumbling. Sun launched a second revolution, which was quickly put down by Yuan's forces. Around the country, local militia leaders began assuming power. In 1914, Yuan disbanded the assembly and attempted to restore the monarchy, proclaiming himself the new emperor. That effort failed to generate any support and in 1916 Yuan died of kidney failure, leaving the country without any effective national leadership. For the next decade, the fragmented country was ruled by regional warlords.

Sun made several efforts to form a national government but lacked political power or military support. In 1923, without any viable alternatives, he reached an agreement with the Soviet Union, in which the neighboring great power pledged to provide support to fight the warlords and reunify an independent China.

This alliance led to the formation of the Chinese Communist Party. Among its leaders was Mao Zedong, the son of a successful farmer and merchant whose initial political support came from rural peasants. From the very beginning, the relationship between Sun's Nationalist KMT and the CCP was strained, held loosely together by Sun to fight regional warlords. But this so-called United Front began falling apart when Sun died of liver cancer in 1925.

The Chinese Civil War began two years later, when KMT leader Chiang Kai-shek's army attacked Communists in Shanghai. The war lasted more than twenty years. In 1934, eighty-six thousand Communists embarked on a year-long, six-thousand-mile Long March, a strategic retreat across eighteen mountain ranges and twenty-four rivers.

The KMT and CCP paused their conflict in 1937, forming the Second United Front to fight the invading Japanese Army. But after the Japanese were defeated in 1945, the war resumed.

Mao's Red Army, with massive popular support, eventually defeated the KMT and installed a strong, repressive central government. Chiang Kai-shek's Nationalist forces fled to the island of Taiwan—which had been returned to Chinese control following World War II—and formed an opposition government that has remained in control since that time.

Sun Yat-sen remains one of the very few people revered on both the mainland and Taiwan. The Communist government considers him a national hero, "The Forerunner of the Revolution," while the Nationalists honor him as "The Father of the Nation." In the more than a century since Sun Yat-sen led the creation of modern China, that nation has continued to play a massive and complex role on the world stage in most areas of human endeavor.

It is certainly a mixed record, including both technological advances and at times a horrific human rights record. The existence of two Chinas, the Communist mainland and democratic Taiwan, remains an unsettled and potentially devastating issue.

China today is a superpower, the world's second largest economy behind only the United States. Through its Belt and Road Initiative, a program of investment and construction in foreign nations, it has established a footprint in at least one hundred fifty countries. While millions of Chinese—many of them in rural areas—still live in poverty, the nation also has large and vibrant middle and upper social classes that now travel throughout the world.

Sun Yat-sen's vision of a Chinese republic on the mainland has certainly not become reality, but the revolution he began that ended imperial rule in 1911 has reached and impacted every country in the world.

SEVEN

1932 and 1940: The Elections of Franklin D. Roosevelt

AS ELECTION DAY APPROACHED in 1932, the political comedian Will Rogers noted, "This President business is a pretty thankless job. Washington or Lincoln didn't get a statue till everybody was sure they were dead."

Few people were laughing. Both Bing Crosby and Rudy Vallee were at the top of the music charts with their versions of the song "Brother, Can You Spare a Dime," although Ted Lewis's "In a Shanty in Old Shanty Town" was also a major hit.

The world was in despair, reeling from the Great Depression. The banking system and stock market had collapsed. The unemployment rate reached an historic 24 percent. Americans literally were starving to death. Hundreds of thousands of families were homeless, living in makeshift shantytowns or "Hoovervilles." Breadlines and soup kitchens sprang up in every city. An army of mostly young men were jumping freight trains to travel across the country searching for work. The combination of low prices for crops and a severe drought across the Great Plains forced many farmers into bankruptcy. There was massive social unrest; food riots took place in some cities, while World War I veterans demanding their promised bonus marched to Washington only to be met by troops with tear gas and bayonets.

The Depression struck every continent, every nation. International trade fell as much as 30 percent. Dictatorships were taking hold in places like Germany, Japan, Spain, and the Soviet Union as people turned to strong leaders who promised some relief.

In the United States, President Herbert Hoover, who had been elected in 1928, was blamed for the crisis. Heading into the 1932 election, there was little chance desperate Americans would reelect him, but he remained the Republican candidate. The question was who the Democratic nominee would be and what policies he would pursue to end the suffering.

The leading candidate was New York Governor Franklin Delano Roosevelt. If it is true that politicians are born, not made, Roosevelt had been born into politics. Americans retained tremendous respect for his fifth cousin and mentor, the late former President Theodore Roosevelt, whose "Square Deal" policies had proved both popular and economically successful.

The Roosevelt name was a political pot of gold. It carried with it instant recognition, respect, and nostalgic goodwill. Franklin Roosevelt had been close with his cousin; when he had married the president's niece, Eleanor, in 1905, TR had given away the bride, responding loudly to the question "who shall give this woman away?" by proclaiming, "The President of the United States!" A decade later, Franklin proved his loyalty by testifying on Teddy's behalf in a sensational libel trial.

Although he shared TR's progressive politics, FDR was a Democrat, while his cousin had been a Republican for most of his career. Their party choices probably were determined as much by the traditional politics of the different branches of the family as political reality. By this point in American history, the Democratic party was considered to be progressive, focused on improving the quality of life for the average American, while Republicans were still strongly identified with business interests. And those business interests, which had helped create a booming economy during TR's administration, were now viewed as the culprit in the economic collapse.

Franklin Roosevelt had used the family name well, even following TR's career blueprint: Like the president, he attended Harvard, went to Columbia Law School, then won election to the New York State government. Just like his cousin, he served as assistant secretary of the navy, "another place which I myself once held," Teddy wrote.

After serving seven years in that post, through the entire Great War, his high public profile led the Democratic Party to nominate him for vice president on the 1920 ticket with Ohio Governor James Cox, just as TR had once run for that office. But Republicans Warren Harding and Calvin Coolidge, who promised a "return to normalcy" after the war, had won a landslide victory.

A year later, while vacationing on Campobello Island, off the coast of Maine, FDR was struck by the dreaded disease, polio, which left him crippled—and reliant on a wheelchair—for the rest of his life. At that time, any physical handicap was a huge political problem—carrying with it a perception of weakness—and FDR began learning how to hide it from the general public, creating ways to appear to be "walking."

In 1928, Democratic presidential candidate Al Smith asked Roosevelt to run for New York State governor, "to strengthen the national ticket." It was an enticing offer, and once again a position Teddy Roosevelt had won. The *Buffalo Times* reported that Franklin was "advised against it by friends, 'the stress of the campaign will break you,' they told him." But Roosevelt and Smith had been close friends for years and he agreed to run. "Leaning heavily upon his invalid's cane, Roosevelt stumped the state vigorously, speaking more for Al than for himself," the newspaper noted.

His political career was at stake—losing that race would have resulted in a stain on his electoral prospects that would be difficult to remove, and for a time on election night it appeared it might be over. At midnight the *Buffalo News* reported that, buoyed by Republican presidential candidate Herbert Hoover's huge lead, it appeared that for FDR's opponent, state attorney general Albert Ottinger, "Victory Appears Likely." But as more returns came in, Roosevelt won an easy victory, becoming New York governor and instantly becoming the leading Democratic presidential candidate for the 1932 election.

The stock market crash in October 1929 scuttled much of FDR's planned progressive program, from support for education to greatly expanding access to public utilities. Instead, he embraced policies that provided aid to New Yorkers, "not as a matter of charity, but as a matter of social duty." The state invested heavily in public works programs, hoping to stimulate employment. The effectiveness of his programs varied—but far more importantly, the public accepted as fact that he was physically capable of doing the job and, unlike many politicians, actually instituting policies that might help them.

The Democratic convention in 1932 was held in Chicago. There were several contenders for the nomination, among them Speaker of the House John Nance Garner and the previous nominee, Al Smith. Roosevelt was favored, having won several state primaries, but lacked sufficient support to clinch the nomination. Walter Lippmann, arguably America's most respected political columnist, spoke for many Democrats when he dismissed him as "A pleasant man who, without any important qualifications for the office, would very much like to be president."

On the fourth ballot, in exchange for receiving the vice presidential nomination, Garner gave his support to Roosevelt. Historically, candidates did not attend the convention, instead being notified of their selection by messenger or more recently, by phone. But Roosevelt's political instincts were sharp; to make the point that he was not tied to tradition he flew to the convention—the first presidential candidate to utilize an airplane in his campaign—to accept the nomination. In response to questions about his physical capabilities, newspapers reported that he entered Chicago Stadium "leaning on his tall son, Elliott. He was helped up the stairs to the platform, his son on one side and another man on the other."

As a pipe organ played "Happy Days Are Here Again," he began laying out his campaign. "The appearance before a national convention of its nominee for president to be formally notified of his selection, is unprecedented and unusual, but these are unprecedented and unusual times . . . in so doing I broke traditions. Let it be from now on the task of our party to break foolish traditions."

Later in the speech, he introduced the phrase that would come to define his presidency. Invoking TR's "Square Deal," he told the convention, "Throughout the nation, men and women forgotten . . . look to us here for guidance and for more equitable opportunity to share in the distribution of national wealth . . . Those millions cannot and shall not hope in vain. I pledge you, I pledge myself to a new deal for the American people . . .

"This is more than a political campaign. It is a call to arms. Give me your help, not in votes alone, but to win in this crusade to restore America to its own people."

Republicans also gathered in Chicago to hand their nomination to Hoover. The party platform essentially warned against the dangers of becoming dependent on government assistance, instead emphasizing the role that charitable community organizations should play in an economic recovery. For example, "The suffering and want occasioned by the great drought of 1930 were mitigated by the prompt mobilization of the resources of the Red Cross and of the government."

Although considered the heavy favorite, Roosevelt campaigned actively, crossing the country by train. In Los Angeles an estimated two hundred thousand people lined the streets to greet him, and another forty thousand jammed into the Hollywood Bowl to hear him. Additionally, he became the first candidate to make extensive use of radio and newsreels throughout the campaign. In a decade, radio had gone from rudimentary crystal sets to the greatest tool available for mass communication. On July 30 FDR made his first national radio address, a forerunner of the "fireside chats" he would later regularly broadcast around the country: "I want you to hear me tonight as I sit here in my own home away from the excitement of the campaign . . ."

It is likely that at some point during that historic evening, ominous news from Germany was reported: "Adolf Hitler, fighting for a Nationalist majority in the Reichstag, made the final speech of his campaign in Munich." On that election day, in Germany, nine members of an organization of veterans were ambushed and beaten by Nazis while distributing handbills while two others were shot to death in another city. As election results filtered in, it appeared the far-right Nazi Party had won the most seats in the Reichstag, the German Parliament. The proverbial storm clouds were indeed gathering over Europe.

Throughout the summer and fall, Roosevelt and Hoover campaigned not only on the economy, but also on two fundamental issues that had been debated since the founding of the republic: the role government should play in the lives of Americans and the balance of power between the central government and the rights the Constitution reserved to the states.

As Hoover had said during his 1928 campaign and repeated in 1932, Republicans believed "It is just as important that business keep out of government as that government keep out of business." During World War I, he explained, "We necessarily turned to the government to solve every difficult economic problem . . . For the preservation of the state, the Federal Government became a centralized despotism which undertook unprecedented responsibilities, assumed autocratic powers and took over the business of citizens. To a large degree we regimented our whole people temporarily into a socialistic state . . . If continued in peacetime it would destroy not only our American system but with it our progress and freedom as well."

In a September campaign speech, Roosevelt reminded Americans that "The creators of national government were perforce ruthless men. They were often cruel in their methods, but they did strive steadily [toward] . . . a strong central state able to keep the peace, to stamp out civil war, to put the unruly nobleman in his place and to permit the bulk of individuals to live safely."

His own belief, he continued, was that "The Declaration of

Independence discusses the problem of government in terms of a contract. Government is a relation of give and take . . . rulers were accorded power and the people consented to that power on consideration that they be accorded certain rights. The task of statesmanship has always been the re-definition of these rights in terms of a changing and growing social order. New conditions impose new requirements upon government and those who conduct government."

Once again, it was Will Rogers who captured the public mood, writing, "The money was all appropriated for the top in the hopes it would trickle down to the needy . . . [but instead that] money trickled up."

Roosevelt was elected in a landslide, receiving 57 percent of the popular votes, 472 of 531 electoral votes, and carrying forty-two of the forty-eight states. Democrats also took control of the Senate and greatly increased their existing majority in the House. Minorities and organized labor, voting blocs that had generally supported Republicans since Lincoln, turned to the Democratic party, a shift in allegiance that would last for decades. Although there was no data compiled by gender, and women still comprised a smaller percentage of the total turnout twelve years into women's suffrage, it was obvious that a substantial majority of women who did vote—many of them drawn to the polls by Eleanor Roosevelt—supported FDR.

It was a mandate for change, and Roosevelt used it to change the role of government.

In his inaugural address, FDR told Americans, in words that would be enshrined in history, "This great nation will endure as it has endured, will revive and will prosper. So first of all, let me assert my firm belief that the only thing we have to fear is fear itself—nameless, unreasoning, unjustified terror which paralyzes needed efforts to convert retreat into advance . . ."

Declaring "This Nation is asking for action, and action now," within weeks his administration began instituting progressive New Deal programs. Establishing the concept of "the first hundred days," his administration and the new Democratic Congress passed fifteen major bills that created an array of new federal agencies, including the Civilian Conservation Corps, which in its ten years of existence employed about three million young men in conservation and resource management projects, planted billions of trees, and created eight hundred parks and recreation areas; the Tennessee Valley Authority, which modernized the region by supplying hydroelectric power; the Agricultural Adjustment Act to assist struggling farmers; and several banking acts—including briefly closing the banks to determine which institutions were sound and guaranteeing federal insurance for depositors.

The New Deal expanded federal government powers far beyond anything previously attempted in American history. The Social Security Act of 1935, for example, provided for a monthly stipend to be paid to Americans over age sixty-five, as well as providing assistance for needy people, all of it funded by a new payroll tax. (Many nations around the world, including most of Europe, already had similar programs in place. Germany had created the first old age insurance program in 1889.) FDR also created the Works Progress Administration, a program that put millions of Americans at work constructing a vast national infrastructure while also supporting the arts.

The New Deal fundamentally altered the power of the federal government by reinterpreting the Constitution. Doing so required deft legal maneuvers and far more importantly, strong public support—although there was also considerable opposition to such drastic change. Business leaders fought against increased regulations, which included protecting workers' rights, workplace safety, and establishing a minimum wage.

Republicans were furious and frustrated but lacked the votes—or public support—to stand in Roosevelt's way. The 1936 election, in which Roosevelt ran for a second term against Kansas's Republican Governor Alf Landon, was basically a referendum on the popularity of the New Deal. "This is the largest tax bill in history," Landon warned. "And to call it 'social security' is a fraud on the workingman . . . I am not exaggerating the folly of this legislation. The saving it forces on our workers is a cruel hoax."

The Republican platform that year claimed: "The powers of Congress have been usurped by the President. The integrity and authority of the Supreme Court have been flouted. The rights and liberties of American citizens have been violated . . . The New Deal Administration constantly seeks to usurp the rights reserved to the states and to the people [and] . . . it has insisted on the passage of laws contrary to the Constitution."

As a result of those excesses, and many more, "To maintain the American system of Constitutional and local self-government . . ." the Republican party invited "all Americans, irrespective of party, to join us in defense of American institutions."

It was a hopeless effort. Americans overwhelmingly approved of FDR's policies. He won forty-six of the forty-eight states (losing only Maine and Vermont), 61 percent of the popular vote, and the largest electoral vote margin of any contested election in history. Only George Washington, who had run unopposed, had a larger electoral vote margin. Democrats also increased their majorities in both the House and Senate.

The final word on whether the federal government could impose these laws on the states was left to the Supreme Court. There were few applicable precedents for the court to rely on. This dispute could be traced back directly to Hamilton and Madison, Jefferson and Adams. Strong legal arguments could be made for both a strict interpretation and the doctrine of implied powers.

Initially, the court struck down several pieces of legislation, ruling that state governments retained the right to regulate commerce and manufacturing within their borders. Specifically, it invalidated the National Recovery Act, ruling that it violated the separation of powers, and the Agricultural Adjustment Act, finding that parts of it were "beyond the powers delegated to the federal government."

Roosevelt responded by threatening to "pack the court," proposing to a friendly Congress that the president be allowed to appoint a new justice to the court for each sitting judge over seventy years old. (At that moment, six of the nine justices were seventy or older.) His message was clear: Those nine old men were preventing him from ending the Depression. The court got the message, voting to uphold various programs that granted far more power to the executive branch—including the retirement benefits and unemployment compensation clauses of the Social Security Act.

FDR had successfully shifted the balance of powers from the states to the central government. The Depression wasn't over, but the country had settled into a slow, stable recovery. Happy days really seemed to be ahead—or so people believed.

While the nation was focusing on that recovery, the world had changed. By the late 1930s, fascism was rising. Desperate people had turned to radical answers. The post–World War I German republic had been transformed into Hitler's totalitarian Nazi state. Japan's parliamentary democracy had become a military dictatorship. In Russia, Stalin had eliminated all opposition and ruled with a brutal fist. The Spanish monarchy had been replaced by a democratically elected government, which was now engaged in a civil war for its survival.

The promise that the Great War had been "the war to end wars" was long forgotten. All of Europe was watching fearfully as the German military grew stronger. By the middle of Roosevelt's second term, a war in Europe seemed inevitable—and the question became whether America could, or should, stay out of the war by remaining neutral.

In those ensuing years Roosevelt had become one of the most beloved figures in American political history—and one of the most despised. Conservatives especially, who believed in small government, reacted bitterly to his broad expansion of federal powers that added tens of millions of dollars to the budget and relied heavily on deficit spending, allowing the government to regulate businesses, create vast new agencies, and pass social legislation. His wife, Eleanor, had become equally controversial; she was an outspoken woman who became a champion of progressive causes like civil rights. When the Daughters of the American Revolution prohibited Black American opera singer Marian Anderson—who previously had sung at the White House—from performing at Constitution Hall, Roosevelt resigned her membership and arranged for Anderson to give a free concert for seventy-five thousand people on the steps of the Lincoln Memorial—and for a nationwide radio audience.

FDR was well aware of his many political enemies. In a 1936 speech he boasted, "They are unanimous in their hate for me—and I welcome their hatred. I should like to have it said of my first Administration that in it the forces of selfishness and of lust for power met their match. I should like to have it said of my second Administration that in it these forces met their master."

He told a joke about his critics. Every day a man bought a newspaper, he began. He would glance at the front page then throw it away. Finally, the news dealer asked him why.

"I buy the paper," the man replied, "because I want to look at the obituaries."

"But the obituaries aren't on the front page, they're in the back section."

"Believe me," the man said, "when that SOB I'm looking for dies, it'll be on the front page."

Indeed, the 1938 midterm elections for the entire House of Representatives and one-third of the Senate had been disastrous for Democrats. Although Roosevelt remained personally popular, the New Deal was faltering. By 1937, the economy had largely recovered; production, profits, and wages were back to pre-Depression levels and unemployment had been greatly reduced. But a series of setbacks, including a reduction in investments, labor unrest, and changing fiscal policies—among them cutting federal spending to reduce the deficit while imposing new Social Security taxes to pay for existing programs—had put the country into a severe recession. Once again, production was down and unemployment was up. Republicans won eight Senate seats and an astonishing eighty House seats; although Democrats still held the majority in both chambers, there was little support for additional New Deal policies.

It appeared that the 1940 election would mark the end of

the Roosevelt administration. Even FDR purportedly acknowledged that the country was tired of looking at the Roosevelts. He also was well aware of the deeply ingrained tradition, though it was not codified in law, that a president would not seek a third term. Both Washington and Jefferson, who could have won a third term, had declined to run. As Jefferson defended his decision in 1809, "If the principle of rotation is a sound one, as I conscientiously believe it to be with respect to this office, no pretext should ever be permitted to dispense with it, because there will never be a time when real differences do not exist, and furnish a plausible pretext of dispensation."

The tradition generally was seen as a defense against any one man becoming too powerful—no matter how popular he was. The fear was he could become a dictator.

But for a year before the election, FDR refused to rule out running again. His reason for even considering it, he told advisors, was the concern that there would be a war in Europe and there was no candidate with sufficient foreign policy skill to deal with it. As he wrote to famed journalist William Allen White, "the situation of our civilization and mine is indeed in peril." He added, "Our world trade would be at the mercy of [Germany and Russia]." And relationships with Latin American countries "would end—unless we were willing to go to war in their behalf."

Whatever the historic consequences, Democrats supported him. A Gallup poll taken in late 1939 showed that he was the first choice of 83 percent of Democrats. Publicly, Roosevelt denied he was planning to run and in fact began moving his presidential papers to his home in Hyde Park, New York. The only thing that might change his mind, Roosevelt told the American people, was the course of the war in Europe.

A week before the Democrats convened in 1940 to select their candidate, the Battle of Britain began. German bombs were dropping on London. Civilians were being killed. Prime Minister Churchill vowed that "We shall defend every village, every town and every city." Watching the seemingly invincible Nazis marching through Europe, increasingly anxious Americans wanted someone they knew and trusted, someone in whom they had confidence, in the White House.

By the time the convention was gaveled to order, there was no doubt Roosevelt would be the nominee. In an effort to deflect criticism for breaking with tradition, his spokesman told the delegates FDR "has never had, and has not today, any desire or purpose to continue in the office of president, to be a candidate for that office . . . or be nominated by the Convention for that office."

In response, Chicago Stadium rocked with the chanted demand, "We want Roosevelt! America wants Roosevelt!" for nearly a half hour. FDR was "drafted" and won the nomination on the first ballot. His two-term Vice President Garner, who had opposed FDR's third term and considered running himself, was replaced on the ticket by secretary of agriculture Henry Wallace.

This time his acceptance speech was broadcast to the nation from the White House. He had not intended to run, he said, but "The normal conditions under which I would have made my public declaration of my personal desires were wholly gone . . . world events had made it clear to all but the blind or the partisan that a great war in Europe had become . . . a probability, and that such a war of necessity deeply affect the future of this nation."

After painting a dire picture of what needed to be done to

protect this country, including the recent institution of the draft, he continued, "My conscience will not let me turn my back upon a call to service. The right to make that call rests with the American method of a free election . . . If such a draft should be made upon me, I say to you in the utmost simplicity I will with God's help continue to serve with the best of my ability and the fullness of my strength."

With that statement, Franklin Roosevelt became the first American president to run for a third term.

The Republican convention had taken place several weeks earlier in Philadelphia. Ten men announced their intention to run for the nomination, but the four viable candidates were Ohio Senator Robert Taft, the son of former President William Howard Taft; highly respected Michigan Senator Arthur Vandenberg, who had supported many of the most popular New Deal initiatives; famed crime-busting Manhattan District Attorney Thomas Dewey, who had put Mafioso "Lucky" Luciano in prison for as long as fifty years; and businessman Wendell Willkie, until a year earlier an avowed Democrat whose regular appearances on the popular radio show *Information Please* and man-of-the-people manner had made him very popular.

Both Taft and Vandenberg were isolationists who opposed any American involvement in the war—including providing aid to Great Britain. Dewey arrived at the convention as the favorite, although he was only thirty-eight years old and had no foreign policy experience. That left Willkie, whose appeal was that he was not a politician, but rather a very smart, very successful businessman with great common sense and charisma. Young voters especially supported his campaign. "Willkie clubs" around the country sent as many as one million telegrams to convention delegates urging them to vote for him. Petitions were circulated. But still, two months before the convention, a poll showed him with a minimal 3 percent support among Republicans.

As the Republican convention opened, no candidate had sufficient support to win the nomination. In fact, the convention seemed so open that former President Hoover offered himself as the compromise candidate. But in what *The New York Times* described as "one of the greatest upsets in the history of the convention system," Willkie won the nomination on the sixth vote. To raucous cheers he delivered his speech in person—and for the first time, in addition to radio, it was broadcast live by a local TV station.

The election of 1932 had been about the immediate future; how people were going to live and eat tomorrow. This election was about how American military power should be used to change—or even save—the world. The decisions made by the next president would determine America's place in an increasingly dangerous future. Soldiers, sailors, and airmen would live or die depending on his decisions. The question was, who should make those decisions?

The only issue that really mattered in the campaign was how America would respond to the fighting in Europe. While Americans strongly supported providing assistance to England, a majority of people wanted the country to stay out of the war. Roosevelt campaigned from the White House; his justification for running, he told an aide, was the international crisis, so he could not run a traditional campaign. He gave few speeches throughout the entire campaign, creating the image he was so busy defending America that he had no time for politics. He simply ignored the debate over a third term, never mentioning it in those speeches or to the press.

Willkie barnstormed by train through thirty-one states. The Republican party platform "firmly opposed involving this nation in a foreign war." Although Willkie personally was not an isolationist, and supported delivering aid to England, he claimed that Roosevelt inevitably would bring America into the war. He also hammered Roosevelt's effort to win a third term, warning that a vote for Roosevelt was a vote for a dictatorship over democracy. "If one man is indispensable," he said, "then none of us is free," and predicted if FDR was elected, it might be "the last free election this nation will ever see."

In response, Roosevelt pledged, "Your boys are not going to be sent into any foreign wars," unless the country was directly attacked. But he continued assisting England and making preparations to join the fight—turning America into an "arsenal of democracy."

Just in case.

In September, he sent fifty aging destroyers to England in exchange for ninety-nine-year leases on military bases in British territories, and enacted the first peacetime draft in history, planning to put an additional four hundred thousand men into military service.

The election appeared to be very close. Two days beforehand, *The New York Times* reported, "Tuesday's Presidential election was in doubt . . . although trends generally are said to be in favor of Mr. Willkie." Whatever the outcome, "the victor . . . will have won a tense battle . . . and he will have been opposed by a very large national minority."

British Prime Minister Winston Churchill watched helplessly from London, believing the continued existence of democracy was at stake. As he would later remember, "No newcomer into power could possess or soon acquire the knowledge and experience of Franklin Roosevelt. None could equal his commanding gifts."

Ironically, it was Hitler's military success that determined the outcome of the election. By November 1940, Poland, Denmark, Norway, Luxembourg, the Netherlands, and France had all been defeated. The Third Reich controlled Austria and Czechoslovakia. George Gallup wrote that his polling showed "Sentiment for a Roosevelt third term rose sharply when the Nazis began their world-shaking invasion of Holland, Belgium, and France." Additional polls taken later reinforced that result, as many voters claimed if the war had not been a factor, they would have supported Willkie.

Roosevelt once again won a landslide victory, receiving five million more popular votes than Willkie and 449 of the 531 electoral votes. So, when the Japanese attacked Pearl Harbor the following year, FDR was in the White House. His decade of experience, his established relationships with world leaders and American politicians, and the reservoir of respect he had earned enabled him to rally the shaken nation. His historic, defiant speech to Congress in which he declared December 7, 1941, "a day of infamy" and promised, "With confidence in our armed forces, with the unbounding determination of our people, we will gain the inevitable triumph—so help us God" roused public support for the long, harrowing days that followed.

Working initially with Churchill and later Soviet Prime Minister Joseph Stalin, he adroitly planned and executed the strategy that led to the Allied military victory in World War II. The election of 1944 was a vote of approval for his wartime leadership. Some Republicans believed he could only be defeated by an equally historic figure and launched a campaign to get the nomination for the greatly admired four-star general Douglas MacArthur, just as Union general George B. McClellan had run against Lincoln, but that effort never garnered popular support. Young, vibrant, popular New York Governor Thomas Dewey became the opposing candidate.

There was no doubt the Democrats would renominate FDR, and it was highly likely he would win an incredible fourth term, but party leaders wanted to replace Henry Wallace as his running mate. It was obvious that Roosevelt's health had declined, and Wallace was considered too liberal, too inexperienced in foreign affairs, perhaps too much of a pacifist and a bit too eccentric to win a national election.

Or lead the country should Roosevelt's health fail.

Roosevelt could have insisted on keeping Wallace as his running mate, but he did not. He may have even been pushing the switch from the political shadows. Southern Democrats despised Wallace's liberal, anti-segregationist views; there was even some discussion from them about organizing a third party headed by Senator Harry Byrd. Personally, FDR favored replacing Wallace with his assistant James Byrnes, Supreme Court Justice William O. Douglas, or the moderate senator from Missouri, Harry Truman, believing that any of them would strengthen the ticket.

It took two ballots to nominate Truman. No one anticipated how soon the vice president would be forced to make one of the most momentous decisions in history.

People were just beginning to wonder what the postwar world would look like. How would Europe recover? What would be expected of the United States? What would be done with Germany, which had started two world wars? Would there be an organization like the failed League of Nations?

In 1943, Roosevelt met with Churchill in the Moroccan city of Casablanca to lay out the Allied strategy to end the war. They agreed on a doctrine of "unconditional surrender," meaning the Allies would take absolute control over the enemy nations—and that none of them would seek a separate peace. FDR also began laying the groundwork for postwar Germany, the "four D's policy": demilitarization, disarmament, denazification, and democratization.

In December of that year, Roosevelt and Churchill met with Stalin in Tehran to plot military strategy and begin discussing how the postwar world would be governed. Although the D-Day landings in Normandy were still six months away, the Nazi advances in Europe had been halted, while in Asia, island by island, the Allied navies were moving closer to Japan. The Allied industrial war machine was grinding down the enemy. The iconic photographs of FDR with the two other men reinforced his image as the leader of the free world. Roosevelt drew on Lincoln's Civil War campaign to remind voters of the dangers in swapping horses midstream and easily won his fourth election.

Only weeks after his fourth inauguration, the physically weakened president once again joined Churchill and Stalin, this time in Yalta on the Crimean Peninsula. It was there that they divided up the postwar world, agreeing to split Germany—and Berlin—into four zones administered by the United States, Russia, England, and France, as well as establish the United Nations. They also reached somewhat vague agreements about how Eastern Europe would be governed. Afterward, critics would contend Roosevelt ceded too much to Stalin, leading eventually to the decades-long Cold War.

Two months later, while at his vacation home in Warm Springs, Georgia, Franklin D. Roosevelt died of a cerebral hemorrhage. One of the biggest secrets he had kept throughout his presidency was the existence of the Manhattan Project, a program to develop the greatest weapon ever produced, the atomic bomb. It finally was ready to be used. The controversial decision of how to utilize it against Japan was left to Harry Truman—who ordered the bomb dropped on the cities of Hiroshima and Nagasaki, leading directly to Japan's unconditional surrender.

The country, both domestically and internationally, and the world that Truman inherited—the good as well as the bad—reflected the New Deal and wartime decisions made by Franklin Delano Roosevelt. Beginning in 1932, his four administrations greatly expanded the role and the powers of the federal government and set the stage for geopolitical divisions that have persisted through the decades.

And there was one final thing for which he was responsible: In February 1951, the nation ratified the Twenty-Second Amendment to the Constitution, affirming that "No person shall be elected to the office of the President more than twice."

EIGHT

1932: The German Elections Result in Adolf Hitler Becoming Dictator

IT WAS PLATO WHO warned in *The Republic*, "The people have always some champion whom they set over them and nurse into greatness . . . This and no other is the root from which a tyrant springs."

It was Adolf Hitler who proved it.

The nation of Germany was created by geography, economics, politics, tradition, a common language—and war. Its history can be traced to 962 AD, when the tribal region east of the Rhine River was named Germania by Julius Caesar, eventually becoming a significant part of the Holy Roman Empire. For almost a thousand years, different areas in the region were ruled by a variety of often harsh and sometimes benevolent government structures as alliances, borders, and leaders changed.

A decade after Napoleon defeated the empire in 1806, the German Federation was formed. It consisted of thirty-nine loosely aligned sovereign states, among them kingdoms, duchies, principalities, and free cities, joined together for mutual economic and defense benefits. The federation had no central government; although it was dominated by Prussia and Austria, each member retained its independence. Advances in communications and transportation brought these regions closer together and the idea, the concept, of a single unified powerful nation began to take hold.

German speakers were reminded how much they had in common by people like brothers Jacob and Wilhelm Grimm, whose compilation of folktales and fables highlighted the similar cultures between regions, and Karl Baedeker, whose guidebooks made travel to new places both inviting and exciting.

The actual unification movement was sparked at an 1817 festival to celebrate the Reformation held in Wartburg. About five hundred university student protestors rallied for change, burning books they believed defended an oppressive government and marching behind black, red, and gold flags, the colors of units that had fought against Napoleon.

In an effort to prevent the formation of a powerful German state, the legendary Austrian prince, Metternich, took steps to crush the growing desire for a central government. Instead, he urged individual states to set up their own local governments based on historic borders—fully aware that any confederation would be dominated by Austria.

The Second French Revolution, which began in February 1848, ignited protests throughout Europe. Rioters in Berlin emulated their French heroes, erecting barricades of rubble and carriages in the streets. But they were too few, too unorganized, and basically unequipped. Hundreds of young revolutionaries were killed before the fighting ended. Finally, to prevent any further spread of nationalist fervor, Prussian King Frederick William IV offered concessions, including a new constitution and the creation of a National Assembly.

Throughout history European monarchs had been considered divine, chosen by God to rule. Now royalty was being forced to cede some power to the people. The question became how to do so. What form of government would satisfy the "rabble"—while allowing the rulers to retain as much power as possible? Generally, it was accepted that it had to be some form of participatory government. There had to be elections, although who would be elected and what power those officials would have was debated. In New York, the Friends of German Liberty, an organization created to support and finance the revolution from across the Atlantic, suggested the establishment of "a free government in Germany, after the model of the constitution of the United States."

As a result of the revolutionary spirit spreading throughout Europe, elections for a German parliament that would create a constitution—granting fundamental rights and freedoms—were held in all the states of the confederation. For the first time, German "adult independent males" were allowed to vote. Each state established its own electoral system; Prussia, for example, adopted a three-class system heavily weighted to the wealthy and vaguely similar to the different voting classes of ancient Rome. Men who paid the highest taxes formed the first class, followed by the middle taxpaying class, and then the lower classes. Each class would elect the same number of representatives to the assembly; but since the first class had the fewest members, each of their votes would have more weight relative to the number of people represented. In some areas, the entire first level consisted of one or two people, ensuring the upper classes would retain the most power to elect officials.

Eventually, the Frankfurt Parliament adopted a constitution. While it did lead to some reforms, it lacked the support necessary to create a unified state. The new assembly was dissolved by individual states and replaced by their own participatory governments. As *The New York Times* reported in 1866, "There is, in political geography, no Germany proper . . . There are kingdoms and Grand Duchies, and Duchies and Principalities, inhabited by Germans, each separately ruled by an independent sovereign with all the machinery of state."

The creation of a unified Germany required the determination, political skill, and military prowess of the widely respected Prussian statesman and diplomat Otto von Bismarck. "The great questions of the times," he said, "will not be resolved by speeches and majority decisions . . . but by iron and blood." After Prussia defeated Denmark, Austria, and France in war, in January 1871 Bismarck proclaimed the existence of a German empire—without Austria—and that Prussian King Wilhelm I would become the first emperor, or kaiser, of the federal state.

Much like America's Congress, the new government consisted of two chambers; the popular assembly, the Reichstag, was elected by all male citizens over the age of twenty-five, controlled the state budget, and had some power over the kaiser, while the Bundesrat consisted of appointed representatives from the twenty-six different constituencies in the state. But the kaiser retained almost autocratic powers, with the right to make the most important decisions without the approval of Parliament.

Bismarck, who had been appointed the nation's first chancellor by the King, began shaping the unified Germany. He created popular social welfare programs, including health, disability, and old age insurance, which further bound the state together. His impact on history ended in 1890 when young and ambitious Kaiser Wilhelm II dismissed him. Wilhelm eventually instituted a world policy, "Weltpolitik," designed to expand Germany territory and economic and military power. By 1914 Germany had the world's second-largest military, behind only Russia, a booming economy—and dreams of European domination.

In an effort to blunt these ambitions, other European nations began to engage in a constantly shifting musical chairs of alliances and conspiracies. It was an extraordinarily complicated political situation. The assassination of Austria-Hungary's archduke Franz Ferdinand in Sarajevo was the excuse Wilhelm II needed to pursue his quest for control of the Continent. Like dominos falling, other countries were brought into the fighting that became World War I.

The war ended in 1918 with the surrender of Germany and Austria-Hungary; thirty-two countries had been in the fighting and at least nine million soldiers had died. There also were millions of civilian casualties, including hundreds of thousands of Germans who starved to death in the final year of the war. Kaiser Wilhelm II abdicated, fleeing the country and bringing an end to the German monarchy.

The ensuing peace treaty, the Treaty of Versailles, required Germany to accept responsibility for causing the war, pay 132 billion gold marks (about $500 billion today) in reparations; surrender significant territories to France, Belgium, and Poland; and maintain an army greatly reduced in size, as well as cease manufacturing certain weapons and military aircraft. The intent was to make certain that Germany was economically and militarily unable to ever wage war on Europe again.

Within the country people began debating what form of ruling body would replace the kaiser-led constitutional monarchy. The National Assembly met in the ancient town of Weimar, the "German Athens" that was the home of Goethe, Schiller, and Liszt, and adopted a new constitution that created a representative form of government. The democratic Weimar Republic consisted of a president directly elected by the people for a seven-year term, the Reichstag, and a chancellor appointed by the president who served as that parliament's leader. On paper, it was a system with checks on power, but in practice, the chancellor eventually became the most powerful government official. The new constitution guaranteed a range of civil liberties, including freedom of speech, the right to assemble, and a free press, granted the right to vote or hold elective office to all Germans—women as well as men—who were at least twenty years old, and ensured a multiparty parliament by establishing a proportional system of election to the Reichstag.

The transitional parliament elected Friedrich Ebert as Germany's first president. According to the Associated Press, on February 12, 1919, "Pealing church bells announced to the people of Weimar at 4:15 this afternoon that the German folk, for the first time in history, had chosen the head of their own state . . . Great crowds massed outside during the session, waiting patiently in the cold for a chance to see the new president."

While Germans cheered, the rest of Europe was wary. Americans also watched with caution, hoping a truly democratic Germany could help stabilize Europe and hasten the world's recovery from the devastation, but knowing from experience that further chaos was possible. Ebert's first speech, according to newspaper reports, "forecasts further and continued engagement with Germany and from first to last was an indication that the war is by no means over . . . When the terms of the armistice were denounced by Ebert as 'unheard of and ruthless' the fact was shown to the world that Ebert and the people whom he represents are not yet able to realize that they have been defeated."

"We warn our opponents not to drive us to the uttermost," he bellowed. "Hunger is preferable to disgrace, and deprivation is to be preferred to dishonor."

And, as it turned out, the harsh terms of the treaty caused massive resentment, which eventually was transformed into political—and military—action.

A proportional elective system, in which a political party earns representation based on the percentage of votes it receives rather than the first-past-the-post winner-take-all system, ensures that a wide variety of beliefs will have a voice. To elect government leaders, the different parties form coalitions in the absence of an outright majority. In a closely divided government, the smallest parties, whose few votes could determine the majority, wield power far greater than their electoral support would indicate. It also ensures that numerous parties with different ideologies will be competing for votes.

While in theory this system might seem to be the purest form of representative democracy, in practice it has often led to fragmented or unstable governments, weakened by a continuous shifting in the combinations of ruling parties. In the Weimar Republic, for example, at various times more than forty different political parties won seats in the Reichstag. Among them were Ebert's liberal Social Democratic Party (SDP), the moderate Centre Party, the Communist Party (KPD), and the far-right German Workers' Party, which evolved into the National Socialist German Workers' Party.

The Nazi Party.

The party was originally formed in 1919 by a small group of men, among them a locksmith and a sportswriter, established to appeal to middle-class workers alienated by the terms imposed on the nation by the Treaty of Versailles and suffering from the inability of the Weimar government to stabilize the economy. Rather than supporting democratic reforms, from the beginning it adopted anti-government, anti-Communist, and anti-Semitic policies. Its weekly meetings were held in the back of a beer hall in Munich.

The German Army, alarmed by the Communist leanings of some of the small parties that had sprung up, assigned soldiers to attend their meetings and submit reports. In September 1919, war veteran Corporal Adolf Hitler was sent to monitor the right-wing Workers' Party. Hitler had been born in Austria-Hungary. After being rejected by an art school in Vienna, he earned a meager living selling small watercolors and drawings. To escape compulsory military service, he had moved to Munich, but when the Great War began, he enlisted and served on the Western Front, where he was wounded. When assigned to report on the meetings in the beer hall, he finally found a place he belonged. He embraced the party's radical, anti-Semitic policies, which fit perfectly with his own racist, ultranationalistic views. He became the fifty-fifth member of the party.

Hitler's extraordinary public speaking skills enabled him to rise rapidly to party leadership, and after being discharged from the army he began working for the party full-time. In his early speeches he began referring to Germans as Aryans, a "pure" master race responsible for all significant human accomplishments. As he later would write in his political autobiography and manifesto, *Mein Kampf*, "My Struggle," "Everything we admire on this earth today—science and art, technology and inventions—is only the creative product of a few peoples and originally perhaps one race."

Aryans.

As the divided Weimar government continued to prove itself incapable of dealing with the myriad economic problems facing the country, more Germans began to search for radical solutions. By 1923 the Nazi Party had attracted more than fifty thousand members, among them the widely admired World War I general Erich Ludendorff. Hitler and Ludendorff believed the party was powerful enough to stage a revolution.

Their attempted coup began in the Munich Beer Hall. The Nazis claimed they had seized control of the Bavarian state government, believing Germans across the nation would rise in support and overthrow the Weimar government. "The government of criminals sitting in Berlin is deprived of office," Hitler boasted. "Tomorrow will see the execution of a nationalist government in Germany, or it will see us dead. There is no middle course."

General Ludendorff was proclaimed dictator. In Berlin, President Ebert declared that Hitler, Ludendorff, and anyone who supported them were traitors. Rather than joining the rebellion, the army remained loyal to the government. The next day Munich police confronted an estimated two thousand Nazis marching toward the center of the city; in a shootout, sixteen Nazis, four police officers, and a bystander were killed. Hitler was arrested and tried for treason. His month-long trial gave him both publicity and a platform to spread Nazi propaganda. As "steel-helmet soldiers reinforced by Munich police" prevented pro-Nazi demonstrations, Hitler was found guilty of treason and sentenced to five years in prison, but the trial had become a great victory for the party.

General Ludendorff was acquitted, perhaps due to the respect he had earned during the war.

Rather than serving five years, Hitler was released from Landsberg Castle Prison after slightly more than eight months. While serving his sentence, Hitler wrote *Mein Kampf*. In it, he left no doubt about his intentions, declaring, "The weapon of ruthless, brute force is of greatest value in war between two diverse views of the world . . . The 1914 frontiers mean nothing to Germany's future. They were not a protection in the past, and they would not mean power in the future."

Many European and American politicians tended to dismiss the threat, believing, as the *Brooklyn Eagle* reported, that his release "indicates that the Bavarian Government has ceased to care about Hitlerites. Their complete defeat in the recent elections indicates popular sentiment has turned against them."

That confidence was shaken in 1925 when seventy-eight-year-old Field Marshal Paul von Hindenburg, the commander of the German military during the war, became the first president of the Reich directly elected by the people. He received nine hundred thousand more votes than his opponent. The conservative, authoritarian Hindenburg was the candidate of the nationalistic right, and many supporters believed he would use his power to destroy the republic from the inside, but in his inaugural address he said, "No war, no inner insurrection, can free our fettered and disunited nation. It needs long, quiet, peaceful work . . . The President is especially called upon to uphold the sacredness of justice."

Despite the challenges he faced, Hindenburg managed to bring a period of calm and some prosperity to Germany. The economy was stabilized by currency reforms and increased foreign investment—although that required borrowing substantial sums from America to pay war reparations and support industry. Several agreements signed with wartime enemies in 1925 to respect the existing borders led to Germany joining the League of Nations, restoring some national pride and allowing the country to begin participating in international affairs. German culture once more began playing a significant role in the arts; the Bauhaus, for example, the renowned school of art, architecture, and design founded in Germany in 1919, significantly influenced creative arts throughout the world. The constitutional liberties also resulted in a vibrant culture that transformed Berlin into a cosmopolitan intellectual center.

But underneath the glamor, the glitz, and the economic recovery, the repressive Nazi movement continued growing in strength and numbers—waiting. When Germany was ravaged—just like the rest of the world—by the 1929 Depression, Hitler was politically well positioned to respond to the needs and desires, but mostly the fears, of the people.

The Nazi propaganda machine that Hitler created with Joseph Goebbels and architect Albert Speer was a masterful mélange of politics and psychology, creating an encompassing culture designed to reinforce the image of the invincible leader. Der Führer, the leader, as he later would refer to himself, was portrayed as a man who understood their struggles in the world.

The party had begun holding meticulously planned rallies every few years in Nuremberg. They were choreographed to evoke emotions, to make people feel they were part of an unstoppable movement greater than themselves—that they mattered. By 1929, the *Chicago Tribune* was reporting that at that year's rally "120,000 uniformed Hitlerites marched past their leader," although other outlets estimated far lower numbers.

Still, before the Depression the radical Nazi Party had remained on the fringes of electoral power. In the 1928 elections, it had managed to win only 12 of the 491 seats in the Reichstag. But when the American Stock Market collapsed a year later, Germany was especially hard hit. American banks demanded the repayment of recent loans to the country, which increased the pressure on the German economy. Just as in the United States, businesses failed, unemployment soared, hyperinflation wiped out savings, and by the middle of 1931, almost all the banks had closed.

The Reichstag struggled and mostly failed to provide any meaningful assistance, so President Hindenburg claimed emergency powers and with Chancellor Heinrich Brüning began issuing decrees allowing the government to institute economic reforms. Nothing helped. The promises of democracy had failed. By 1932, more than six million workers were unemployed and industrial production had fallen an estimated 42 percent. Desperate Germans again began looking for other solutions, and the extremist political parties, the Nazis on the right and the Communists on the left, gained significant support. Hitler's National Socialists became the second-largest party in the Reichstag. It was no longer possible to dismiss its influence.

During a crisis, people often look for scapegoats, desperate to blame someone, anyone, any entity for their problems. The Nazis had always preached German racial purity, accusing Jews, Communists, liberals, and non-Aryans of weakening the nation. As misery spread, so did the virulent anti-Semitism.

The presidential election of 1932 pitted eighty-four-year-old Hindenburg, representing the anti-Nazi centrist parties, forty-two-year-old Hitler, Communist Ernst Thälmann, and Theodor Duesterberg, the head of a large veterans' organization, against each other. Hitler campaigned across the nation, becoming one of the first politicians to utilize a chartered airplane, which enabled him to attend as many as four rallies a day. And the rallies were spectacles, staged with dramatic lighting and music, featuring bold symbols like the eagle and swastika. A *Toronto Star* reporter wrote:

> Adolph Hitler entered the arena. Eight thousand men and women leaped erect, stretching their hands in the Fascist salute. The roar of 'Heil Hitler' penetrated far beyond the walls and were echoed back by the multitude standing in the streets of Munich . . .
>
> Inside the arena Hitler spoke. He was an evangelist speaking to a camp meeting . . . his converts moved with him, laughed with him, felt with him. They booed with him the French. They hissed with him the republic. The 8,000 were an instrument on which Hitler played a symphony of national passion . . . Hitler, the evangelist, could found a new religion. Hitler, the actor, could sway packed theatres. Hitler, the orator, could make a revolution.
>
> Adolph Hitler is the hero a million people worship; the threat that Europe fears.

Hindenburg ran a more traditional campaign, positioning himself as a national hero who could bring together the moderate parties to form a stable democratic government. Thälmann also campaigned heavily, blaming the capitalist system for causing the economic disaster and promising to replace it with a government modelled after the Soviet Union, in which land and industry belonged to all the people and the wealth of the nation was spread to the middle and lower classes.

The German electoral system provided for two rounds of voting; if no candidate received a majority of votes in the first round, a runoff would be held several weeks later. American newspapers forecast that "it would be a close race, with the idolized Hindenburg stemming the Fascist tide by a narrow margin, although not by enough to re-elect him . . . Frequent public references in the campaign to the danger of civil war . . . if Hitler is not elected served to heighten the national tension."

In the first round Hindenburg received 49.6 percent of the vote, tantalizingly close to a majority but still requiring a runoff weeks later. Hitler lost by more than seven million votes, getting only about 30 percent. But the possibility existed that a Fascist could still win the presidency. *The Des Moines Register* cautioned, "If Hitler wins in April the future of the nation and even of Europe is to a great extent uncertain."

The world was temporarily reassured in April 1932 when Hindenburg won the runoff with 53 percent of the vote, even though Hitler increased his support by more than two million votes. After the results were known, Hitler claimed he had achieved "a great victory. Despite persecution and oppression . . . you have proved yourselves worthy to carry further the banner of national freedom. Tomorrow a new battle begins."

To try to quell the increasingly militant right wing, Hindenburg appointed conservative diplomat Franz von Papen the new chancellor. Papen was an ambitious monarchist who believed an authoritarian government, with the power to make and impose decisions, was necessary to bring Germany out of the Depression.

Hitler had lost his election, but was winning the electorate. In many parliamentary systems, under certain conditions the leader of the government, the president or prime minister, can dissolve the assembly and call for new, unscheduled elections. Hindenburg made a huge mistake; believing he could restore confidence in his government, he called for another round of elections in late July. Rather than reinforcing support for Chancellor Papen, the election allowed the Nazis to solidify their April gains; they won an incredible 230 of the 608 seats with 37 percent of the vote, more seats than any party had won in the brief history of the Weimar government. Suddenly, the Nazis were the most powerful party in the Reichstag. The Social Democrats lagged well behind with 21 percent, and the Communists trailed with 14 percent.

As the leader of the dominant party, Hitler demanded that Hindenburg appoint him chancellor. The idea repulsed the president. It was well-known that he despised Hitler, and purportedly responded, "That man for a Chancellor? I'll make him a postmaster and he can lick the stamps with my head on them."

Bold words, but it had become obvious that Hitler could not be ignored. As yet another parliamentary election in November demonstrated, Papen had lost whatever credibility he once had; the desperate Hindenburg replaced him as chancellor with another right-winger, General Kurt von Schleicher, in a last-ditch attempt to deal with Hitler. That proved to be politically disastrous; Schleicher's effort to split the Nazi Party by supporting Hitler's main rival was a dismal failure.

German politics had become confusing, complex, and highly combustible. Hitler did not hold an elective office, although arguably his ability to control his mass following made him as powerful as any elected official. But while the army remained loyal to the Weimar government, as shaky as it was, his options were limited. To achieve his objective of destroying the government, he first had to become part of it.

Hindenburg finally decided he had to deal directly with the

threat posed by Hitler. He was persuaded by Papen to bring Hitler into the government, where he could be controlled.

It was a remarkable gamble: By giving Hitler power, Hindenburg believed, he could contain his power.

On January 30, 1933, after several days of negotiations, Hitler was named chancellor. The United Press service reported, "President Paul von Hindenburg has insisted on a cabinet wherein the Nazi leader and his colleagues shall have only a minority of available places. It is obvious the old Field Marshall does not intend to . . . allow Hitler to install Fascism and a permanent dictatorship of his Brown Shirts, if it can be prevented.

"The question is, can it be prevented?"

The reporter doubted it, adding, "This insignificant appearing little man with a Charlie Chaplin moustache is one of the world's greatest demagogues and a first-class politician."

Adolf Hitler had never personally won election to any government office. Instead, he had successfully plugged into the zeitgeist, the prevailing mood of the German people, and used their support to rise to the pinnacle of the republic. As the *Chicago Tribune* explained it at the time, "Hitler restored to the millions of his followers faith in themselves, faith in their own country, faith in their future. For this, millions of Germans idolize him."

And after Hindenburg invited him into the government, Hitler moved rapidly to transform Germany into a dictatorship. His first action was to convince the president to hold another round of parliamentary elections the following March. The campaign was marked with violence, as Nazis intimidated and beat people, broke up meetings, and ransacked newspaper offices and printers with absolute impunity.

The legal takeover of the nation began five days before those elections were scheduled to take place when a massive fire broke out in the Reichstag. A twenty-four-year old Dutch Communist, Marinus van der Lubbe, was caught at the scene, supposedly carrying plans to set additional government buildings and palaces on fire. According to reports, this was to spark an uprising, a "bloody Bolshevik revolution and civil war."

Almost immediately questions were raised about this claim; it was considered unusual for an arsonist to have his passport and planning documents with him when committing his crime, and how one man could carry so much gasoline into the building was never made clear. There was considerable speculation that Nazis had actually set fire to the Reichstag. While van der Lubbe was convicted of high treason and arson and executed by guillotine, historians have never found sufficient evidence to determine what actually happened that night.

Whoever instigated the attack, the fire provided the excuse the Nazis needed to seize additional power. While firemen were still battling the flames, the cabinet drafted an emergency decree "for the protection of the Germen people against the Communist danger," which allowed the government to basically impose martial law. Civil liberties were suspended and political opponents were imprisoned. The Communist Party was essentially outlawed; about one hundred Communist members of the Reichstag were arrested, opposition rallies were banned, and leftist newspapers were prohibited from publishing. Six thousand Nazi storm troopers were given guns and truncheons and granted police powers. In the following days, as many as four thousand people were imprisoned.

The right-wing members of Hindenburg's cabinet had failed to exercise any control over the Nazis. Europe feared the outcome. *The Times of London* wrote that the Continent "is facing a calamity as great as that which came with the declaration of war nineteen years ago."

The outcome of the parliamentary elections was assured. The vote totals didn't matter: The Nazis had taken control. "The German democracy, after a precarious life of 15 years, has succumbed," the AP reported. "Chancellor Adolph Hitler, by ruthless suppression of the opposition parties, by occupying Communist headquarters and breaking up political meetings, and by mustering his Brown Shirt volunteers in every important city to terrorize the voters, has negated in advance whatever vote the German people may emit tomorrow."

As Chancellor Hitler demanded, within weeks the new Parliament passed the Enabling Act, which gave the cabinet—over which he had total control—dictatorial powers. "Hereafter," it read, "the Chancellor will simply proclaim laws decided upon by the cabinet. These laws will not require the approval of the Reichstag . . . Laws proclaimed by the chancellor may deviate from the constitution."

Speaking from a balcony, as the huge jubilant crowd roared "Heil Hitler," he said, "The first chapter of our movement is closed. Now we begin the second."

Throughout the rest of 1933 Hitler consolidated his power. He abolished all the other political parties and trade unions, he arrested opponents and sent them to the first concentration camp, Dachau, which became a training camp for guards and a model for the thousands of additional camps that would be established. He began systemic persecution of Jews, including starting a nationwide boycott of Jewish-owned businesses and prohibiting them from holding government jobs, teaching in universities, or practicing law. He appointed governors to exercise control over the various state parliaments. And he took the first steps toward rearmament by withdrawing from the League of Nations, which had limited the nation's military.

The only person who could have stopped him was the aged Reichspräsident Hindenburg. But for a variety of complex reasons, he failed to act. When Paul von Hindenburg died in August 1934, his son, Colonel Oskar von Hindenburg, announced that just before his death his father had designated Hitler as his "direct successor as head of the German State."

Hitler named himself president and chancellor, declaring himself Der Führer, the unrestrained leader of the nation, and held a referendum to confirm that this was the will of the people. Although he received almost 90 percent of the forty-two million votes cast, American newspapers, perhaps searching for some positive news, noted that this was fewer votes than he had gotten only months before.

The number of votes for or against him made no difference. Hitler had used the tools of democracy to destroy it. The election was neither free nor fair.

In addition to fraud, throughout history, powerful men have intimidated voters to deliver the election results they demanded. Fear is an effective political tool. The Nazi party had proved that dissent was dangerous, sometimes deadly. Political enemies had been imprisoned or killed. The 1933 Law against the Founding of New Parties had essentially ended any organized opposition.

Conversely, the Nazi Party had begun restoring the German pride that had been surrendered in the Treaty of Versailles. Ebert's plea to the victorious Allies to treat his nation with respect and economic decency after the Great War had been ignored. So, while some voters were intimidated into supporting

Hitler's referendum, many others did so to celebrate Germany's return to the world stage as a powerful nation that had to be respected.

The results of that election—while certainly not legitimate—made the world pay attention.

During the next few years, he rebuilt the German military and instituted more and stronger racial and anti-Semitic laws. He created an oath to the Führer, in which Germans pledged their unconditional allegiance to him rather than the state. In late 1934, more than seven hundred thousand people attended the now annual Nazi rally in Nuremberg, which became a massive propaganda victory when the documentary made by Leni Riefenstahl, *Triumph of the Will*, introduced the rebuilt militant Germany to a global audience. The 1936 Berlin Olympics provided a platform to show the world how Germany had emerged from the ruins of the Great War to once again become a powerful nation whose rights and desires had to be recognized and respected by the rest of the world.

Europe did not know how to deal with this new Germany. During the ceremonial march of nations into the Olympic stadium, for example, the *Atlanta Constitution* reported, "Sensational enthusiasm was evoked by the French squad, which not only dipped its colors but gave the Nazi salute during the entire circuit of the track. Hitler stood, returning the salute." But that same newspaper informed readers, "France, alarmed by Hitler's reoccupation of the Rhineland and the disintegration of the Versailles and Locarno pacts, built a monster line of subterranean forts along the Rhine and speeded her munitions factories."

Hitler truly began pursuing his dream of a vast German empire, a Third Reich that would last for a thousand years, when he annexed Austria in 1938. World War II began on September 1, 1939, when German troops attacked Poland, causing England and France to declare war. By the time the Führer committed suicide in his bunker beneath a Berlin street on April 30, 1945, and Germany surrendered a week later, more than seventy countries had been involved in the conflict. As many as fifty million civilians and twenty-five million soldiers—including 5.3 million German troops—had been killed. In hundreds of concentration camps in Germany, Poland, Austria, and other occupied countries, six million Jews, more than a third of all the Jews in the world, had been murdered. It was the deadliest war in history. Vast parts of Germany and much of Europe were reduced to rubble, traditional borders across Europe had been erased, and an estimated twenty million people were homeless. The chaos created by Hitler resonated for decades. In the years following the war new political alliances had been forged, new nations had been created, a Cold War between the Western Allies and the Eastern Communist bloc had begun, bloody border disputes erupted in Europe and the Middle East, and regional wars had become almost common.

Beginning in the back room of a beer hall, with only a few other men, Hitler has become a symbol of evil equal to the most reviled villains of history. But his life, and his rise to power, remain a vitally important lesson of how democratic institutions can be perverted for individual gain.

NINE

1945: Clement Attlee Defeats Churchill

IN MAY 1940, WINSTON CHURCHILL accepted appointment as prime minister of the besieged United Kingdom with his historic, defiant pledge, "I have nothing to offer but blood, toil, tears and sweat . . . You ask, what is our policy? I will say: It is to wage war, by sea, by land and air . . . against a monstrous tyranny never surpassed in the dark and lamentable catalogue of human crime . . .

"You ask, what is our aim? I can answer in one word: it is victory, victory at all costs, victory in spite of terror, victory, however long and hard the road may be, for without victory there is no survival."

His task was to take a battered, bloodied nation and lead it to that victory over the seemingly invincible Nazi military that had conquered much of Europe.

Incredibly, he achieved just that. With unflinching courage, with unfailing fortitude, tenacity, and determination he had rallied the British Empire and led it through, as he gallantly defined it, "their finest hour." There had been terrible times—the evacuation of Dunkirk, the Battle of Britain, hundreds of thousands of military and civilian casualties, the devastation of the economy—and Churchill's words and decisions through those most perilous challenges had created and maintained a national pride as great as any country had ever experienced. During the entire war his approval rating never fell below 78 percent. Few men in history had earned as much love, respect, and admiration from the people that he commanded. Years later, the English people would name him the Greatest Briton of all time.

Years later.

But in May 1945, the Nazis had surrendered. Hitler was dead. And the wartime loyalty was about to be tested. The wartime government he'd led for the course of the war had been dissolved. A national election was going to be held for the first time in a decade. The question was, could that adoration be turned into votes?

Churchill's Conservatives were running on a different view of Abraham Lincoln's 1864 campaign: Don't change the horse that got you across the stream. While the opposing Labour Party, in its campaign against Churchill, was saying: You're safely across the stream, the horse is tired, and you need a fresh horse to carry you into unexplored territory.

At stake was the future of the British Empire as it was rebuilt from the devastation of the war. And there could not have been two more starkly different choices.

England's prime minister is appointed by the King or Queen, but by tradition, it is the leader of the political party holding the most seats in the House of Commons. Unlike some democracies with a fixed period of time between national elections, the duration of a Parliament has varied throughout history from a few weeks to as long as twenty years. The Parliamentary Act of

1911 established the term between general elections at a maximum of five years, although the monarch retained the right to dissolve the government sooner than that upon the request of the prime minister. That was not always practical. In 1915, for example, during World War I, the "Prolongation Bill" had temporarily postponed the election. As war once again raged in 1940, the political parties agreed that the scheduled election should be postponed and a national coalition government would remain in power.

That agreement had led to Churchill's elevation to prime minister. The minority Labour Party had agreed to let Conservatives form the wartime cabinet—but only if Prime Minister Neville Chamberlain was replaced. He was viewed by members of Parliament (MPs) as too weak to lead the fight against Hitler.

With the support of Parliament, Churchill formed a cabinet of Conservatives, Labourites, and Liberals. He kept for himself the post of defense minister. The two posts made "Two Gun Winston," as the *Daily Express* dubbed him, the "lord of the war lords," the most powerful prime minister in the nation's history.

Churchill eventually named Labour party leader Clement Attlee England's first ever deputy prime minister. That decision surprised Conservatives, many of whom had little respect for Attlee. "He looked and spoke like an insignificant little clerk," said economist Beatrice Webb, a founder of the London School of Economics, "without distinction in the voice, manner or substance of his discourse. To realize that this little nonentity is the Parliamentary Leader of the Labour Party . . . is pitiable."

But this "little nonentity" and the rest of the coalition cabinet worked together through the war. Attlee, in fact, had strongly supported Churchill's controversial decision to pursue the war to the end rather than attempting to negotiate peace with Hitler after France surrendered. The two men apparently respected each other, although they were never close friends. In fact, while newspapers claimed Churchill had once described Attlee as a "modest little man with plenty to be modest about," he would strongly defend him against public criticism.

Every year during the war Parliament had "prolonged" the wartime government, postponing the election. The coalition had worked so successfully that after Germany's surrender, both Churchill and Attlee agreed it should remain intact until Japan was defeated—possibly another year. Labour leaders refused to accept that, quoting Churchill's own words, "I have myself a clear view that it would be wrong to continue this Parliament beyond the period of the German war."

The prime minister turned down Labour's compromise offer of waiting until the legal end of Parliament in the fall, instead offering his resignation to King George VI, who immediately scheduled new elections. The election would be held in three weeks, although the results would not be announced for an additional three weeks to ensure that ballots from service members stationed around the world had been received and counted.

While officially this was an election between the Conservative, Labour, and Liberal Parties, in reality it was a choice between Churchill and Attlee. Throughout the war, polls had shown that Attlee's Labour Party, which supported significant social reforms, was far more popular, but history made Churchill the immediate favorite.

A similar situation had come about at the conclusion of World War I. A postwar election was scheduled for 1918; all men over twenty-one years old, soldiers at least nineteen, and, for the first time, women over thirty, were eligible to vote. The entire campaign lasted only three weeks and was held during an outbreak of the Spanish flu pandemic. The immensely popular wartime prime minister, the Liberal Party's David Lloyd George, was considered "the man who won the war."

The nation rewarded him for his wartime leadership. Although the Conservative Party won a majority of seats in Parliament, a coalition of Conservatives and Liberals made Lloyd George prime minister. But what people who cited that election to predict Churchill's victory failed to note was that his peacetime leadership was a failure, his coalition fell apart, and he lost the next election.

It had been Lloyd George who helped save a young Winston Churchill's political career by bringing him into his cabinet as minister of munitions. The comparisons between the two men were obvious; even the tenor of Churchill's use of the English language reflected the eloquence of Lloyd George's phrasing at the beginning of War War I: "We shall need all our qualities, every quality that Britain and its people possess. Prudence in council, daring in action, tenacity in purpose, courage in defeat, moderation in victory, in all things faith and we shall win."

When the 1945 campaign began, polls that showed Labour was far more popular were ignored. It was almost impossible to imagine that Churchill, the "British Bulldog," the man who had sat with FDR and Stalin, would be turned out of office. Rather than Churchill losing, newspapers speculated on the size of his majority. Churchill fueled those predictions, warning that if he did not receive massive support, "it's no use people thinking I can continue to serve."

It was a campaign of personality vs. policy. Churchill the

icon vs. Labour's detailed plan for the future. Although some journalists described Churchill's campaign as a victory tour, the situation facing the country was quite different. The war had almost bankrupted the nation. There were tremendous shortages of food and housing, there were piles of rubble in the streets, and the tens of thousands of soldiers coming home needed jobs and assistance. The two main parties proposed very different scenarios for rebuilding the nation—capitalism vs. socialism. Private enterprise vs. nationalized industry and social services.

The Conservative platform was based firmly on the ability of free enterprise to motivate progress, believing the profit motive provided the best path to success. "This is the time for freeing energies, not stifling them," read the party's policy statement. "Britain's greatness has been built on character and daring, not on docility to a State machine. At all costs we must preserve that spirit of independence."

Or, as *The Guardian* explained it, "The Conservative party believes that the basis for our economic activities must be what they call private enterprise, inspired by the motive of private profit . . . They seemed to hold that if every individual seeks his own interest somehow or other the interests of all will be served."

Labour offered a very different vision. Attlee supported radical social reform, based on the widely approved 1942 Beveridge Report. The report, sponsored by the coalition government to initiate discussion about postwar policies, had created a mild sensation. People had actually waited in line to buy a copy of this "blueprint for the future." Officially titled the bland "Social Insurance and Allied Service," it laid out a program of social welfare to fight the "five giants" the postwar nation would be facing—Want: ensuring a minimum standard of living. Disease: universal healthcare. Ignorance: making education accessible to everyone. Squalor: providing safe housing. And idleness: creating new jobs paying a living wage. It was an almost utopian proposal that suggested the government would repay the sacrifices made to win the war by creating a new world of benefits. Among its significant elements were proposals that working people make a weekly contribution from their paychecks to create a social safety net for people in need and that the government create a free, national health service that would benefit everyone.

The broad concepts outlined in the report proved extremely popular. People still remembered the widespread unemployment, food lines, and economic stagnation following World War I—under Conservative governments—and feared history would repeat itself. The plan offered an enticing alternative. The respected archbishop of Canterbury, William Temple, called it "the first time anyone had set out to embody the whole spirit of the Christian ethic in an Act of Parliament." It was, lauded *The Times*, "a momentous document which should and must exercise a profound and immediate influence on the direction of social change in England."

Even Churchill supported elements of it, describing it as a program that would provide security for every citizen "from the cradle to the grave." However, he remained strongly against the state becoming too strongly involved in the economy and maintained people needed "freedom of choice" in their healthcare.

Meanwhile, Attlee ran on a promise to implement major portions of the report, to make radical changes to British society—to lay the foundation for a new England.

Labour's support for it made it easy for Conservatives to

attack Attlee as a socialist, which they casually equated with Russian Communism and even Hitler's Nazi Party. The fact that Attlee had briefly been a member of the Socialist Party early in his career helped them make that political leap. And they reminded voters that when the report was issued, the Nazis had claimed it was evidence Britain supported the concept of national socialism.

Churchill set the tone in his very first radio address of the campaign. "Socialism," he told them, "is abhorrent to the British ideas of freedom . . . There can be no doubt that Socialism is inseparably interwoven with totalitarianism . . ."

The portrait of Attlee's socialism he painted was ominous and threatening. "There is to be one state to which all are to be obedient in every act of their lives . . . once it is in power it will prescribe for every one of them where they are to work, what they are to work at, where they may go and what they may say; what views they are to hold and within what limits they may express them."

But then he went even further, declaring there had never been a Socialist system that had survived without the support of a political police force. "No Socialist Government . . . could afford to allow free, sharp or violently-worded expressions of public discontent. It would have to fall back on some form of Gestapo."

That charge, on the first day of the campaign, ignited a political firestorm. The electorate knew Clement Attlee. They liked him. Respected him. Admittedly, he was not the most dynamic or charismatic man, but he had quietly played a significant role in the successful wartime cabinet. And for Churchill to compare the political party that had cooperated so completely with him throughout the entire war to Hitler's hated monsters was beyond outrageous. Labour leader Herbert Morrison called the charge "crazy." Rumors spread that Churchill's wife, Clementine, had read the speech and strongly urged him to remove that phrase, but he refused.

Attlee responded with calm, reasoned words the next day. "When I listened to the Prime Minister's speech last night in which he gave such a travesty of the policy of the Labour party I realized at once what was his object. He wanted the electors to understand how great the difference between Winston Churchill, the great leader in war of a united nation, and Mr. Churchill, party leader of the Conservatives. He feared lest those who had accepted his leadership in war might be tempted to follow him further."

As for the dire threats of socialism's impact on the nation, Attlee continued, "He has forgotten that Australia and New Zealand . . . and the Scandinavian countries have had Socialist governments for years, to the great benefit of their people with none of these dreadful consequences."

In fact, his plans to nationalize England's basic industries would lead the country to a "happier and securer future."

Churchill was an experienced, brilliant campaigner. Almost immediately he set off on a one-thousand-mile tour, reinforcing the image of the beloved but tough-when-necessary leader the British people could trust to protect their future. Between appearances in Essex, for example, he stopped by a children's victory party and while news photographers recorded it, "delighted the youngsters by putting on a clown's hat—and making a brief speech." At another rally, he showed the working-class crowd that he was one of them by drinking a pint of beer. Standing on a podium at another stop he sang the opening bars of "Rule, Britannia" to the raucous cheers of the crowd. There could be no doubting his personal popularity; everywhere he went he was "our Winnie," "dear old Winnie," although no one could guess if that would translate into votes.

The Conservative campaign consisted basically of emphasizing that the great wartime leader Churchill had earned the right to lead the nation into peacetime, that Britons knew him and could trust him to make the right decisions, and that the Labour's Socialist policies would destroy the nation, and . . . and. The party offered few specifics about the postwar policies it would pursue. To explain that, Churchill boasted, "I will offer no bribe flung out there to catch a vote here or there . . . We shall move forward where we consider it right to move."

In contrast, Labour pointed out smartly, "The party which sees the Gestapo under every Socialist's bed endorses the totalitarian idea of one leader, one party, one people."

Attlee seemed to revel in his perceived drabness, sensing that after a decade of careening from crisis to bigger crisis, the people wanted the calm he represented. He did not object when his own secretary reinforced that image, calling him cautious and colorless, a speaker he "wouldn't walk five yards to hear." But, another advisor told a reporter, "I should always expect to see his job competently performed with no loose ends left behind." He told a rally of Yorkshire women, "I am not going to appeal to your fear. That happens at every election from the Conservative side."

As polls continually reported strong support for the Beveridge Report, he repeatedly offered safe, broad generalities to packed halls and overflowing rallies: Questioned about nationalizing the coal mines, he pointed out, "The history of this industry . . . shows it must be better managed." Asked about nationalizing the railroads, he said, "It's got to be run as a great service for the benefit of the whole community. When monopoly gets into the hands of a few men, then the only safe monopoly is a monopoly of the community." As for foreign policy, he was confident his Labour government could get along better with Stalin's Russia than the Conservatives, and about the colonies aspiring for independence: "We want to see self-government for India . . . We as the Labour party are particularly concerned with the great masses of the people."

While the national Churchill/Attlee campaign captured most of the front pages, the inside pages of newspapers were filled with reports on the local campaigns that actually would determine the composition of Commons—and thus the choice of prime minister. Both the Conservatives and Labour were running more than five hundred candidates, David Lloyd George's Liberal Party had nominated three hundred people, the Common Wealth Party had thirty-two, and Communists were running twenty-two candidates. The same issues being debated by Churchill and Attlee were discussed every day in the towns and villages across the nation. Among those Liberal Party candidates running for Parliament was William Beveridge, the author of the report, who had been appointed to Commons from Berwick-upon-Tweed after the incumbent had been killed in Normandy.

In the closing hours of the campaign, Churchill once again gave rise to the specter of the Gestapo, telling his audience that if socialism "were established here in its totalitarian form," there would have to be political police in Britain.

This time that claim received audible boos. Undeterred, the prime minister said, confidently, "We are winning. There is little doubt in my mind that the nation intends to vote for the government which is pledged to carry through the great purposes for which we fought this war." *The Daily Telegraph* agreed, writing that "Reports received up to last night promise a majority for Mister Churchill . . . There are indications that the heavier the poll the more strongly is Mr. Churchill's victory assured."

More than twenty-four million men and women went to the polls on election day, 72.8 percent of the electorate. And then they waited three weeks as the ballots trickled in from service members around the world as well as some districts slow to report. During that time government business proceeded normally; in the middle of that odd waiting period Prime Minister Churchill asked Attlee to join him as an observer at a conference with Stalin and new American president Harry Truman held in Potsdam, Germany, to determine Germany's fate and begin laying out plans for the postwar world.

Churchill and Attlee returned for the announcement of the election results, joining, as *The Guardian* wrote dramatically, "the rest of the seventeen hundred candidates in waiting for the sword of life or the sentence of death."

The results were shocking. As *The New York Times* reported, "In one of the most stunning election surprises in the history of democracy, Great Britain swung to the left today in a landslide that smothered the Conservatives and put Labour into power with a great majority.

"Winston Churchill has resigned."

It was an outcome no one, "not even the wildest prophets," the *Times* continued, "had anticipated." In one of the greatest landslides in British history, Labour gained almost two hundred fifty seats in Commons, its first parliamentary majority. While Churchill won his own seat, his son, his son-in-law, and numerous members of his cabinet lost their elections.

Leaders around the world, unprepared for this outcome, struggled to make sense of it. In America, a republican senator warned, "We are confronted by the greatest attack on [a] free economy in history." Russia celebrated this "new chapter . . . in the life of Britain." Spain saw it as "a defeat . . . for the Franco regime." French and Italian leftists welcomed the new government, while a leading Swedish newspaper wrote that Churchill had been "betrayed by his people."

As soon as the results became obvious, Churchill went to Buckingham Palace and resigned. Within minutes Attlee arrived and told the King, "I've won the election."

"I know," King George VI replied, "I heard it on the six o'clock news."

Churchill was stoic in defeat, announcing, "I have laid down the charge which was placed upon me in darker times. I regret that I have not been permitted to finish the [war] against Japan." Privately though, when Clementine suggested this defeat might be "a blessing in disguise," he responded that if that were true, "At the moment it seems quite effectively disguised."

Naturally, the experts who had not foreseen this electoral outcome immediately began trying to explain it. There obviously were many reasons for it. But the message sent by voters was clear: The war was over, and it was time for change. Big change. The change in the entire thousand-year social fabric of England that was promised.

Churchill had asked for overwhelming support basically to do whatever he wanted; instead, voters gave their support to

Attlee to do what *they* wanted. And he did, creating a new social structure for England, dismantling large parts of the empire and altering the map of the world.

The Attlee government's effort to nationalize British industries began in 1946 by bringing both the Bank of England and civil aviation under government control; rather than being profit driven, they were going to operate for the benefit of the general population. Within the next few years, the railroads, coal mining, power companies, and other major industries also had been nationalized. In most of those areas, wages and working conditions, especially safety, were improved.

Major aspects of the Beveridge Report were turned into reality. In return for paying a flat rate for the new social safety net, people were provided with pensions, unemployment and disability payments, maternity and funeral benefits, aid to children, the elderly, and the handicapped, and assistance for people living in poverty; as Churchill had described it, literally covering the needs of the individual "from cradle to grave."

Among the most beneficial changes in the lives of Britons was the creation of the National Health Service, the publicly funded healthcare system created in 1948 against strong opposition from the entrenched medical establishment. Although not without controversy, the NHS has made access to medical care a right of every British citizen.

The nation's educational system was revamped, new schools were constructed, and existing schools were refurbished, thousands of new teachers were recruited and trained, food and clothing were provided to needy students, grammar school fees were eliminated, and free secondary education became a right, enabling thousands of returning veterans to obtain a university education never previously available to them.

Every decision had to be balanced by its effect on the economy. The cost of fighting the war had left the nation close to bankruptcy. Soldiers returning to civilian life needed jobs. Restocking the country after the war with everything from basic home supplies to weapons had added to the massive trade deficit. A series of monetary crises forced the government to take painful steps to minimize disruption. For instance, wartime rationing had to be continued for a considerable period, but such measures allowed the government to keep both unemployment and inflation at an acceptable 2 percent. The average workweek was slightly shortened, but due to new, modernized equipment production output rose. The economy grew at an average rate of 3 percent, the best economic recovery in Europe.

Domestically, Attlee had substantially fulfilled his campaign promises.

Measuring success in foreign affairs is considerably more difficult, and many of the problems Attlee's administration sought to deal with continue to plague the world. By far the most dangerous problem Attlee inherited was the creation of the Iron curtain—as Churchill had described it—and Stalin's expansionist dreams. The fact that he and Truman had to deal with the Soviet Bear rather than the far more experienced Roosevelt and Churchill made the situation even more difficult. Attlee relied on the new United Nations to contain Stalin and sought to build a working relationship with him. When that strategy proved essentially worthless, he played a key role in the creation of the North Atlantic Treaty Organization, a coalition that pledged military support to any member attacked by Russia, essentially turning much of Europe, the United States, and Canada into a single entity to fight the Communists.

Attlee viewed the growth of Communism inside Britain as

a serious threat and did as much as legally possible to restrain it. Among other actions, he allowed intelligence services to target and surveil members of the Communist Party of Great Britain and purportedly restricted the free movement of suspected subversives.

He also made extraordinarily difficult decisions that fundamentally altered the British Empire. In 1947, after trying and failing to deal with Mahatma Gandhi's decades-long freedom movement that galvanized India, his government finally acceded to independence for the so-called "Jewel in the British crown," creating two nations by partitioning the Hindu-majority India from the Muslim-majority Pakistan. While bringing freedom from colonial rule to as many as four hundred million people, the result was a hostile relationship between those countries that at several different times has descended into warfare. He also gave independence to Burma, now Myanmar, and Ceylon, now Sri Lanka, while preparing other British possessions for an eventual change in their status.

By far the most complex situation facing the victorious Allies was how to deal with the area of the Middle East known as Palestine, the ancestral home of both Muslims and Jews. Since the end of World War I, it had been administrated by the British following a mandate from the League of Nations. After World War II, an estimated 250,000 displaced Holocaust survivors were living in camps in Europe and needed to be resettled. Thousands of them tried to reach Palestine, but most of them were stopped by British troops. In 1947 the new United Nations voted to partition the region, creating the State of Israel.

Britain abstained from the vote—but withdrew its forces from that area.

The decisions made by Attlee in the years following World

War II have continued to reverberate for decades. The Empire was being dismantled while domestically a vast social welfare net had been put in place. But political fatigue had set in as well, and the Labour Party seemed to be running out of new initiatives. Fighting had broken out on the Korean Peninsula and more than fifty thousand British troops were sent there, raising anxiety about another major war—this time against the Communists.

In the scheduled elections that year, Labour retained only a slim majority of seats, making it extremely difficult to govern. Desperate to add to that majority, in 1951 Attlee called for "snap" elections. That gamble failed. Although Labour received the highest number of votes overall ever cast for a party, Conservatives won a majority in Parliament—and once again, Winston Churchill became prime minister of England.

TEN

1955: Dr. Martin Luther King Jr. Elected Leader of the Montgomery Improvement Association

JULY 16, 1854, WAS A warm Sunday morning in New York City, and a young Black teacher named Elizabeth Jennings was late for church, where she played the organ. Streetcars were segregated, but the Blacks-only car was full, so in desperation she boarded the whites-only car. The conductor told her to get off his car, and when she refused, he pulled her out of the car onto the platform. A crowd gathered. Indignantly, she got back on—and this time she was physically removed by a police officer. The furious Jennings found a lawyer, twenty-four-year-old Chester A. Arthur, and sued the company.

The case got national attention, sparking an organized movement to end segregation on New York's public transit. Eventually, a circuit court ruled in Jennings's favor, awarding her about $250, plus expenses. The next day, the company desegregated its cars. It took another decade, but eventually segregation on public transit in the city was ended.

Almost exactly one hundred years later, Rosa Parks boarded a bus in Montgomery, Alabama, and sat down in a seat reserved for white people. The driver ordered her to move to the back of the bus. She had been preparing for this moment for a long time. "No," she said.

And a revolution began.

The Civil War and the resulting constitutional amendments freed enslaved people to become second-class citizens. The promises of Reconstruction had ended in the presidential election of 1876. As a result, in 1955 the American South remained strongly segregated. An entire parallel Black society existed; Jim Crow, as it was known, led to a large-scale suppression and separation of almost all human activities for Black people. African-Americans lived in often inferior segregated areas of cities and towns; they had their own culture, their own movie industry, their own baseball league, their own newspapers, churches, clubs, and restaurants. They had their own school system and colleges. Black men and women like heavyweight champion Joe Louis, Olympic star Jesse Owens, and entertainers Paul Robeson, Sammy Davis Jr., Hattie McDaniel, and Marian Anderson became celebrated throughout the country—but were not allowed to stay in most hotels or eat in many restaurants or diners.

An endless stream of racial attacks had been mostly ignored by the white media. A 1908 race riot in Springfield, Illinois, and a 1923 race massacre, in which the entire prosperous Black section of Tulsa, Oklahoma, was burned, became mostly forgotten footnotes. Lynchings were common throughout the South. While the first major American civil rights organization, the National Association for the Advancement of Colored People, had been formed in 1909, the horrors of racism had overwhelmed attempts to fight for equal rights. Beginning with the former slave turned brilliant orator and writer Frederick Douglass, there had been several high-profile Black men and women leading the cause in the post–Civil War era; among them Ida Wells, W.E.B. Du Bois, Marcus Garvey, A. Philip Randolph, and Thurgood Marshall. But none of them had been able to generate sufficient support to command the respect of the nation's Black population. It was a growing movement in search for a leader.

Montgomery, Alabama, the first capital of the Confederacy, was typical of segregated communities across much of the country. Almost 40 percent of its estimated 120,000 residents were Black, and they were allowed to live in only certain areas of the city. A significant number of those people worked in menial jobs in the white areas, everything from housekeepers to store clerks, commuting to those jobs on the city's segregated bus system. The Black citizens of Montgomery were not even permitted to try on shoes in a shoe store; instead they would outline their foot on a brown paper bag and wait outside while a salesperson found their correct-sized shoe.

Through the years, there had been a number of failed efforts to increase equality in the city. Among them were Edgar D. Nixon, the president of both the Alabama state chapter of the NAACP and the Montgomery branch of the Pullman Porters Union; Rufus Lewis, a former head football and track coach at Alabama State Teachers College who was deeply involved in voter registration efforts—he owned a popular nightclub that only admitted registered voters—and whose wife, Jewel, owned the largest Black funeral chapel in the city; Jo Ann Robinson, a professor of English at Alabama State and president of the militant Women's Political Council; Rosa Parks, E. D. Nixon's assistant and secretary of the NAACP, who had been actively involved in several previous efforts; Ralph Abernathy, the pastor of the First Baptist Church and dean of students at Alabama

State; and Fred Gray, one of only three Black lawyers in the city, who intended to destroy segregation by using the legal system that had created it.

All of these people were determined to end racial oppression. But it was so prevalent in every aspect of daily life that the question was where to start. However, as Parks later explained, "I don't think any segregation law angered Black people in Montgomery more than bus segregation." By law, Black passengers had to sit in the rear of the buses. If no seats were available there, they had to stand in the back section, even if there were empty seats in the front.

The Black community depended on city buses; but the city depended on those passengers to keep the system solvent. More than thirty-five thousand Black residents used those buses every day, comprising about 70 percent of total ridership.

Segregation on Montgomery's public transit had begun in 1900, when city ordinances were passed forcing Black passengers to sit in the back of the electric streetcars. Within days of those rules being instituted, Black ministers organized a boycott of the streetcars, during which Black city residents walked, rode horses, or used wagons to reach their destination. After several weeks of growing losses, the city relented, agreeing that Black passengers could be forced to surrender their seat to a white person only if there was an empty seat in the rear. Otherwise, they could remain seated.

But even that compromise lasted only briefly, ending when the state legislature passed laws mandating that Black riders had to sit or stand in the back.

Over the decades as the streetcars were replaced by buses, the system evolved; white people sat in the front of the bus, Black people sat in the back, and a section in the middle could be used by both races—although Black riders had to give up their seat to whites if no seats in front were available—and if there were no seats in the back they had to stand.

There had been many confrontations and incidents, but the police department always supported the white citizens. Jo Ann Robinson, who had been fighting for civil rights as president of the Women's Political Council, had her first encounter with the system after moving to Montgomery in 1949. On her way to the airport to visit relatives in Cleveland, she boarded a mostly empty City Lines bus and inadvertently took a seat near the front. The furious driver ordered her to "Get up from there," she recalled, "with his hand drawn back."

She was furious and frightened. "I felt like a dog. And I got mad . . . and I realized that I was a human being, and just as intelligent and far more trained than that bus driver . . . It was then that I made up . . . my mind that whatever I could do to that organization that would help bring that practice down, I would do it."

The situation had grown progressively worse. On the sweltering afternoon of August 12, 1950, a twenty-two-year-old army veteran named Hilliard Brooks had boarded a bus, put his dime in the meter, and started walking down the aisle to the rear. The driver stopped him, telling him that when whites were standing, a Black had to get off the bus and reboard in the back. Spectators agreed Hilliard, who may have been drinking, told the driver he would get off the bus—but he wanted his dime back.

An argument started. The driver summoned a nearby police officer, who cursed at the soldier and ordered him off. The situation escalated. A fight started. Brooks was knocked to the floor of the bus. He got up, pulled the officer's whistle off his chain, and started to get off. The officer fired his weapon. The bullet tore through Brooks's body and struck two bystanders. He died in a hospital.

A week-long protest march was organized but accomplished nothing. The Black residents needed the buses—but as a small group of activists began to understand, white people needed them too, and without Black riders the bus system would collapse. E. D. Nixon had made several efforts to negotiate improved conditions with the company, but his efforts were rejected.

In 1954 the Supreme Court announced in its decision in *Brown vs. Board of Education* that the long-established doctrine of providing separate but equal facilities in education was unconstitutional. Schools had to be integrated. It was a momentous decision, an upheaval in the social structure. Segregation was wobbling. People began wondering how far the court would extend these rights—both those who viewed the *Brown* decision as a direct attack on their traditional way of life, and those who sought a legal route to racial equality.

In Alabama, the NAACP began searching for the right case to legally test the city bus restrictions. While that was going on, attorney Fred Gray and Rosa Parks began meeting several times a week during her lunchtime break from her day job as a clerk at a local department store to lay out a strategy.

In March 1955, teenager Claudette Colvin, who had been studying Black history at her segregated high school, decided to make a stand. Or, more accurately, refused to stand and give up her seat to a white person. "We'd been studying the Constitution," she said. "I knew I had rights." As police officers dragged her off the bus, she resisted and was arrested for assault and battery as well as violating the segregation laws.

E. D. Nixon arranged for Fred Gray to represent her. Under Gray's direction, she became the first person known to plead not guilty to violating the city bus ordinance. But Colvin was fifteen years old, unmarried, and pregnant. While it was never revealed exactly why the movement decided against making her the test case, her age and personal situation made her a less than ideal choice. Fred Gray later denied that was the reason, explaining, "It was simply that the community wasn't ready."

Eventually, the judge dropped the civil rights charges, meaning the ordinance couldn't be challenged. Colvin was convicted of assault and placed on probation.

In their almost daily meetings, Parks and Gray carefully outlined the legal steps that had to be followed. Parks told him, if she was in that situation, "I would just sit there and wait for the police to take me away."

On December 1, 1955, that's precisely what happened. She was seated in the front row of the "colored" section of the bus when the driver ordered her to give up her seat to a white man. Three other people complied, but she remained seated. People later suggested she simply was tired after a long day at work. "No," she wrote, "the only tired I was, was tired of giving in."

She was arrested. The community had its test case. That night, Robinson and Gray met in Robinson's living room and began planning a one-day boycott of the bus system for December 5. The Women's Political Council joined the effort. The intention was to try to force the city council to eliminate segregation on public transit by demonstrating the economic power of the Black community to the city.

They had no way of knowing if that community would support them. For thousands of people the buses were an absolute necessity. In many instances, jobs were at stake. Thirty-five thousand handbills were secretly printed literally overnight and handed out at schools so children could take them home to their parents. The message was simple: "Don't ride the buses to work, to school, or anywhere on Monday."

It was impossible to predict the success or failure of the protest. Every Black resident of Montgomery had to make his or her own decision: Was it time?

America's African-American community was a movement in search of a leader. Only four months earlier fourteen-year-old Emmett Till, visiting family in Mississippi, was abducted, tortured, and murdered for supposedly flirting with a white woman. At his funeral, his mother insisted on keeping his coffin open, so people could see what was done to her son. Photographs of his mutilated body were printed in Black magazines and newspapers. His accused killers were tried and acquitted—then bragged about the murder.

It was time.

On Monday morning, December 5, both Black and white people waited anxiously to see the outcome of the protest. Men gathered in a Black barbershop across the street from a bus stop saw one well-dressed Black man apparently waiting there for the bus. He became symbolic of what would happen. As they watched, the bus arrived; for several seconds the man was hidden from view. But when the bus pulled away, he was still standing there. That scenario was repeated throughout the city. Thousands of people stayed off the buses. The protest was far more successful than anyone had imagined.

That morning, a large crowd also filled the courthouse and the surrounding streets to support Rosa Parks. As she and Gray had planned, she pleaded not guilty to charges of disorderly conduct and violating a city ordinance. She was convicted and fined $10 plus $4 court costs. That allowed Fred Gray to appeal the conviction to a higher court, hoping that eventually it might reach courts with the authority to determine whether the segregation laws should stand, or be found unconstitutional.

The overwhelming response to the boycott inspired its leaders to extend it from one day to . . . to as long as it took. Managing that was a massive task that would require creating an organization. The entire effort had to be coordinated. Daily transportation for thousands of people had to be arranged, responsibilities assigned, money raised, legal issues resolved.

Robinson, Gray, Abernathy, and fifteen other people, most of them ministers, met that afternoon at the Mount Zion AME Zion Church on Holt Street. The announced purpose of the meeting was to make a schedule for the mass rally that would take place that night at the Holt Street Baptist Church. But the discussion quickly became focused on the stunning success of the boycott and the need for an organization to run it. There was some conversation about enlisting the aid of the NAACP, but there was general agreement that this had to be run locally. That would avoid any charges that the movement was being controlled by "outside agitators," and at that time, the NAACP did not have an especially strong presence in Alabama. Other people suggested the local Interdenominational Ministerial Alliance could take control, but Ralph Abernathy strongly urged them to form an entirely new organization. After a brief discussion they created the Montgomery Improvement Association. Now they needed someone to lead it.

The two best-known and respected civil rights leaders in the city were Nixon and Lewis. Both men had their supporters, so rather than alienating a sizeable segment of the population, neither was chosen. Instead, Jo Ann Robinson suggested the pastor of her church, the small, upscale Dexter Avenue Baptist Church—Dr. Martin Luther King Jr. Dr. King was not in the room at the time because he had a three-week-old baby at home and was late for the meeting. King had one substantial advantage: Many of the people at that meeting, including Fred Gray, did not know him. Several of them barely knew his name. As Rosa Parks later wrote, "He hadn't been there long enough to make any strong friends or enemies." E. D. Nixon put it more directly, "He had not been there long enough for the city fathers to put their hands on him."

He was simply the young pastor of a small church. Later that evening, Gray asked Robinson why she had suggested King. He never forgot her response: "Because he can move people with his words."

Rufus Lewis nominated Martin Luther King Jr. for the office of president of the Montgomery Improvement Association. The nomination was seconded. All those in favor were asked to raise their hands. The vote was unanimous. Dr. Martin Luther King Jr. was elected president. Other officers were elected. According to the minutes of the meeting, "It was agreed that the protest be continued until conditions are improved."

The twenty-six-year-old Martin Luther King Jr. had been born in Atlanta, where his father was the widely respected pastor of the Ebenezer Baptist Church. In 1944, during his first visit to the North he wrote to his father that he "saw some things I had never anticipated to see. After we passed Washington there was no discrimination at all." After serving as associate pastor of his father's church for three years, in 1954 he had moved to Alabama to become minister of the Dexter Avenue Baptist Church. Among the conditions under which he accepted the position was that every church member must be a registered voter and a member of the NAACP. He and his wife, Coretta, had been living in Montgomery for less than a year when the MIA was formed.

Rather than a national election involving millions of people and costing millions of dollars, or the highly structured regular elections held by large organizations, unions for instance, with nominations and campaigning over a period of time, this was a simple, foundational election. It was the kind of election held every day by school boards, teams, and small groups throughout the world. It was the essence of the democratic process. Even those people present in the room did not consider it special, and certainly not historic. They were sure it soon would be forgotten. What happened afterward proved them wrong.

The rally that night was Dr. King's official introduction to the public. Hundreds of people filled the church and stood outside. Loudspeakers were set up so everyone could hear. The main issue was how long the boycott should continue. A few more days? It was doubtful it could last longer than a week. The logistics that would be required to transport an entire community twice a day defied logic. It just wasn't possible.

The church was hushed as Dr. King stood to deliver the first significant speech of his career. He discussed the protest and warned of the hard days that might be coming, urging people to protest peacefully and with love in their hearts, then said if they do so, "when the history books are written in future generations the historians will pause and say, 'There lived a great people—a Black people—who injected new meaning and dignity into the veins of civilization.'" That was, he concluded, their challenge and their responsibility.

The crowd roared!

Rather than ending after a few days, the Montgomery Bus Boycott began growing. In only a few days, a massive, functioning transportation system was in operation. Thirty thousand people were driven back and forth from work by a fleet of taxis, private cars, and even hearses every day. Other people walked miles or rode bicycles. Initially, the MIA did not demand an end to segregation on the buses, but rather a compromise that would make the system more palatable for Black riders. The white city government refused to negotiate seriously, terrified that if they lost the battle, this strategy would spread to other areas—in particular, schools.

As the protest stretched into weeks and began attracting national attention, Dr. King, an obscure pastor at the beginning of December, was becoming more widely known—earning respect for his calm, reasonable, commanding approach, coupled with his extraordinary use of the English language. He preached the doctrine of nonviolence, of passive resistance, both as a tactic and a way of life.

The city did not know how to deal with the situation. Each attempt made to respond to the protest just raised King's profile. The mayor and several members of the city council announced they had joined the racist organization the White Citizens' Council. The mayor described the protest as "an attempt to destroy the social fabric." One night in late January a man walked up to the King home and tossed a small bomb on the front porch; no one was hurt, but there was damage to the property. When a large crowd gathered outside the house, King pleaded with them, "Don't get your weapons; he who lives by the sword will perish by the sword."

In early February, the increasingly desperate city used an obscure, decades-old city statute essentially prohibiting organized boycotts to indict 115 people, including Rosa Parks, Nixon, Lewis, Abernathy, and Dr. King. They all went peacefully to the police station and stood in line to be arrested. E. D. Nixon pointed out the irony. "You stopped riding buses when you were arrested. Now you're arrested for not riding."

Reporters from more than thirty-five media outlets around the country attended a massive rally held that night. Dr. King told more than five thousand people who crammed into Abernathy's First Baptist Church, or listened outside, that decades of being humiliated, of being cursed at, had sent them into "the abyss of oppression." And in response, "we have decided to rise up only with the weapon of protest . . . This is not a war between the white and the Negro but a conflict between justice and injustice."

He moved people with his words.

Rather than conducting more than ninety separate trials, Fred Gray and other attorneys representing the protestors agreed that one trial would be held and the verdict in that trial would be applied to all the other defendants. Martin Luther King Jr. would be put on trial for the community.

This was now a national story. As the trial began, *The New York Times* reported on its front page, "The Rev. Martin Luther King Jr. was the first of ninety-three persons, including twenty-five ministers, arrested in connection with the movement to be tried."

Numerous Black witnesses testified about the abuse they had suffered mostly in silence for years. For almost all of them, it was their first opportunity to speak directly to white men and women about their lives. Or, as one woman said, "Well, now, since y'all got me up here, there's a lot of things I want to tell you about this whole mess." And then she did.

Among the highlights of the trial was the testimony of Georgia Gilmore, who was asked who made the decision to stop riding the buses. The courtroom was rocked with cheers when she replied, "Fifty thousand Negroes of Montgomery."

Days later the *Times* profiled King as its Man in the News, writing, "Dr. King is a Baptist preacher in a great southern tradition of resounding, repetitive rhetoric. And he can build to his climax with a crescendo of impassioned pulpit-pounding that overwhelms the listener with the depth of his convictions."

He began accepting invitations to speak around the country. At a news conference in Chicago, he told reporters he was there to give an unbiased account of life for Black Americans in the South to the northern media. In New York he delivered a sermon about Moses fleeing oppression to ten thousand parishioners at the massive Cathedral of St. John the Divine. In Boston, he received the Unitarian Association Award as "an uncompromising champion of enduring principles." The national Black magazine *Jet* wrote that he "has become a symbol of divinely inspired hope, a kind of modern Moses who has brought new self-respect to southern Negroes."

The media attention continued to escalate. More than sixty outlets literally from around the world covered the trial, including all the major TV networks. "If this movement is successful," editorialized the *Hartford Courant*, "the Reverend Dr. King will become . . . the continuing spearhead in the fight against segregation."

At the conclusion of the trial Dr. King was found guilty by

the judge and fined $500 plus an additional $500 court costs, which the judge said was less than it could have been because "the defendant had discouraged violence." The verdict was appealed. But that verdict did not end the boycott, which continued for an astonishing 381 days.

While the protest was still ongoing, Gray and attorney Charles Langford had challenged bus segregation in federal court. The Montgomery Bus Boycott ended only after the Supreme Court, citing the precedent set by *Brown*, upheld a lower court ruling that segregated seating on Alabama's buses was unconstitutional. On December 20, 1956, Black passengers on Montgomery's buses could sit in any seat. It was the beginning of a cascade of legal decisions attacking Jim Crow. But by that time, Dr. King had become recognized and respected around the world as the leader of the Civil Rights Movement.

In 1957, he founded the Southern Christian Leadership Conference to coordinate the activities of numerous other civil rights organizations. Throughout the next decade the SCLC played a significant role navigating the roiling waters of racism to achieve equality of rights in every aspect of society. He later worked closely with both the John F. Kennedy and Lyndon Johnson administrations in the attempt to end centuries of racial discrimination in America, culminating with Congress passing the landmark Civil Rights Act in 1964 and Voting Rights Act a year later.

A year earlier, in August 1963, King had galvanized the nation when he spoke to 250,000 people during the historic March on Washington for Jobs and Freedom. His iconic "I Have a Dream" speech given on the Washington Mall remains a momentous event in the struggle for equal rights.

In 1964, less than a decade after being elected president of the Montgomery Improvement Association by a group of angry people meeting in a small Alabama church, for "his nonviolent struggle for civil rights for the Afro-American population," Dr. Martin Luther King Jr. was awarded the Nobel Peace Prize.

While America was fighting a war in Vietnam, Dr. King continued his efforts to ensure equal rights for all people. In April 1968, while in Memphis, Tennessee, to lead a protest march by striking sanitation workers, he was assassinated as he stood on a balcony of a local motel. By that time, he had already secured his place in history. Like Mahatma Gandhi, he has become a legendary figure, a global symbol of nonviolent protest in the fight for human dignity.

ELEVEN

1958: The Election of Pope John XXIII

VERE PAPA MORTUUS EST. "Truly, the pope is dead."

With that announcement begins the process of electing the next Bishop of Rome, Successor of the Apostles, Supreme Pontiff of the Universal Church, Patriarch of the West, Primate of Italy, Archbishop and Metropolitan of the Roman Province and Sovereign of the State of the Vatican: The Pope.

The title itself is from the Latin *pater* and Greek *pappas*, both meaning "father," but to the estimated five hundred million Catholics living around the world in 1958 he was simply the Holy Father. The Pontiff, or "bridge builder," is the leader of the Catholic Church, in addition to serving as the ruling monarch of Vatican City, the world's smallest city-state, making him the world's only elected sovereign.

On October 9, 1958, after almost twenty years of service, Pope Pius XII murmured, "Pray. Pray that this regrettable situation for the Church may end," and died at his summer residence in Castel Gandolfo, Italy. Immediately, a process dating back almost one thousand years began, the highly structured ritual of electing his successor, who would be the 261st Pope.

Or 262nd, depending on who was doing the counting.

Eugenio Pacelli, Pius XII, had been elected on March 2, 1939, and skillfully guided the Church through the terrors of World War II, the postwar creation of the Communist bloc, and the beginning of the Cold War. The Catholic Church is a religious institution, but its massive size and global presence also give the Pope tremendous political influence, making the selection of a new Pope a significant world event.

There is no other electoral system anywhere else in the world so imbued with tradition, so dependent on pomp and circumstance as the one that has developed over nearly a millennium to determine the new leader of the Catholic Church. Unlike any other elective office, there is no set term, the man chosen by his peers will serve for the remainder of his life—or until he voluntarily resigns.

The new Pope is elected by a conclave, a gathering of cardinals, although only those men under eighty years old are eligible to vote. The process has been roughly the same since the college of cardinals was created in 1059. Prior to that time, there was no accepted standard way to choose a new Bishop of Rome. The system has changed regularly through the centuries to fit the political reality of the times. In the earliest years, for example, a layman could be picked for the post. But kings, emperors, and powerful Roman families—those whose fortunes would be affected by the decisions of the new Pope—played a significant role in the Church's choice.

The first Pope was St. Peter, who was appointed by Jesus Christ to rule in His name. According to Matthew 16: 18–19, "I will give thee the keys to the kingdom of heaven; and whatever thou shalt bind on earth shall be bound in heaven, and whatever thou shalt loose on earth shall be loosed in heaven."

Ironically, when called upon by Jesus to spread his message, St. Peter was Jewish.

Since St. Peter was crucified by the Emperor Nero, sometime between 64 and 68 AD, there has been an unbroken line of succession. The precise number of Popes has long been debated; Stephen II died two days after being elected in 752—but before he could be consecrated. One Pope initially was listed twice, under two different names. Between 1378 and 1417, the Church had two, at times three, different men claiming the papacy, each of them having a significant following.

The often-chaotic process of selecting the Pope also led to some unusual choices. Eighteen-year-old Pope John XII was essentially given the post in 955 by his powerful Roman father and became known for his scandalous behavior. Pope Benedict IX supposedly sold the papacy to his godfather, Pope Gregory VI, in 1045, although he later would reclaim it by force.

The transformation of that erratic system into an orderly procedure began in 1059 when Pope Nicholas II established then empowered the college of cardinals to elect one of their members to serve as Pope. There was no designated number of cardinals necessary to conduct an election. For many years, the difficulty in making the long trip to Rome limited the size of that group; in 1254, for example, there were only seven cardinals. The procedures to be followed changed drastically through the ages; because conclaves often lasted for months or even years, in 1274 Gregory X issued a papal bull, a decree, instituting a secret ballot, which required the cardinals be secluded behind locked doors with their food rationed until they reached a decision.

There have been many efforts to formalize the selection process. At the Lateran Council of 1179, a gathering of bishops to debate and determine church doctrine and practice, it was agreed that two-thirds of the votes would be required for election, which has continued with occasional changes since then.

These attempts were not always successful. In 1294, for example, after rival factions had spent two years trying to agree on a compromise candidate, Pope Celestine V, a seventy-nine-year-old hermit living in a cave, was chosen.

Additional reforms instituted by Gregory XV in 1621 firmly established step-by-step procedures to be followed from the moment a Pope died until his successor formally accepts his new position. Additional changes have been made or introduced to deal with developing technology and strengthen the role and image of the Church. For instance, while ballots have been burned following each conclave vote since the 1400s, it wasn't until 1914 that the popular tradition of emitting smoke from the roof of the Sistine Chapel—black if no one had been elected, white to announce a new Pope—was introduced.

By 1958, what once was an unruly, unpredictable, mercurial system had slowly developed into a highly structured, carefully delineated process.

The actual duties of the Pope have also evolved. He is the unquestioned authority in matters of faith and morals of every member of the Church, able to make and interpret laws. He canonizes saints, appoints bishops, establishes new dioceses and has the resources of the Church at his disposal. However, the well-known claim that the Pope is infallible, that he cannot be wrong, in actuality applies only to a very narrow range of issues specifically concerning faith and morals, and does not include other papal statements. It sometimes may be conflated with St. Augustine's statement in about 417 AD, "Rome has spoken. The cause is finished," but that was never the intent. In fact, the doctrine of infallibility has only been invoked twice in church history.

The seat of the Catholic Church and the Pope's residence, Vatican City, was recognized as an independent state by Italian dictator Benito Mussolini in February 1929. It is the smallest independent state in the world, about 0.2 square miles, or about 110 acres, located entirely inside the city of Rome. The Pope is the head of state, although the Holy See, the governing body of the Church, also rules Vatican City.

As a result of his religious and secular duties, the Pope occupies a unique position and is considered one of the most important men in the world. Pius XII had positioned the Church as an anti-Communist bastion, which obviously impacted millions of Catholics living in Eastern Europe. He also had come out strongly against racism, warning the world only weeks before his death, "One knows too well, alas, to what excesses racial pride and racial hate can lead." He even gave the strongly questioned use of nuclear energy for peaceful purposes "our blessing together with the approval and the congratulations . . . of all civilized people." So, when Pius XII died the world paid attention. The conclave to elect a new Pope began sixteen days after his death. Fifty-three cardinals were eligible to vote, but two of them were prevented from attending by the Communist governments of Hungary and Yugoslavia.

On Saturday morning, October 25, the fifty-one cardinals moved slowly in a procession into the Sistine Chapel, chanting "*Veni, Creator Spiritus*," "Come, Creator Spirit." There were representatives from twenty-one different countries, among them seventeen cardinals from Italy, the smallest percentage in five hundred years. For the first time, cardinals from China, India, and Africa were part of the conclave. The doors were doubly locked behind them. Throughout the entire conclave, no communication with the world outside those doors was permitted. Reading newspapers, watching television, phone calls, even conversations with any laypeople were prohibited. The shutters on the windows were closed to prevent communication by lights or mirrors. Earlier that morning, the cardinals had attended a mass in St. Peter's Basilica, at which they were urged to elect a supreme pontiff "who will be a teacher, a bridge between social classes, peoples and nations and, above all, a saintly man." In contrast to Pius XII, who had been considered cold and aloof, the next Pope "will freely receive and welcome the bishops . . . He will be prepared to give them counsel in their doubts, to listen and comfort them in their anxieties and to encourage their plans."

As this conclave began no candidate was favored. There have been times at which the popular choice is clear; in 1939, that had been Eugenio Pacelli, who became Pius XII. There was little question he would be elected. But not this time. Almost all of these men had been made cardinals by Pius XII; only four of them had participated in the conclave that had elected him. Theoretically, the campaigning and maneuvering was done beforehand. While lobbying is not permitted once those doors are shut, informal conversations take place during social gatherings and meals in which views and opinions can be exchanged. Because participants are sworn to secrecy, with harsh penalties, exactly what takes place inside a conclave is more rumor than substance, although it is known that making deals, trades, promises, and agreements is not allowed.

Following Pius XII's long reign, the college of cardinals had to decide what type of Pope would serve the present needs of the Church; someone young who might lead it in a more modern direction? An older man capable of guiding it smoothly until a consensus about the future of the Church could be reached? There was even serious discussion about electing a non-cardinal—a suggestion that elicited such an angry response from one cardinal that he pounded a table so vigorously he smashed the ruby in his ring.

As in most elections, voting blocs formed. The cardinals who had been working together in Rome knew each other well and wanted to ensure continuity. The French cardinals valued their independence and wanted to protect it. Others believed it was time to look beyond the Holy See.

Among the strongest early candidates was Cardinal Giuseppe Siri, the conservative fifty-two-year-old archbishop of Genoa. He was known in the Church as the "minestrone cardinal" because of his volunteer work in Genoa's soup kitchens. What made his election problematic was his age; one prelate, or high church official, warned that he could serve as Pope for forty years, which would eliminate any dreams held by young, ambitious men. "What we need is an old man," that official suggested, "a transitional Pope. He won't introduce any great innovations and will give us time to pause and reorganize." And leave plenty of opportunity in his wake.

There was also support for sixty-three-year-old cardinal Gregory Peter Agagianian. While he had spent most of his career in Rome, he was an Armenian and it was highly unlikely that a non-Italian would be selected.

The sixty-seven-year-old archbishop of Bologna, Cardinal Giacomo Lercaro, had many supporters who had long admired his commitment to a simple life of service, his belief that local clergy should have more decision-making authority, his commitment to social reform, and that, in the words of Cardinal

Angelo Roncalli, "He knows how to create at once an atmosphere of happiness."

Other possibilities included seventy-nine-year-old Cardinal Benedetto Aloisi Masella, sixty-eight-year-old conservative cardinal Alfredo Ottaviani, and the seventy-seven-year-old Roncalli, who had served as the patriarch—the leader—of Venice since 1953.

It really was a wide-open competition. *The New York Times* profiled twelve possible candidates. *Life* magazine ran photos and brief bios of eight men. Cardinal Roncalli's name appeared on every list. There was substantial gambling on the selection, and some oddsmakers listed him as the two-to-one favorite. The cardinal was noncommittal, telling friends before the conclave began, "It's true that we're all saying, 'Not me, Lord, not me,' but the Holy Spirit's tongues of fire have to fall on one of us."

Cardinal Roncalli's supporters believed he would be a reliable, calm caretaker through a transitional period—as the Church moved from Pius XII to a younger leader more reflective of the changing times—that, given his age, clearly would not last long. There was little in his past to raise concerns he would become anything beyond a sensible manager for the immediate future.

Angelo Giuseppe Roncalli was the fourth of thirteen children born to sharecroppers in a small village in Lombardy. He had entered the priesthood as a twenty-three-year old in 1904. During World War I he had served as a stretcher-bearer and chaplain, then spent most of the early years of his career representing the Vatican in Turkey, Greece, Bulgaria, and post–World War II France. His tenure in France was especially notable; it was reported by newspapers that "he had endeared himself to political leaders with his diplomatic skill and to the people with his love of France, French wines and cuisine." It was rumored, perhaps humorously, that his robes of office had been made for him by Christian Dior. When he left France in 1953 to become patriarch of Venice, he received the coveted Commander of the Legion of Honour and was feted by the eight men who had served as prime minister during his time there.

His actions as archbishop of Venice had reassured other cardinals that he respected the traditional values. At one point, for example, he barred tourists wearing shorts from visiting that city's churches, explaining, "Italy is not on the Equator, and even there, by the way, lions wear their coats and crocodiles are lined with their most precious hides."

It was later revealed that during World War II, he had used his position to save the lives of numerous refugees, especially Jews. His efforts included delivering lifesaving "immigration certificates" to Palestine, sending baptismal certificates "of convenience" to priests in Europe, and in several instances he also interceded to help liberate people from concentration camps.

Although Roncalli knew he was papabile, a legitimate candidate for the papacy, he did not believe he could win the election. While he had the support of the French cardinals, he had spent too many years away from Rome to have made the presumed necessary strong connections with the powerful men there. So he had packed just a few clothes in a small overnight bag, feeling confident he would quickly be returning to his duties in Venice.

It had taken only three votes over twenty hours to elect Pope Pius XII, the shortest conclave of the twentieth century. No one expected the election to replace him to be brief. By tradition, one ballot, one vote, can be taken on the first afternoon and after that four votes—two in the morning, two in the afternoon—are taken each day, until someone receives the necessary two-thirds plus one or, in this instance, thirty-five votes. Voting in a conclave is an elaborate procedure. It is done by secret ballot. Until this election each cardinal had been given a paper ballot on which he wrote his choice, signed his name, folded the ballot over his signature, and then sealed it with wax. Pius had changed the ballot in 1945, eliminating the need to sign and seal it.

The actual voting procedure is a ceremony that has been refined and ritualized over a thousand years. Each cardinal, after writing his choice on his ballot, holds it up so it can be seen by everyone, then walks to the altar and recites the pledge, "I call as my witness Christ the Lord, who will be my judge, that my vote is given to the one whom I believe should be elected according to God," places his ballot on a plate, then tips it into the chalice, the sacred vessel.

As a round of voting is completed three cardinals, known as scrutineers, shake the container and count the votes. The name on each ballot is read aloud. When the tally is concluded the ballots are stitched together with red thread and burned in a small stove, emitting white or black smoke.

On the first day of this conclave no vote was taken. Four ballots took place on the second day. After each round, the votes were burned, sending a message to the tens of thousands of people gathered in St. Peter's Square. The smoke should have been black, indicating a Pope had not been chosen. There had been a brief problem that morning when the first puffs of smoke appeared to be white, although within a few seconds they turned dark.

That was a hint of what was to happen after the fourth

ballot. *The Irish Independent* reported, "As the sky over Rome was becoming a velvet Black, and as the 200,000 Romans and Pilgrims . . . who thronged St. Peter's Square were beginning to feel the chill of the evening air, the searchlights beamed on the chimney emerging from the Sistine Chapel caught a puff of smoke which seemed to be white . . . Then there was cheering, singing and clapping and loud cries of 'Viva il Papa.'

"A little while later it was seen that the smoke was undoubtedly black."

Vatican Radio announced gleefully, "There is absolutely no doubt. A Pope has been elected."

But it was a mistake. A huge mistake. The error raced around the world. It took almost twenty minutes before the joy—and the white smoke—dissipated. While the precise reason this happened was never fully explained, one official claimed it was caused by problems lighting the straw in the stove; another official suggested the lack of the wax seal used previously on the ballot had somehow changed the color of the smoke. The marshal in charge of conclave logistics had contacted the cardinals "by means of communications which I cannot disclose" to inform them of the issue and provide them with correctly colored smoke torches from a local fireworks factory.

Few highly contested elections remain free of controversy and intrigue. Even church elections. This strange episode launched a conspiracy theory which claimed Cardinal Siri actually had been elected on that first day of voting and chosen the name Pope Gregory XVII, but outside forces had threatened the Vatican into submission, forcing them to rescind his election. Siri himself dismissed this wild claim.

At the end of that day, Roncalli led with twenty votes, Agagianian had eighteen, while the remaining votes were split between several men. Four more ballots taken on the third day of the conclave were equally inconclusive. The voting between Roncalli and Agagianian, Roncalli later revealed, "went up and down like two chickpeas in boiling water."

The conclave was deadlocked. Cardinal Masella was briefly suggested as a compromise candidate, but that idea was rejected. More ballots were held. While electioneering is not allowed, quiet discussions took place as the cardinals glanced toward the heavens for guidance. Slowly, vote by vote, the conclave moved toward Roncalli. Finally, on the eleventh ballot, Angelo Roncalli was elected Pope. "One would say it is like a dream," he wrote in his diary, "and yet, until I die, it is the most solemn reality of my life. So, I'm ready, Lord."

Another series of rituals followed his election. During the conclave, the cardinals sat on chairs beneath a purple canopy; after the choice was made, the junior cardinal deacon lowered all the canopies—other than the one covering the new Pope. Then the dean of the college of cardinals asked Roncalli in Latin, "Do you accept your election as Supreme Pontiff, which has just been canonically concluded?"

"Accepto," he said. "Seeing the sign of God's will in the votes of my brother Cardinals of the Holy Roman Church, I accept the decision they have made."

The dean continued, "By what name do you wish to be known?"

A newly elected Pope can choose any name he desires, but Roncalli's response came as a surprise. It was the first indication that he was not going to be the docile place-holding pontiff most people expected him to be. "I will be called John," he replied. He picked that name, he later explained, because it was his father's name, the name of the parish church where he was baptized, and that "It is the name which has been most used in the long series of Roman Pontiffs." He did not mention that the name had not been used since 1413, when one of three anti-popes, illegitimate claimants for the papacy, had claimed to be John XXIII. (It was acknowledged that John XXII had served from 1316 to 1334.) Roncalli's decision briefly confused historians, who wondered if he was John XXIII or John XXIV, eventually agreeing that he was the legitimate John XXIII.

The last thing he had to do before greeting the hundreds of thousands of people waiting in the square was put on the pontifical robe. The newly elected Pope John XXIII went into the small room next to the Sistine Chapel known as the "Room of Tears"—called that because it is the place the newly elected Pope can freely express emotion. Robes in three sizes had been prepared to fit whomever was elected. He was a big man and unfortunately, even the largest robe was too small. Using safety pins and a strategically placed surplice, a vestment, a tailor was able to hide the problem. When it was done, he looked at himself in the mirror and joked that the loosely hanging garments would be a "disaster for television."

After being properly outfitted John XXIII returned to the Sistine Chapel and was seated on a papal chair; the Fisherman's Ring—symbolic of the fisherman St. Peter—was brought to him on a velvet cushion and placed on the fourth finger of his right hand.

Then, like victorious politicians all over the world greeting supporters on election night, Pope John XXIII stepped out on the balcony. He did not give a speech, remembering later, "Dazzled by the television lights, I could see nothing but an amorphous, swaying mass. I blessed Rome and the world as though I were a blind man."

Although Roncalli became John XXIII at that moment, several days later a five-hour-long coronation ceremony took place on the balcony, during which the papal tiara was placed on his head. As he acknowledged, it took him a few weeks to get used to his powerful position. "It often happens," he admitted, "that I wake up at night and begin to think about a serious problem and I decide I must tell the Pope about it. Then I wake up completely and remember that I am the Pope."

His election was popular within the Church. While there was hope he would allow clergy more freedom to make local decisions and would listen to their concerns and suggestions, they took comfort in his respect for tradition. As the Vatican newspaper noted, "He is endowed with clear qualities and well-tested virtue," which was why "observers were apt to regard his forthcoming reign as 'transitional,'—conservatively following the policy lines laid down in the last 19 years by Pius XII."

But the new Pope destroyed the notion that his was going to be a caretaker reign in January 1959 when, reported the United Press International news service, he "launched the Catholic world on a new offensive . . . calling the Church's 1,800 cardinals, archbishops, patriarchs and other top spiritual leaders to the Vatican for the first Ecumenical Council in 89 years.

"An Ecumenical Council is the most important meeting of church leaders in Catholic dogma. Only 20 have been held in history."

It was a churchquake. A totally unexpected, unanticipated momentous announcement. Ecumenical councils were rare and resulted in fundamental changes in the foundations of the Church. The First Ecumenical Council, held in 325, set the date for Easter. Subsequent gatherings declared Mary the mother of God and resolved the schism that challenged the very existence of the authority of the Pope in Rome; the eighteen-year long Council of Trent condemned the beliefs of Martin Luther and other Protestants; and the most recent meeting, Vatican I, which ended prematurely in 1870 with the beginning of the Franco-Prussian War and the unification of Italy, established the supremacy of the Pope and defined papal infallibility.

His unexpected announcement stunned church leaders. While there was some indication that Pius XII had laid the groundwork, John XXIII explained that the concept came from a higher authority, that he had felt his soul "illuminated with a great idea."

While the announced objectives of the gathering were intentionally vague, the reality was that it was going to be an effort to modernize the Church, to make it more accessible to more people and more relevant to their lives. It was an extraordinarily ambitious agenda. *Time* magazine wrote, "John's historic mission is fired by a desire to endow the Christian faith with . . . a new spirit . . . He set out to adapt his church's whole life and stance to the revolutionary changes in science, economics, morals and politics that have swept the modern world."

It was an ambitious undertaking. Strong opposition to it came from the ultraconservative Roman Curia, the administrative body essentially running the Church. It took several years to turn the concept of the council into reality, but in October 1962, almost three thousand religious leaders gathered in St. Peter's Basilica—built over the ruins of Nero's circus, where Christians had been fed to lions and St. Peter had been crucified—to reform the Church.

By the time Vatican II ended three years later, Pope John had died and been replaced by Pope Paul VI, but his desire to make the Church relevant in the modern world had been achieved. Among the council's accomplishments were allowing the Latin mass and other sacraments to be conducted in local languages; changing the way of life and dress of nuns, monks, and friars; declaring Jews could no longer be blamed for the crucifixion of Christ and promoting harmony with Jews and other non-Christians; declaring that all men should have religious freedom; and issuing guidelines for dealing with contemporary challenges facing the Church like nuclear war, social justice, and updating the moral doctrines on sexuality and marriage.

Vatican II revolutionized the Church in significant ways. While not straying from its essential religious message, it modified the methods used to deliver it. As many had hoped, the Vatican had ceded more responsibility to local authorities. The media suggested it was similar to the State Department allowing embassies in different nations to determine foreign policy in those areas.

The council's decrees and declarations certainly were not universally popular. More conservative members of the clergy strongly objected that the reforms had rejected centuries-old traditions; that rather than strengthening the Church, these proposed changes "watered it down," especially the decision to conduct Mass in regional languages.

If the council was all Pope John XXIII had accomplished in his brief (four years and seven months) papacy, it still would have been enough to make him an historic figure. Not only did he demystify the Church by literally changing its language, he also gave it a human face. As *Time* wrote in 1962 when it honored him as the first Pope to be selected its Man of the Year,

"John XXIII is the most popular Pope of modern times—and perhaps ever."

He also embraced change, increasing the college of cardinals for the first time in more than 370 years, from the traditional maximum of seventy to ninety, naming the first cardinals from Japan and the Philippines, and encouraging the growth of the Church in Africa by elevating Cardinal Laurean Rugambwa of Tanganyika.

He pursued a joyous papacy; telling people he wanted to be known as "the good shepherd defending trust and goodness," he made himself publicly accessible. He had an intrinsic understanding of the media and took advantage of new technologies to showcase the warmth and caring attitude that he was injecting into the Church. In Venice he had been ordered by Pius to stop strolling freely in the streets, talking to everyone, but after becoming John XXIII he ventured out far more than any other Pope. He went places no Pope had ever been seen, visiting schools and prisons, parish churches and orphanages. When visiting one prison, he told the inmates, "You could not come to me, so I came to you." He was the first twentieth-century Pope to travel by train, making a whistle-stop tour across Italy; tens of thousands of people surrounded his car when the train stopped for one minute in the seaport of Ancona. He also welcomed more world leaders and commoners to the Vatican than had ever visited before; when granting a papal audience to a traveling circus, he cautioned a lion cub, "You must behave here. We are used only to the calm lion of St. Mark."

On June 3, 1963, the UPI informed the world, "Pope John XXIII, one of the greatest Popes in the history of the Roman Catholic Church, died today." The AP reported, "When

Angelo Giuseppe Cardinal Roncalli was elected Pope in the autumn of 1958 some observers thought his reign would mark time . . . But the Pope promptly ended such notions . . . He studded his reign with landmarks in every area of papal activity."

In honor of his many contributions to the Church and the world, in April 2014 Pope John XXIII, "The Good Pope," as he has become known, was declared a saint.

TWELVE

1967 and 1969: Women Become World Leaders—Indira Gandhi and Golda Meir

IN 1940, THE LEGENDARY comedienne Gracie Allen announced that she was the Surprise Party's candidate for president of the United States. She ran a well-publicized mock campaign, popping into the most popular radio shows and embarking on a thirty-four-city whistle-stop tour, during which she held rallies from the rear of her train that attracted hundreds of thousands of people. Running without a vice-presidential candidate (because she vowed there would be no vice in her administration), she told doubters, "A woman can and will be elected if she is qualified and gets enough votes."

America got the joke. The whole world did. The ancient Greek playwright Aeschylus wrote in 467 BC, "Let the women stay at home and hold their peace," and throughout history, most societies had embraced that notion. Women were appreciated, lauded, and admired for a great variety of skills, but politics was not among them. Women kept the house and raised the kids; running governments and making decisions were a man's job. In fact, simply being able to vote in elections was a relatively new development for women; New Zealand became the first country to allow women to vote in national elections in 1893 and other countries followed cautiously.

Even Eleanor Roosevelt, Franklin Roosevelt's greatly respected First Lady, was hesitant about women running and holding political office, saying, "There are some women who have the same type of mind as men. That used to be considered the highest compliment that a man could pay a woman . . . [It meant] her mind was analytical, non-emotional and objective . . . And less credit will always be given for her intelligence. She will be constantly proving herself and if she makes a mistake it will injure not herself alone, but all women."

It was a deeply ingrained belief, though there were occasional exceptions. In 1872, stockbroker, newspaper publisher, and former traveling fortune-teller Victoria Woodhull became the first female presidential candidate when she was nominated by the Equal Rights Party. Several others followed her. In 1916—four years before the Ninteenth Amendment granted American women across the nation the right to vote—Jeannette Rankin became the first woman to hold federal office, when Montana elected her to the House of Representatives. In 1932 Arkansas made Hattie Caraway America's first female to be elected to the Senate. In England, American-born Nancy Witcher Astor became the first female Member of Parliament in 1919.

But those and other similar campaigns were isolated events, rare examples of strong-willed women making themselves heard while providing a hint of what was possible. The fight for women's suffrage had actually begun in the American colonies in 1647, when Mistress Margaret Brent, heir to Lord Calvert's estate, demanded a seat in the Maryland legislature. "I've come to seek a voice in this assembly," she announced. "And yet because I am a woman, forsooth I must stand idly by and not even have a voice in the framing of your laws." The governor rejected her request.

While John Adams was at work in the Continental Congress creating a system of laws, his wife Abigail Adams wrote to him, warning, "If . . . in the new laws . . . particular care and attention are not paid to the ladies, we are determined to foment a rebellion and will not hold ourselves bound to obey any laws in which we have no voice."

An organized campaign for women's right to vote was initiated by Elizabeth Cady Stanton and Lucretia Mott at the Seneca Falls Convention in upstate New York, in 1848. What would eventually become the Nineteenth Amendment, granting full women's suffrage, was drafted by Susan B. Anthony in 1875 and introduced in Congress three years later—although it would not be finally ratified by the necessary three-fourths of the states until August 18, 1920.

In 1869, the Territory of Wyoming had become the first political entity to allow women to vote in local elections and by the time the amendment was ratified, numerous states had some form of universal suffrage.

Long before the United States permitted women to vote in presidential elections, twenty-one foreign nations had granted them that right, among them England, Germany, the Scandinavian countries, Poland, Australia, and Czechoslovakia.

But the right to vote did not necessarily include the right for women to run for an elective office. It wasn't until 1902 that Australia became the first modern nation to allow women to run for federal office. And while throughout history legendary queens, czarinas, pharaohs, and empresses had led empires, states, and nations—among them Cleopatra, Catherine the Great, and

Queen Victoria—and Native American tribes had female chiefs, in modernity, a woman had never been elected to head a major government. That began to change in July 1960, when the island nation of Ceylon, later to become Sri Lanka, elected the first female prime minister in modern history, forty-four-year-old Mrs. Sirimavo Bandaranaike, the widow of an assassinated leader. As newspapers reported, "Crowds, mostly women, cheered when she appeared on a balcony . . . 'Victory to our lady' the throng cried as she acknowledged the tribute."

Bandaranaike was essentially a replacement for her husband, who had been killed months earlier. She "campaigned largely on her personal appeal and the promise to continue the domestic policies of her husband, which at the end were vague." Her political experience, it was pointed out, consisted primarily of serving as a hostess for her husband and an informal advisor; the nation's media nicknamed her "the weeping widow" for her skillful use of sympathy about her husband's murder for her own political gain.

The real importance of her election, according to the *Herald Tribune*, was that "voters will be grateful to the Ceylonese voters for the chance to see at last what a democratically elected female ruler is like . . . no country has really considered the possibility."

During the next four decades, she served three different terms as prime minister, leading the nation's difficult transition from Ceylon to the fully independent Republic of Sri Lanka in 1972. During her sometimes turbulent years in office, she instituted socialist policies and land reforms and nationalized major industries. She actually was appointed to her third term in 1994 by her daughter, Chandrika Kumaratunga, Sri Lanka's first female president.

Other women soon followed Bandaranaike down the path

she pioneered as a national leader. In 1966, India's Indira Gandhi became the first female leader of a major international power when her party picked her to replace Prime Minister Lal Bahadur Shastri, who had died in office. In 1969, Israel's Labor Party nominated Golda Meir to replace Prime Minister Levi Eshkol, who also had died in office.

The initial elevations of both Gandhi and Meir were essentially accidents of history. In all probability, neither one of them would have been elected to national leadership by popular vote—that was not a woman's position—but instead were voted into office by the male leadership of their party to serve as malleable caretakers until the next elections could be held and a qualified man took control.

And then those next elections were held.

These two women had considerably more than opportunity and good fortune in common. Both of them had been deeply enmeshed in the political movements that led eventually to India's independence and Israel's creation. In addition to being well positioned to take advantage of the situation, they were extremely well prepared.

Indira Nehru had been born into Indian politics. If she had been a man, she would have been groomed for high office. When she was born in 1917, India was a British colony, ruled by a viceroy appointed by the king. But an independence movement had started to take hold, led by men like Mahatma Gandhi, who staged his first nonviolent protest that year; her grandfather Motilal Nehru; and father, Jawaharlal Nehru. Her family remained at the center of the freedom movement; Gandhi was a frequent visitor in their home and her grandparents and parents were arrested several times.

Her own involvement began as a teenager, carrying messages

between members of the movement. "I grew up with the idea that courage was the most important thing," she later wrote. "My mother fought for all sorts of rights for women, while she was fighting for independence . . . Gandhi felt the struggle for independence had to involve the women as much as men."

In 1942 Indira married Feroze Gandhi—no relation to Mahatma. That year she was beaten at a ceremony raising the flag of independence, then arrested for her anti-British activities. She served eight months and her husband spent a year behind bars. "Mud entered our souls in the drabness of prison," she remembered. "When I came out it was such a shock to see colors again I thought I would go out of my mind."

When India finally won its independence in 1947, it established a parliamentary democracy, in which elected representatives in the lower house, the Lok Sabha—the House of the People—choose the prime minister. Indira's revered father, Jawaharlal Nehru, became the new nation's first prime minister. Indira became his personal assistant and, because her mother had died years earlier, fulfilled the duties of the First Lady—while also advocating for increasing women's rights as head of the women's division of the majority Indian National Congress Party.

There were no role models for her, or her husband, to emulate. The traditional bread-winning husband and housekeeping wife relationship was challenged, and both of them had to figure out how to deal with it. Feroze Gandhi was a successful politician, a Member of Parliament, but his wife sat at her father's side at the center of the nation's government and became a well-known figure. There were rumors that she had to choose between her country and her marriage, which she denied. "We were happy at times," she told American journalist Betty Friedan. "We quarreled tremendously at times . . . I wouldn't have gone into public life if he had said no. But when I did . . . and became successful he liked it and he didn't like it. [When other people] would say, 'How does it feel, being so-and-so's husband?' he would get upset, and it would take me weeks to win him over. To hurt the male ego is, of course, the biggest sin in marriage."

When Feroze Gandhi died of a heart attack in 1960, Indira was serving as president of the Congress Party—a role, she said, party leaders "bullied me into taking"—while continuing to work with her father. Jawaharlal Nehru was the dominant figure in Indian politics; during his sixteen years as prime minister he shaped a new, progressive, secular India as it established a strong footprint as one of the world's most powerful nations. His death from a heart attack in 1964 left a huge political void.

The new prime minister, Lal Bahadur Shastri, recognizing the power of Gandhi's name and growing political influence, appointed her to his cabinet as minister of Information and Broadcasting. While not an especially significant position, it gave her a public platform. Throughout the world, women's roles were slowly evolving. In the United States, in 1960 the federal government approved an oral contraceptive, "the pill," which provided easily available birth control for women. In 1963, Betty Friedan's book *The Feminine Mystique*, which envisioned a more equitable role for women, sold more than a million copies. And significantly more women began pursuing a college education and career paths previously entirely dominated by men.

In 1966, Prime Minister Shastri died suddenly while visiting Tashkent in the Soviet Union. The Congress Party faced a leadership crisis. Rather than supporting the leading candidate, Morarji Desai, party leaders elected Indira Gandhi India's third prime minister and the first woman to head a major nation.

Party leaders believed that rather than the independent Desai, who would be a strong leader, they could exercise control over Gandhi's decisions while benefiting from her popularity in parliamentary elections scheduled for the following year. Political opponents and the press criticized her as "Goongi goodiya," Hindu for "dumb doll."

The Indian public largely supported her election. Although she was not a member of the parliament when elected by the party, which was not a requirement, she brought considerable government experience to the position. The AP reported that thousands of people "filed past, offering the clasped-hands 'namaste' greeting or placing garlands of flowers around her neck" as she stood in her garden welcoming them. "Some dropped to their knees and kissed Mrs. Gandhi's shoes."

Other countries celebrated this historic choice. "Can it happen?" asked *The Boston Globe*. "A woman in the prime minister's palace, why not in the White House?" A female Canadian columnist noted, "Mrs. Gandhi's election has created an interest that pinpoints the need of more women in government. More women to help decide the future of their children and play a part in governing this country . . . Laugh if you wish," she added, "but don't laugh too loudly."

Indira Gandhi stated firmly she did not intend to be an inspiration; early in her political career she wrote to a friend, "I am in no sense a feminist, but I believe in women being able to do everything." In fact, when elected leader of the Congress Party in 1959 she quoted a Hindi song, "We are the women of India. Don't imagine us as flower maidens . . . We are the sparks in the fire."

Years later, after her election as prime minister, she said pointedly, "I am not a woman. I am a human being." Rather than being the caretaker her party desired, she quoted a letter her father had written from prison, "Don't let making history scare you." Then she set out to make history.

The real test would take place in February 1967, when Indians would go to the polls to elect their new government.

Golda Mabovitch was also a pioneer, playing a vital role in Israeli history—decades before Israel existed. Born in Kyiv, Ukraine, her parents brought her to America, settling in Milwaukee, Wisconsin, in 1906. After she married Morris Meyerson in 1917, the couple emigrated to British-controlled Palestine, where she spent three years working on a kibbutz, a collective farm, learning how to raise poultry by day and immersing herself in politics at night. Eventually, Morris and Golda and their two children settled in Jerusalem, where "Meyerson" became Hebraized to "Meir."

The British Mandate for Palestine, which governed the region beginning in 1923, had been established by the League of Nations following World War I as the world struggled to figure out how to satisfy competing claims between Arabs and Jews for those Biblically historical lands. It was an almost impossible task: two cultures had lived in the area for thousands of years, and fighting frequently had broken out in the region.

Golda became active in the Zionist movement, which had been created to establish and support a Jewish state. She attended international conferences, raised more than $50 million to help finance the movement, and smuggled Jewish immigrants into Palestine—but also learned how to use weapons. As a member of the Jewish Agency, a sort of shadow government preparing for the creation of the Jewish state, she worked closely with its legendary leader, David Ben-Gurion.

As a result of Hitler's Holocaust, millions of Jews were driven from their homes in Europe, many of them to be murdered in concentration camps. After the war there was no place for survivors to go. To create a homeland for these displaced refugees, in 1947 the United Nations partitioned Palestine into two states, the State of Israel and an independent Arab state, which never materialized. A third area, a "Special International Regime," was to be established to govern the city of Jerusalem and the surrounding lands.

The greater Arab world furiously rejected this decision and was determined to prevent it from being implemented. When war between Arabs and Jews appeared inevitable, Golda Meir disguised herself as a veiled Bedouin woman, then risked her life by sneaking through guerrilla lines to meet secretly with King Abdullah, the king of newly created Jordan and leader of the Arab armies. When the king asked her not to hurry to proclaim the state, she supposedly replied, "We have been waiting for two thousand years. Is that hurrying?" Efforts to reach an agreement failed and in May, the day after the State of Israel declared its independence, the war erupted.

Ben-Gurion sent Meir—or Meyerson, as she still identified herself—to America on a month-long tour to raise desperately needed financial support. In addition to becoming, according to Ben-Gurion, "The Jewish woman who got the money which made the state of Israel possible," her appearances introduced "Golda" to the American public as the matronly "former Milwaukee schoolteacher" who somehow had become a leader of the new state.

While working in the Jewish Agency, Golda Meir helped persuade Russian dictator Joseph Stalin to allow Czechoslovakia to supply vital weapons to Zionists, and after the State of Israel was created, Ben-Gurion, its first prime minister, appointed her its ambassador to the Soviet Union. "Stalin expected a swayable woman who would help him put Israel under socialist rule," the *Chicago Daily News* reported, "but found Mrs. Meir a strong-minded Zionist who urged Soviet Jews to come to her country . . . Stalin switched to denouncing 'bourgeois Zionist deviationism.'"

Like India, upon its creation Israel adopted a parliamentary democracy, headed by a prime minister selected by the legislature. As Israel fought several wars through two decades, Meir served in a variety of government posts; she was the labor minister, the foreign minister, and the leader of the Labor Party, all while creating a remarkably warm image. She was known for holding important government meetings in the kitchen of her modest Tel Aviv apartment, while chain smoking and serving endless cups of coffee. "She seems like a Sholom Aleichem grandmother who could soothe most upsets with a glass of tea and a wise Yiddish saying," wrote a columnist. "But the grandmotherly gray bun, sensible shoes and shin-length coats disguise a tough diplomat, politician, fund raiser and labor leader."

Perhaps David Ben-Gurion best summed up her contributions when he described her as "The only man in my cabinet."

That was an ironic comment, considering Meir was the only woman to serve in his cabinet.

Like Indira Gandhi, Golda Meir did not consider herself a role model for women. "I am not a feminist," she said flatly, adding, "I am not a great admirer of the kind of feminism that gives rise to bra burning, hatred of men or a campaign against motherhood . . . The fact of being a woman has never, never, I say, been an obstacle." In another interview she said, "That woman business doesn't mean anything. The question is one of doing a capable job."

While she took great pride in her two children, her marriage broke up some time in the early 1940s. She never disclosed the reasons for it, although she once explained, "There is a type of woman who does not let her husband and children narrow her horizons."

President Richard Nixon, who had great respect for her, said, "she acted like a man and wanted to be treated like a man." No one seems to have doubted her strength, though; an Israeli columnist once wrote, "She is the headmistress of a political school and those who have been bad boys tremble as she grabs her ax."

After her long career—she was on a first-name basis with the world, everyone knew who "Golda" was—in 1968, the combination of health problems and political defeats at the hands of the next generation of Israeli politicians led to her quasi-retirement, although she did keep her seat in Parliament.

In January 1969, when Prime Minister Levi Eshkol died suddenly of a heart attack, Israel once again faced a political crisis: Two strong candidates, acting Prime Minister Yigal Allon and Defense Minister Moshe Dayan, were competing for the job. Both men were former generals who enjoyed extensive support. General elections for Parliament already were scheduled for the following October. To avoid a potentially damaging collision before that election, the majority Labor Party elected Golda Israeli's fourth prime minister as, Israeli media explained, "a compromise candidate to prevent a power struggle."

"Her appointment was widely viewed as another interim measure to keep the government going," reported the *New York Daily News*, ". . . until general elections next fall and a final choice then between Deputy Prime Minister Allon and Defense Minister Dayan for the leadership."

Although Dayan was furious and walked out in protest, threatening to start a new political party, Meir was a popular choice. This seventy-one-year-old grandmother had an extraordinary approval rating among Israelis of almost 90 percent, and a Gallup poll would later name her the most admired woman—in America! On March 17, 1969, she became only the third woman to lead a major world nation. Everyone assumed this was a temporary situation and that in a few months she would return to her apartment.

The real test would take place the following October, when Israelis would elect their new government.

Two years earlier, in the spring of 1967, while Americans sent increasingly large numbers of troops to fight in Vietnam and debated if the most desirable woman's shape was the fully-formed figure of movie star Sophia Loren or the skeletal British supermodel Twiggy ("She's not a picture," said social commentator Marshall McLuhan, "she's an X-ray"), millions of Indians had gone to the polls.

While Gandhi originally had been elected mostly as a placeholder, until either of the two strongest male candidates could secure a majority, she had solidified herself as a viable leader. But her ruling Congress Party faced an angry electorate. Although the country had won a 1965 war against Pakistan, the economy had stagnated. Parts of the country were suffering from severe food shortages. While speaking to fifty thousand people in the city of Bhubaneswar, Gandhi was hit in the face by a rock; her nose was fractured and started bleeding, but she refused to seek safety. Instead, she told the crowd, "This is an insult, not to me but to the country. I am agonized over your future and the future of democracy in this country."

She later told reporters, "I'm as tough as ever," but had to cancel several campaign appearances.

She campaigned on history and hope, reminding voters that Indians had fought British oppression with little but determination, they had defended their borders with unity, and now they needed to join together to fight the real enemies: poverty, backwardness, and ignorance. They had to conquer inefficiency and bureaucracy to produce more food, and build not only an industrial base but additional schools. She had become a stirring speaker: "In the old days," she reminded the huge crowds that gathered to hear her, "the maharaja would dictate like father to a family and all accepted his decisions. The only way we can really move ahead now is for people to think things out for themselves, to take responsibility. The danger . . . comes from being insecure, from having been poor and deprived and dependent, ruled by others for so long."

In the election, the Congress Party, which had held a large majority in Parliament since independence, was rebuked. It lost seventy-eight seats, including those of several top party leaders, and while it still held a majority, its power was greatly reduced. Still, she retained her seat and was elected prime minister for a full term. That marked the beginning of a remarkable, sometimes controversial career during which she led the nation for almost sixteen years, establishing herself as one of the most powerful women in the world. She quickly erased any question that she was a so-called puppet and in 1971 was rewarded with a landslide electoral victory.

During multiple terms in office, she earned worldwide respect for her toughness, so much so that America's Secretary of

State Henry Kissinger once admiringly described her as an "Iron Lady." Among her numerous accomplishments were the Green Revolution, which transformed India from a country forced to rely on food imports to feed its population to achieving complete self-sufficiency in wheat and rice production, as well as an anti-poverty campaign, launched in 1971, that made measurable gains and laid the groundwork for later programs. As a military leader, she successfully repelled Chinese incursions in the Himalayas and led several operations against Pakistan, including supporting the 1971 independence movement of Bangladesh. In 1974, under her direction, India successfully tested a nuclear weapon and became the world's sixth nuclear nation. Even at the height of the Cold War between NATO and the Soviet bloc, she managed to maintain working relationships with both sides, deftly navigating a nonaligned course that protected India's political independence.

But there had been costly failures too. Failures for which she was responsible—and controversial policies she had instituted. India had won the 1971 war against Pakistan, but at the cost of creating millions of refugees and crippling the economy; when an extended drought made the situation worse, food riots took place in some parts of the country, and the nation's standard of living had declined. Her political opponents pounced, claiming that she had violated election laws: In June 1975 a state court, the Allahabad high court, found her guilty of using local officials to erect platforms and loudspeakers at public expense, and allowing her secretary to illegally campaign for her. She was acquitted of equally technical charges like spending more than $4,500 on campaign expenses; that her campaign symbol, a cow and a calf, was an illegal appeal to the Hindu majority; and that her supporters had tried to bribe voters with free blankets and clothes. The Allahabad court barred her from office for six years.

It was a true constitutional crisis. She refused to leave office. The order was suspended temporarily until the Supreme Court could meet. Opposition parties announced they would resort to civil disobedience to force her from office. *The Guardian* wrote that these charges "would have been the subject of amusement from one end of India to the other" at the height of her popularity, but now that events had weakened her, India was literally on the verge of losing its democracy.

In response Gandhi proclaimed a state of emergency. Her government suspended basic constitutional rights including freedom of speech, the rights of habeas corpus and assembly; it was estimated that more than one hundred thousand political opponents, journalists, students, and protestors were arrested and imprisoned; newspapers were censored or prevented from publishing; and elections were postponed. In an address to the nation, she said, "There is nothing to panic about . . . It is not important whether I am prime minister or not. However, the institution of the prime minister is important and a dangerous political attempt to denigrate it is not in the interest of democracy or the nation."

The Times of India responded by printing an obituary, claiming "Democracy, beloved husband of Truth, loving father of Liberty, brother of Faith, Hope and Justice, expired on June 26."

The state of emergency lasted twenty-one months, during which time the government amended the constitution, enabling Gandhi to rule mostly by decree. Among the most unpopular actions was a sterilization program run by her son, Sanjay, in which several million men, mostly poor, many minorities, were pressured or even forced to be sterilized in an effort to deal with overpopulation. In 1977, she suddenly and completely unexpectedly ended the state of emergency, releasing some political prisoners and calling new elections. There has never been a satisfactory explanation for this. But it proved to be a disastrous political decision; the opposition Janata Party won in a landslide, and she lost her own seat by fifty-five thousand votes. Her longtime rival, Morarji Desai, replaced her as prime minister.

Three years later, the Janata government was in tatters. *The Los Angeles Times* reported that "fed up with rising prices, deteriorating law and order and petty political feuds, Gandhi's image as a non-nonsense leader who promised to restore economic and social order had strong voter appeal." Her party easily won the 1980 general election and Indira Gandhi once again became prime minister. The opposition leader said the best way to explain the results was "magic or a miracle."

Indira Gandhi's gender had ceased being an issue years earlier. She had become a powerful world leader as she guided India through an extraordinary range of domestic and international challenges. In June 1984, when Sikh separatists, seeking to form an autonomous state, took control of the revered Golden Temple, the holiest site of Sikhism, Gandhi dispatched Indian Army troops to remove them. In fierce fighting, several hundred Sikhs were killed. Five months later, as she stood outside her home, she was assassinated by Sikh members of her own security detail.

"This despicable act has robbed India of a great and courageous leader," England's first female prime minister, Margaret Thatcher, told Parliament. "We shall all feel the loss of her wise counsel and deep humanity."

In Israel, Golda Meir had to deal with her own crises. Rather than stepping down from her interim post, as had been expected, she instead became the choice for prime minister of a coalition of the four leading parties under the Labor Party banner. Unlike other democracies, because of its small population Israel's elections by law are "universal, nationwide, direct, equal, secret and proportional." That means there are no individual states, districts, or even candidates—instead, all citizens over eighteen years old cast their single vote for a political party. Seats in the legislature, the Knesset, are allocated based on the percentage of votes each party receives.

The most significant issue at hand was the continued security of the nation, in particular how to deal with the vast territories captured during the 1967 Six Day War. Israel's "Iron Lady," as the media occasionally referred to Meir, refused to consider returning any of that land until Arab leaders agreed to serious negotiations about peace. As with Gandhi, any doubts about her toughness had disappeared long ago. During a visit to America just before the elections, she bluntly told a small gathering, "If we have to have a choice between being dead and pitied, and being alive with a bad image, we'd rather be alive and have the bad image."

Years earlier she had expressed a similar philosophy, memorably pointing out, "We have our doves and our hawks. Most Israelis are neither. But we do refuse the role of clay pigeon."

In the 1969 elections, the Labor Party won 56 of the 120 seats in the Knesset, which remains the most substantial victory in Israeli history. That near majority gave Labor a mandate to rule and made Meir the country's undisputed leader. But while her positive image as the world's most unusual Jewish grandmother continued to grow, at home Israelis were frustrated by the lack of any meaningful progress toward peace. Her resolve was tested during the Olympics held in Munich, Germany, in 1972, when terrorists captured eleven Israeli athletes, killing two of them immediately and holding the others hostage. In exchange for those nine men, "Black September" demanded Israel release 234 imprisoned terrorists. While furtively making preparations to attempt a rescue, Meir publicly refused, saying later, "We have learnt the bitter lesson. One may save a life immediately only to endanger more lives. Terrorism has to be wiped out."

A rescue effort by German authorities failed, and the remaining nine hostages were killed. Israelis did not blame their prime minister, who secretly authorized an assassination program to kill those behind the attack. But confidence in her leadership was largely destroyed the following year, on October 6, 1973, the high holiday of Yom Kippur, when Egyptian and Syrian armies launched a surprise attack on Israel. The nation's vaunted intelligence agencies and the Israel Defense Forces were stunned by this offensive. Israeli forces on the Suez Canal and in the Golan Heights were overrun. More than twenty-five hundred soldiers died, and as many as twelve thousand were wounded in the nineteen days of fighting.

When Meir appealed directly to Kissinger for desperately needed weapons, he replied, wary of offending the oil-producing states of the Middle East, that he was an American first, Secretary of State second, and a Jew third. To which Meir supposedly replied, coldly, "You forget in Israel we read from right to left."

The United States sent Israel the weapons it needed to blunt the attack.

Golda Meir's political reputation never fully recovered from that debacle. Critics later claimed she bore significant responsibility for the war because she had refused offers to negotiate with Egyptian President Anwar Sadat, but facts often tend to blend with opinion and rumor to create differing perspectives. One thing was irrefutable: The government had been caught unprepared, and Israelis had died because of it. Meir could not overcome that reality, and the following April, as news wire services reported, she announced, "'I have come to the end of the road. I cannot go any longer.' Then, holding a cigarette in one hand and waving away newsmen, the stooped, craggy-faced grandmother headed back to her Jerusalem home."

That was then. In many nations the possibility of a female leader, once unique, has become common. Since Bandaranaike became Sri Lanka's head of state in 1960, the governments of more than 80 of the 193 members of the United Nations have been led by a woman. In 1979, the British elected Margaret Thatcher their prime minister; this other "Iron Lady" was reelected twice, becoming the longest-serving English prime minister in the twentieth century—in addition to proving to be a widely respected world leader. In 1980, Iceland's Vigdís Finnbogadóttir became the first democratically elected female head of state, defeating three male candidates with almost 34 percent of the vote. She eventually served four terms as the nation's president, running unopposed twice and winning reelection in 1996 with 94.6 percent of the vote. In 2024, Mexico elected its first female president, Claudia Sheinbaum, who received almost 60 percent of the votes, the highest percentage in that nation's history.

When Gandhi and Meir were elected, they were considered groundbreakers; the phrase "the glass ceiling," meaning an invisible barrier that prevented women and minorities from rising, did not come into use until the 1980s. But in reality, they had accomplished something far more historic: They had proved women could play with the biggest boys.

THIRTEEN

1966: Ronald Reagan Wins the California Gubernatorial Election

THE FIRST RETURNS IN the 1964 presidential election from the tiny town of Dixville Notch, New Hampshire, were eight votes for the Republican candidate Barry Goldwater against none for the Democrat incumbent Lyndon Johnson.

That brief moment was the only time Goldwater led.

Johnson won the '64 election with an historic landslide. He received an incredible 61.1 percent of the popular vote, the highest percentage since widespread popular voting had begun 140 years earlier. He won forty-four states, 486 of 538 electoral votes, receiving fifteen million more votes than Goldwater. Analyzing the massive victory, *The New York Times* claimed, "Voters Rejected [Goldwater's] Candidacy, Conservative Cause and the G.O.P.," explaining "Barry Goldwater not only lost the Presidential election yesterday but the conservative cause as well. He has wrecked his party for a long time to come . . . It seemed fairly obvious from the returns that the will of the majority was clearly against extreme conservatism."

The Republican Party had picked that path at its convention in

San Francisco, when Goldwater had won the nomination over the far more moderate New York Governor Nelson Rockefeller. According to the *Times*, "The Goldwater campaign had posed a sharp challenge to almost the entire trend of national policy, domestic and foreign, since the Great Depression and World War II. He had proposed a sharp curtailment of government activities . . ."

Throughout the campaign Democrats had portrayed Goldwater—and his conservative movement—as dangerous, quasi-racist radicals, pointing out that he had voted against the Civil Rights bill while endlessly repeating his words when accepting the nomination: "Extremism in the defense of liberty is no vice and moderation in the pursuit of justice is no virtue."

To emphasize the danger of electing Goldwater, who had suggested using small nuclear weapons in Vietnam, Johnson's campaign created the "Daisy ad," one of the most memorable and controversial commercials in American political history. It depicted a little girl picking the petals off a daisy as a deep voice counted down from ten—and the child is replaced by the explosion of a nuclear bomb, as Johnson warns, "We must either love each other . . . or we must die."

The reporting was accurate; the massive election loss left the American conservative movement in shambles. LBJ's liberal "Great Society," which echoed Roosevelt's New Deal and promised even more government assistance to Americans, had proved to be overwhelmingly popular.

The philosophical battle over the role of government in the lives of Americans that had been waged since the founding of the nation appeared to be resolved: By huge numbers, Americans supported the concept of an expansive federal government.

The definition of conservatism is broad and subject to individual interpretation. American conservatism has a long and proud history. Historians find elements of it in every stage of the nation's political development. John Adams, James Madison, and Alexander Hamilton, even at times Abraham Lincoln, have been called conservatives. But generally, and often with exceptions, it is accepted that an American conservative is someone who supports a limited federal government that remains faithful to the original principles—and rights—enumerated in the constitution; a person who believes in free markets, a strong national defense, individual freedoms, and traditional values.

As American politics evolved, conservatives tended to find a home in the Republican Party, which supported business interests against government regulation, a strong military, a bold and assertive foreign policy, and the rights of individual Americans to exercise control over their own lives. Nobel Prize–winning economist Milton Friedman, known for advocating limited government and free markets, defined his version of the philosophy in bestselling books and a TV series as "Free to Choose."

Supposedly, Goldwater's defeat was a repudiation of modern conservatism. In the 1964 election, rather than it being the intellectual heritage of a John Adams or a Milton Friedman, who created and advocated a viable political philosophy, Democrats had instead successfully linked contemporary conservatism to disgraced politicians like Senator Joseph McCarthy, far-right organizations like the John Birch Society, and Deep South white supremacists.

While Democrats celebrated the demise of conservatism, Republicans already were beginning to sift through the ashes. It wasn't conservatism that was defeated, they contended, it was Goldwater, whose campaign, wrote columnist Holmes Alexander, "was so badly managed . . . that he forfeited all but the hard core conservative votes which he couldn't have chased away with fire hoses and police dogs. He left us with an accurate measurement of the irreducible granary of anti-liberalism. He found well over 25 million Americans who declared themselves ill-pleased, ill-reconciled and unreconstructed after three decades of almost unbroken liberal government."

The chairman of Goldwater's campaign said, "He started slipping the moment he made that remark on extremism in his acceptance speech." What was needed if they were going to survive, leaders of the party agreed, was a new way of presenting the traditional conservative values. Rather than an extremist, they needed a friendly, nonthreatening person who could represent those values in a reasonable manner that resonated with the public. They were starting with twenty-five million voters; they had to find someone who could remind millions more people that they shared those values—even if they didn't yet realize it.

As it turned out, that standard-bearer had been right in front of them, both larger and smaller than life, for decades.

Ronald Reagan was well-known to movie and television audiences. After working at a variety of jobs, among them construction work and doing color commentary on Chicago Cubs baseball games for an Iowa radio station, he had become a successful movie actor. He appeared in fifty-three movies over the course of his career, from the classic *Kings Row* to the campy comedy *Bedtime for Bonzo*, in which he costarred with a chimpanzee. He was considered a versatile, handsome, and likeable actor who moved easily between genres, from emotional dramas to light comedies. Among his best-known roles was ill-fated Notre Dame football star George Gipp in *Knute Rockne, All American*, which earned him the nickname "the Gipper." As a movie critic once described him, he was "everybody's best friend in the old movies." And while often described as a "B movie actor," in fact he was one of the first Hollywood stars to sign a million-dollar contract.

While working in Hollywood, he became active in the Screen Actors Guild, the actors' union, being elected its president in 1947. When his larger-than-life big screen career faltered in the early 1950s, he moved into television, becoming the amiable host of the highly rated weekly anthology series *General Electric Theater.* He also became a spokesperson for the company, traveling around the country giving speeches to employees.

At the beginning of his Hollywood career Ronald Reagan had been a Democrat, considering Franklin Roosevelt a hero and fighting strongly against racism. But after seeing the Communist influence growing in the entertainment industry—and being threatened with having acid thrown in his face so he would "never be in pictures again" for opposing a strike—he began moving to the political right. The fact that he was in the 94 percent tax bracket, meaning "the government took most of what I earned," also increased his political awareness and activity. He embraced a bedrock principle of conservatism: low taxes stimulate spending and investment, which fuel the economy. By 1952, he was supporting Republican General Dwight Eisenhower for president.

Although he didn't change his party registration from Democrat to Republican until 1962, by then he had made the political conversion, becoming a strong supporter of Richard Nixon in both his 1960 presidential campaign against John F. Kennedy and 1962 California gubernatorial race against incumbent Pat Brown. In 1964 he became cochairman of Goldwater's campaign in California. As he remembered later, "I spoke at many fundraising functions . . . [giving] basically the same talk I'd been giving for years . . . I recounted the relentless expansion of the federal government, the proliferation of government bureaucrats who were taking control of American business and criticized liberal Democrats for taking the country down the road to socialism."

As a public speaker, Reagan was able to combine his natural gifts; he was a handsome man with a warm, commanding voice and comfortable demeanor, with the skills developed by spending years in front of cameras and audiences to bring that "everybody's best friend" image to life.

Late in the Goldwater campaign, he taped a half-hour version of his speech to be broadcast on national television. "The Speech," as it became known, was his political introduction to America. "I have spent most of my life as a Democrat," he began. "I recently have seen fit to follow another course." Few politicians have ever had Reagan's ability to relate to his audience, to speak to them, to make his point in language they understood. This was the same man they had been welcoming into their living room for more than a decade, albeit technologically. The speech went on, "We have so many people who can't see a fat man standing beside a thin one without coming to the conclusion the fat man got that way by taking advantage of the thin one. So they're going to solve all the problems of human misery through government and government planning. Well, now, if government planning and welfare had the answer . . . shouldn't they be telling us about the decline each year in the number of people needing help? . . . But the reverse is true . . .

"Actually," he pointed out, "a government bureau is the nearest thing to eternal life we'll ever see on this earth." He concluded the speech with stirring words cribbed from his one-time idol, FDR, "You and I have a rendezvous with destiny," then added a dash of Lincoln, "We will preserve for our children this, the last best hope of man on earth" and finished with his own warning, "or we will sentence them to take the last step into a thousand years of darkness."

The overwhelmingly positive reaction to "The Speech" proved that Reagan might successfully make the transition from movie star to politician. Vernon Christina, the chairman of Goldwater's San Francisco campaign, later recalled standing in a parking lot after that election loss with several other Republican party leaders and wondering, "Why doesn't he—run . . . for governor? He's got all the ingredients to make a goddamned electable person."

The timing was perfect. The party was in disarray. Neither Goldwater's conservative faction nor Rockefeller's moderate group had enough support to control the party. While former Eisenhower Veep Nixon was attempting a miraculous comeback after two devastating defeats, there was plenty of room—and a desperate desire—for attractive new candidates. And few of them were more attractive than an actual movie star.

There was already strong evidence that an entertainer could be elected to political office, at least in California. In 1964, while Goldwater was being pummeled nationally, veteran actor George Murphy had defeated Democrat Pierre Salinger for a California Senate seat. Murphy, who had starred in more than thirty films and actually had preceded Reagan as president of the Screen Actors Guild, had run as a moderate Republican, casting himself as a strong anti-Communist and supporter of civil rights legislation, successfully setting himself apart from Goldwater. In fact, Murphy and Reagan had worked together in Irving Berlin's 1943 musical, *This Is the Army*.

A small group of influential California Republicans, led by wealthy Los Angeles automobile dealer Holmes Tuttle, tried to convince Reagan to run for governor in 1966, claiming he might be the only person capable of beating the powerful two-term incumbent Pat Brown. Reagan initially turned them down. "After doing as much research as I had on the operations of government," he later wrote, "the last thing I wanted was to become a part of it. I'm an actor, not a politician . . . I'm in show business."

Besides, even considering Murphy's upset victory, it was an almost hopeless situation. California was a Democratic stronghold; there were almost 1,400,000 more registered Democrats than Republicans, and twenty-four of its thirty-eight House members were Democrats. Even more challenging, Reagan had campaigned actively for Goldwater in '64, and Goldwater had lost the state by almost 20 percentage points. Chances of a political novice, a man closely associated with rejected extremist policies, beating a reasonably popular governor were basically nonexistent.

But Tuttle's group persisted, and months later Reagan agreed to run. "California isn't a place," he said as he announced his candidacy, "it's a way of life." In his folksy manner he explained that he shared his neighbors' concerns. "Even when we've been here 30 years, as I have, we still refer to ourselves as being from 'someplace.' We're from Illinois, or Iowa . . . But we're here to stay . . . and California's problems are our problems.

"Some of those problems have grown faster than the population, and in that we're number one in the nation." This was a theme he would return to time and again throughout his entire political career: A bloated government doesn't solve problems; it causes them.

The Tuttle group began the campaign with a revolutionary decision; it hired one of the nation's first political consulting firms, Spencer-Roberts, and essentially gave that company total control of the campaign. Their challenge was to transform Reagan into a polished politician without appearing to actually be a polished politician. Spencer-Roberts was responsible for everything from scheduling appearances to crafting the message that would resonate most with persuadable listeners. In some ways, Reagan's 1966 effort was the beginning of the modern political campaign.

It was obvious, for example, that Reagan's opponents would highlight his inexperience in government. Rather than trying to refute that fact, they embraced it: You couldn't attack government as he intended to do if you were part of it. "I'm not a politician," he said in his opening remarks in that first speech, "in the sense of ever having held public office, but I think I can lay claim to be a citizen-politician." That phrase, "citizen-politician," had been selected to help shape his image as someone who was not part of a failed system.

He continued, presenting himself as a reasonable fellow, "Believing as I do that the Republican Party is the party of limited government, individual freedom and adherence to the constitution . . . I supported all the party nominees because the choice today is not one of men but basic and widely differing philosophies." Of course, he then went on to explain that he also had extensive experience in union management and knew how to put honest and experienced people in administrative positions.

Not surprisingly, there was considerable doubt about his candidacy. "In all charity," decided the *San Francisco Chronicle*, "let us agree that if Mr. Reagan's gallant performance as an amateur politician who decides to run for governor remains unconvincing, it was, in the final analysis, not his fault. It was simply a flagrant example of miscasting."

Reagan's first challenge was to win the party's nomination. That was not going to be easy. His opponent was San Francisco's popular former mayor, moderate Republican George Christopher. Early polls gave Christopher a strong lead, both in gaining the nomination and then in defeating the incumbent Democratic Governor Pat Brown, who was running for a third term.

Believing Reagan would be much easier to defeat in the general election, Brown's campaign began maneuvering behind the scenes to help him get the nomination. They fed negative stories about Christopher to sympathetic journalists. Nationally syndicated political columnist Drew Pearson, for example, informed readers that more than two decades earlier, Christopher had been convicted of a misdemeanor and fined for violating milk pricing laws. It was a minor infraction, but when Christopher failed to respond aggressively it left a major negative impression. It also was revealed that while serving as mayor, Christopher had made a substantial profit on a (completely legal) bank stock deal.

The implication was clear: Christopher was just another shady politician.

And, as Christopher was learning, besides being able to cast himself as a nonpolitician, Reagan had another significant advantage. The Kennedy-Nixon 1960 presidential campaign supposedly had turned toward Kennedy when Nixon's five o'clock shadow made him look tired during their TV debate. Reagan had spent his entire career wearing makeup and looking good in front of a camera. "Every time we'd meet in Los Angeles . . . and they would put us in a line for a photograph the same thing happened," Christopher later remembered. "As soon as the photographer was ready to snap the picture, Reagan would put up his hand . . . and make it appear that all of us were deferring to him and looking to him for advice. Well, that was an actor's ability to steal the scene."

Brown faced his own primary challenge, from Los Angeles Mayor Sam Yorty. It was a nasty campaign; Yorty accused Brown of being supported by Communists, while Brown responded that Yorty was a "fright peddler" who had failed to prevent or properly respond to the horrific racial riots that had destroyed much of the Watts section of the city.

On primary night, a bold headline in *The Los Angeles Times* reported: "Reagan Landslide; Brown Winner." "Ronald Reagan scored a smashing victory over former Mayor George Christopher . . . But while Reagan had a breeze in his bout with Christopher, Brown had trouble with his principal opponent."

Ronald Reagan's political career had begun.

Polls taken before the primary campaign had shown Brown with a small lead over Reagan, but after the primaries, that lead had mostly disappeared. Brown had been governor for two terms and his popularity was sagging. Although he had some significant accomplishments, he was caught in the controversial tides of civil rights riots and student free speech demonstrations at state universities, especially Berkeley. Yorty's attacks, and his subsequent refusal to support Brown in the campaign, also inflicted political damage.

Brown made the mistake of trying to run a conventional campaign against an unconventional candidate. Initially, at least, he didn't take Reagan especially seriously, believing that liberal Californians would not elect an inexperienced, conservative actor. One of his commercials showed him in a classroom telling two very young Black children, "You know I'm running against an actor. Remember this: You know who shot Abraham Lincoln, don't you? An actor shot Lincoln." That commercial backfired, hurting Brown, who continued to struggle to find an effective way to attack his elusive opponent.

At the beginning of the campaign, most people assumed Brown would employ the same strategy Johnson had used so successfully against Goldwater—portraying Reagan as an extremist. During his first press conference after winning the nomination, he told reporters he was facing "the toughest fight of my career [against] the crown prince of the extreme right." A document issued by the state Democratic party entitled "Ronald Reagan Extremist Collaborator" claimed that while "he pretends he is a moderate . . . the record belies him. It shows that he has collaborated directly with a score of top leaders of the super-secret John Birch Society."

Realizing the danger, Reagan took steps to distance himself from Goldwater. Saving the conservative movement in America meant ignoring conservatives. At least temporarily. At his own press conference after the primary, he said, "I wouldn't call myself ultra-conservative . . . I don't think there's anything in my philosophy that doesn't cross party lines." To emphasize the point that he was a new kind of Republican, he did not invite any out-of-state politicians to campaign for him—especially Barry Goldwater. Instead, he flew to former President Dwight Eisenhower's home in Gettysburg, Pennsylvania, to receive his advice and endorsement. And to be photographed with the widely respected former president. In response to the attempt to associate him with radical Birchers, he issued his own statements: "I am not a member [of the John Birch Society]. I have no intention of becoming a member. I am not going to solicit their support." However, he added that if members of that group accepted his views, he welcomed their support, successfully defusing a potentially very serious problem.

Although Reagan was well prepared and packaged by Spencer-Roberts, he also relied on the public-pleasing personality that had marked his entire career. Legendary comedian George Burns once said, "The most important thing in life is sincerity. And if you can fake that . . ." One of the most important challenges Reagan faced was convincing voters that he wasn't faking anything, that he wasn't an actor playing a politician, but that he was an honest guy telling them what he really believed, and if that made sense to them, they should think about supporting him.

To counter stories that he was simply reciting memorized lines, that he was following a script, he began taking questions from the audience during every appearance, turning them into a combination of rally and town hall. If he made a mistake or didn't know an answer, which happened, he reacted in a nonpolitical manner—he admitted it. For example, when he did not know the location of California's Eel River, which was involved in a controversial dam project, rather than making up an excuse he sighed and responded, "Here I am, up the wrong river again." Then he joined the audience in laughing at his lack of knowledge.

He even found a way to make his conservative views far less threatening than Goldwater's. Like Goldwater, Reagan was opposed to most civil rights legislation, including a California Fair Housing Act that made racial discrimination illegal when selling property. Although he claimed he was against restrictive covenants, the Brown campaign found evidence that many years earlier he had signed one, prohibiting the sale of his own property to non-whites. It was a potentially devastating revelation—but Reagan once again turned it around, putting his response in aw-shucks words voters could identify with. "I was the first member of my family ever to own property," he explained. "I never read the deed and would not have known how to interpret the legal terminology."

As a result of all that maneuvering, wrote the newspaper syndicate NEA, "Smiling Ronald Reagan may be a Hollywood actor, as his adversaries charge, but he has become a very plausible candidate for the governorship of California . . . He has risen high on the political scale largely because millions of Californians are looking for something new, for a face and voice that promise fresh attacks on Watts style riots, crime, taxes, university chaos. With a blend of boyish candor and good-natured plausibility Reagan is managing to suggest that promise."

Appearance by appearance, rally by rally he grew as a politician, learning what people were concerned about, what they responded to, and what they cared about. The campaign featured all the same issues that were being debated across the nation: the Vietnam War, civil rights, taxes, welfare policies, education, law and order, jobs, the economy, and the role of big government. But it was an unanticipated issue that boosted Reagan's chances: "In every q and a," Stuart Spencer later recalled, "somebody would stand up and say, 'What are you going to do about those bastards at Berkeley?'"

At that moment in history, America was going through a generational upheaval. All over the country, college students were passionately and loudly rejecting the values of their parents. Traditional ideals were under attack. An embryonic counterculture was developing; crew cuts were replaced by long shaggy hair, slacks became jeans, Sinatra was replaced by the Beatles and Rolling Stones. Drugs, especially marijuana and psychedelics like LSD, were becoming easily available. The approval of the birth control pill in 1960 had sparked a sexual revolution. Racial barriers were coming down. Anti–Vietnam War students had begun burning their draft cards, stunning their patriotic parents who had lived through World War II.

For many Californians, the youth protests taking place at the state university at Berkeley symbolized the rejection of their values. What to do about Berkeley unexpectedly became a central issue in the campaign. Reagan's position was clear; he demanded the state legislature investigate "Communism and sexual misconduct" at the university. The problems, which he said were being caused by "beatniks, radicals and filthy speech advocates," had begun "a year ago when so-called free speech advocates, who in truth have no appreciation for freedom, were allowed to assault and humiliate the symbol of authority, a policeman in uniform, and that was the moment when the ringleaders should have been taken by the scruff of their neck and thrown off campus."

It was easy to blame Brown for the situation—and Reagan did. Brown was the governor when the protests began; his efforts to control them had failed. In 1964, more than eight hundred students had been arrested for occupying the administration building—which had only made the situation worse.

Berkeley made it easy for voters to see the difference between the two candidates: Reagan was going to defend traditional American values, he was going to restore law and order, and while Brown did not align himself with the antiestablishment students, he certainly didn't know how to stop them. Reagan had successfully turned what had initially been a longshot campaign into a competitive election.

By the last few weeks of the campaign, Reagan had moved slightly ahead in the polls, but almost 20 percent of voters—

the majority of them registered Democrats—remained undecided. Republicans had coalesced behind him, while Democrats remained fragmented as Yorty refused to endorse Brown and unions offered only tepid support. Perhaps most importantly, voters had been exposed to Reagan and rather than the right-wing extremist Brown had warned them about, he seemed like a pretty decent guy. As columnist David Lawrence wrote, "it is the character of the man, rather than the position he takes on public issues, which so often wins an election. In fact, there are many cases where the candidate who says less than his opponent on specific issues and sticks to general principles turns out to be the victor—very largely because of a winning personality."

In endorsing Reagan, *The Los Angeles Times* praised his campaign, describing it as "vigorous, clean and positive" and adding that he had "ignored attacks upon his political integrity and personal motives. He has comported himself with dignity and courage in the face of brutal name-calling and guilt-by-association tactics."

By election day, Reagan's victory no longer was considered an upset. Californians voted for change. A massive turnout gave Reagan an overwhelming show of support; he received 58 percent of the votes, winning fifty-five of fifty-eight counties and beating Brown by almost a million votes. Republicans won five of the six statewide offices and drastically cut down the Democratic margins in the state Senate and Assembly. This massive Republican victory in a Democratic state not only revived the conservative movement, it instantly turned Ronald Reagan into a viable candidate for the presidency.

Three weeks after Reagan took office, the California Board of Regents fired Clark Kerr, the president of the University of

California. Although Reagan lacked the power to make this decision directly, for their own political survival legislators could not risk ignoring the massive public support he had received. It was the first demonstration of his ability to fulfill his campaign promises.

Ronald Reagan made his first attempt to win the Republican nomination for the presidency in 1968. But he was upstaged by Richard Nixon, who engineered one of the greatest comebacks in American political history to defeat Reagan on his right and Nelson Rockefeller on his left. The Republican party had learned important lessons from Reagan's California victory, embracing some of the conservative values that had proved popular and appealing directly to once-solidly Democratic Southern states. Reagan campaigned tirelessly for Nixon throughout the entire campaign, and the Republican victory further cemented his own position as a powerful and popular voice.

In 1970 he won a second term as governor, beating centrist Democrat Jesse Unruh. By then he had established himself as the plain-speaking, pragmatic leader of the conservative movement, well positioned to follow Nixon into the White House when the president's second term ended in 1976. After finishing his own second term in the statehouse, he began writing a syndicated newspaper column and making speeches outlining his approach to governing in preparation for '76. In his own words, "My theme on the campaign stump was familiar to anyone who had heard me speak over the years. It was time to scale back the size of the federal government, reduce taxes and government intrusion in our lives, balance the budget and return to the people the freedoms usurped from them by the bureaucrats."

Then came Watergate.

Nixon's attempt to cover up the attempt to break into Democratic headquarters in the Watergate complex had blossomed into an historic scandal that ended with his resignation. Gerald Ford, the vice president Nixon had appointed after his elected running mate Spiro Agnew had been forced out for accepting bribes years earlier while serving as Maryland's governor, became president and served the remainder of his term. As the 1976 campaign began, Ford and Reagan battled for the Republican nomination. Reagan adopted a familiar strategy. He had won in 1966 as a political outsider; in 1976 he campaigned as a Washington outsider, fighting against career politicians. It was almost enough. After a hard-fought state-by-state primary battle he lost to Ford at the Republican convention by 117 votes of the 2,258 votes cast. But the dark shadows of Watergate proved too much for Ford to overcome, and he lost the election to former Georgia Governor Jimmy Carter.

Throughout Carter's presidency Reagan traveled around the country, supporting elected Republican officials and candidates, and becoming a respected spokesperson for the party. That work paid off. With the exception of two very early polls that favored Ford, Reagan dominated the entire campaign for the 1980 Republican nomination. In winning it, he received more than double the number of popular votes cast in Republican primaries than his closest contender, George Bush.

Once again, critics dismissed him. The liberal magazine *The New Republic* described him as an "ex-movie actor, darling of the rabid right . . . an international innocent and an economic extremist."

But during a debate against incumbent President Carter, Reagan famously asked the question that has continued to resonate through the political spectrum, "Are you better off now than you were four years ago?" The public answered with a resounding No! and elected Ronald Reagan president of the United States.

From the somewhat reluctant candidate who had been cajoled into running for governor in 1966, he had become the sophisticated leader of a rejuvenated conservative movement—and the free world.

Four years later he ran for a second term; his Democratic opponent this time was former Vice President Walter Mondale. A second term campaign is always a referendum on the first term: Reagan won reelection in one of the largest landslides in American history, beating Mondale with more electoral votes than LBJ had received in his 1964 victory over Goldwater. Mondale won only one state and the District of Columbia.

During his eight years in the White House, Ronald Reagan's policies brought fundamental changes to this country and the entire world. Among numerous accomplishments, the "Reagan Revolution" is credited with bringing an end to the decades-long Cold War against the Soviet Union. By increasing defense spending to record levels—which the Russian economy could not afford to duplicate, initiating programs like "Star Wars" to create a missile shield, and building a realistic relationship with Soviet leader Mikhail Gorbachev, he was able to force the Russians to make fundamental changes in their military, political, and domestic policies. His declaration to Gorbachev, while making a speech in then–West Germany in June 1987, "Mr. Gorbachev, tear down this wall," has echoed through history—and slightly more than two years later, the Berlin Wall that had separated East and West for decades indeed came down. He also strengthened existing bonds with America's allies, building relationships with leaders like Britain's Margaret Thatcher, Germany's Helmut Kohl, and Canadian Prime Minister Brian Mulroney.

Domestically, his conservative fiscal policies, known as Reaganomics, which featured drastically lowering tax rates, successfully lowered inflation, and stimulated economic growth. While that strategy was criticized for favoring the wealthy and adding substantially to the national debt, during his two terms the economy grew at an average of 3.5 percent annually, unemployment was cut in half, and the stock market continued growing. He launched a war on drug abuse and instituted immigration policies that improved border security while granting legal status to almost three million undocumented immigrants.

Reagan also made certain the conservative constitutional beliefs would continue long after the end of his presidency by appointing more than 380 federal judges, among them the nation's first female Supreme Court Justice, Sandra Day O'Connor.

As with most administrations, his eight years in the White House also included significant failures, questionable policies, economic challenges, and even scandals. Among them was Iran-Contra, in which his administration sold weapons to the religious fanatics that had overthrown the Iranian government in exchange for the release of the American hostages they held, then violated a congressional ban by funneling the proceeds of those sales to right-wing rebels trying to overthrow the Nicaraguan government. The administration also was widely criticized for essentially ignoring the rapidly growing AIDS epidemic, refusing to acknowledge it or commit the necessary funds for research and prevention until tens of thousands of people had died or were infected. Financially, large tax cuts generally favoring the wealthiest Americans caused the national debt to soar, and Reagan's deregulation of the banking industry led to the so-called "savings and loan crisis," which required a massive bail-out. To fund those policies, his administration cut several social welfare programs, including food stamps and school lunches.

While the results of most of his programs could be measured, analyzed, and debated, there also were significant intangible achievements that marked his administration. When he took office the country had been ripped apart by the Vietnam War, Watergate, and the clash of generational cultures. Through the strength of his personality and his command of the language—even though he became widely known for his verbal blunders, gaffes that forced his staff to issue explanations and excuses—he was able to communicate his hope, pride, and eternal optimism in the essential goodness of the country. "It's morning in America," he said, imagining America as a "shining city on a hill," a beacon of hope where dreams might still be fulfilled.

He left office in 1989 having completely revived American conservatism, and his incredible approval rating of 63 percent was second only to FDR.

FOURTEEN

1985–1991: Gorbachev and Yeltsin Dissolve the Soviet Union

IN DECEMBER 1937, *TIME* REPORTED "94,138,000 Russians registered to vote and at least 96.5% had voted. All votes counted for the Stalin regime . . . 'The first envelope is slit,' exclaimed *Pravda*. 'All eyes are directed to it. The Chairman takes out two slips—and reads loudly and distinctly, "Comrade Stalin!" Everyone in the room jumps and applauds joyously.'

"There was no other name printed on the ballots . . . 'The result is 100 percent—100 percent!' exulted *Pravda*. 'What election in what country for what candidate has given a 100-percent response?'"

Sham elections—referring to elections which have all the trappings of a legitimate election, except that voters do not have the opportunity to choose among several candidates or policies—have been the hallmark of dictators throughout recent history. They have been held for a variety of reasons: to demonstrate the power and control of the government, to create a public display of support for the leaders, to expose potential opposition, to foster a sense of patriotic unity, and at times, simply for the vanity of the dictator. There is no doubt about the outcome; the government prints and distributes the ballots, monitors the voting, and counts the votes. The result is whatever they announce it is.

In 1939, Winston Churchill described the USSR as "a riddle wrapped in a mystery inside an enigma." In terms of territory, the USSR was the largest country in the world, then consisting of eleven republics—including Russia and Ukraine—spanning eleven time zones and comprised of more than 100 different nationalities and ethnic groups speaking more than 120 native languages. While theoretically those republics retained some level of autonomy, in fact they all remained under the firm control of the central government in Moscow. But the country remained politically unpredictable, subject to the whims of Stalin—especially after he suddenly signed a nonaggression pact with Nazi Germany.

As the twentieth century began, there actually had been free elections in Russia. Between 1906 and 1917, as the czar struggled to retain power, the Russian people had gone to the polls four times to elect four Dumas, or legislatures. The 1906 election, known as the Duma of Public Anger, had produced the first truly representative body in Russian history. Even the election in 1917, following the abdication of Czar Nicholas II, was at least quasi-democratic. More than 45 million people—out of an estimated population of 125 million—voted that year for a national assembly, choosing freely among at least four political parties. At that time this marked the largest electoral turnout in history.

That multiparty assembly met only once before Lenin's October Revolution overthrew the government and, on December 30, 1922, after a long civil war established the Marxist one-party Union of Soviet Socialist Republics. According to newspaper reports, "M. Stalin, commissar for national minorities declared the event was of historical importance to united Russia and marked a new turn in the progress of the soviet regime."

The word *soviet* has several meanings in the Russian language, but generally this usage refers to a body of advisors, a group or council that comes together to debate and discuss various matters.

After Lenin's death in 1924 Joseph Stalin, whom he had appointed general secretary of the Communist Party, successfully used that position to gain total control of the government. Constitutions passed by the ruling Communist Party in 1924 and 1936 supposedly enshrined the right to vote for representatives to the national legislative assembly, the Supreme Soviet—but the candidates had to be approved by the party and often ran unopposed, the only names on the ballot.

Stalin recognized the value of elections for propaganda and personal purposes. In 1936, his new constitution created a bicameral legislature. The people's house, the Soviet of the Union, was to be made up of one representative for every three hundred thousand citizens, to be directly elected by all adults over eighteen years old. At first, it appeared Stalin actually was going to allow contested elections, elections in which voters were presented with multiple candidates for seats in the legislature. Procedures were established for runoffs if no candidate received a majority.

When the Supreme Soviet tried to limit the right to vote in this election to approved social classes, Stalin wondered, "What is there to be afraid of? If you are afraid of wolves keep out of the woods." The danger of candidates who did not support the regime could be minimized, he said confidently, "if our propaganda work is conducted in a Bolshevik way, the people will not let hostile persons slip into the supreme governing bodies."

Among the candidates was Comrade Stalin himself, who gave a rousing speech at a campaign rally. "Never in the history of the world have there been such really free and really democratic elections," he boasted. "The point is not that our elections will be universal, equal, secret, and direct . . . The point is that our universal elections will be carried out as the freest elections and the most democratic elections in any country in the world." While the "so-called democratic countries" also held universal elections, they take place "in an atmosphere of pressure brought to bear on the electors by the capitalists, landlords, bankers and other capitalist sharks. Such elections . . . cannot be called altogether free and altogether democratic elections."

Perhaps he actually did intend to hold free, competitive elections. But local officials, many of them terrified they would lose their own positions, advised strongly against it, claiming they would be replaced by "overt anti-Communists . . . enemies . . . alien elements . . . friends of Hitler." Stalin certainly was aware of that threat. Beginning in 1936, he unleashed The Great Purge, arresting and often executing literally millions of people whom he considered a threat to the Communist state.

At the same time these mass arrests were taking place, preparations for free elections continued. But only days before they were scheduled, Stalin canceled them. His reasons were never explained; no one knew if this had been a strategy to expose and eliminate opponents, a public relations effort, or a genuine attempt to involve Russians in their political future. *The New York Times* reported, "People cannot help wondering, as they do in the case of Hitler's and Mussolini's unanimous plebiscites, what is the use of it all? . . . These shotgun plebiscites . . . demonstrate to the outside world that there is unity in Nazi Germany, in Fascist Italy, in Soviet Russia. It is not the unity of assent but of compulsion, yet a unity of some kind it is. A 100 percent electoral victory for Stalin does not demonstrate popular solidarity, but it does show that Stalin is strong enough to make his people vote solidly for him . . . it is sufficiently firm to be taken into account by any foreign power with designs against Soviet Russia."

The point was made. It would be the last pretense at free elections in the Soviet Union for five decades.

By the time Stalin died of a cerebral hemorrhage in 1953 he had transformed the Soviet Union into a world power, becoming only the second country to possess nuclear weapons. The Cold War, as it was named by George Orwell in 1945, between West and East, between the United States and the Soviet Union and their Allies, was being fought indirectly and in the shadows. Russia, which had come to mean the entire Soviet Union, served as the model for the totalitarian state described by Orwell in his dystopian novel *1984*. The central government in the Kremlin controlled all aspects of society, both public and private, including the entire economy, the military, and the educational system. It was a totalitarian state with few civil liberties; freedom of speech, the press, assembly, or the right to practice a religion did not exist. Individual behavior was monitored by a secret police force. Dissent or even deviation from approved Communist Party positions could result in harsh punishments.

The country actually was run by two separate structures, the Communist Party and the official government. It was a unique, confusing, sometimes overlapping system, consisting of different levels with different responsibilities and powers. But final decisions were made by the Communist Party—the only political party in the Soviet Union.

Unlike other countries in which a citizen could simply join

their chosen political party, the Communist Party was more of an exclusive club. It took several years before an applicant might become a member. At its height, less than 10 percent of the entire population belonged to the party. Generally, young people would begin their quest to eventually be approved by joining the Komsomol, the Communist Youth League, which both vetted and trained young people for future membership. When it became time to actually join, applicants had to provide recommendations from party members, pass background checks, and prove their knowledge of Marxist-Leninist theory and their loyalty before being admitted.

The representative body of the Communist Party was the Central Committee, whose members were elected by the party. But that election was essentially a formality. The real decision-making body was the political bureau, the politburo, a small group of less than twenty men who "approved" candidates for the Central Committee and determined the country's policy. There was an official process to elect new Central Committee members, but generally the politburo decided who would be granted membership. The next level down was the secretariat, which managed party operations and implemented the will of the politburo. The presiding officer of the secretariat, the First Secretary—who also was a member of the politburo—became the leader of the nation.

At least on the surface, the government structure of the USSR was roughly comparable to other parliamentary systems. The Supreme Soviet, the legislature, consisted of two chambers, which turned the decisions of the politburo into law. Members were elected—but candidates were approved by the party and there was only one name on the ballot.

Elections were held sporadically, and voting was basically

mandatory. Officially, the turnout was always around 99 percent of eligible voters; in 1950, for example, the government reported that 111,090,010 of the 111,116,373 eligible voters had cast their ballots—close to 100 percent—for the approved candidates.

By the time someone (almost always a man) was elected to the politburo, their entire life had been shaped by the Communist Party; they had proven their unfailing loyalty to it through many decades. Knowing that, appreciating the difficulty of rising to a leadership position in the party, makes it even more incredible that Mikhail Sergeyevich Gorbachev, who was raised in that system, was able to work through every level of the party to eventually become the First Secretary, the most powerful man in the Soviet Union—then use his power to institute both policies and elections to cause its dissolution.

Stalin had built a self-perpetuating closed system held together by terror. No one will ever know how many millions of people Stalin ordered killed or sent to labor camps. Gorbachev was born in 1931 in the North Caucasus, into Stalinism. His parents were poor peasants, living in a rural area, on occasion using straw from the stables as insulation against the biting cold, working long hours on a collective farm. His family suffered under Stalin: Two of his uncles and an aunt died during the famine that swept the country in the early 1930s, and during The Great Purge both of his grandfathers were arrested and sent to labor camps. His paternal grandfather, an early member of the party who had helped create the region's first collective farm, was tortured for being a member of a subversive Trotskyite group.

But Gorbachev believed in the system. He followed a traditional path through party ranks. In 1946 he joined the Komsomol, eventually becoming the leader of his local group and a member of the district committee. The system rewarded initiative, intelligence, hard work, and perhaps most important, loyalty, qualities he displayed in abundance. In the summers, he worked with his father on a combine harvester, earning the Order of the Red Banner of Labor for harvesting eight hundred metric tons of grain. He was distinguishing himself and people were noticing.

In 1950, while studying law at Moscow State University, he applied for party membership, writing, "I would consider it a high honor to be a member of the highly advanced genuinely revolutionary Communist Party . . . I promise to be faithful to the great cause of Lenin and Stalin, to devote my entire life to that party's struggle for Communism." Two years later he became a full member of the party.

On March 6, 1953, the Associated Press reported Stalin's death, claiming "He dominated a third of the world's peoples as the most powerful dictator in history." Following a complex power struggle, Nikita Khrushchev, a rotund veteran of both World Wars and staunch Stalinist who had been a loyal party member since 1918, emerged as the Russian leader. Although Khrushchev was a fiercely loyal follower of Stalin when he was alive, after gaining power he made a deft pivot, eventually denouncing him, and launched an anti-Stalin campaign to "liberate Party officials from the fear of repression." The party, the government—and young, ambitious people like Gorbachev—learned how to move easily with the flow of time and changes in leadership, when necessary retreating to their unshakable loyalty to Karl Marx. Or, if beneficial, Vladimir Lenin.

Being politically flexible was an important skill in a system so responsive to the policies of a single person, policies that changed as state leadership changed from Khrushchev to Leonid Brezhnev to Yuri Andropov to Konstantin Chernenko.

Throughout those decades, Gorbachev remained loyal to the party, working his way through the ranks, gaining favor and making friends. By nature neither flamboyant nor boastful, his accomplishments and his intelligence attracted attention. As a colleague who knew him for decades once remarked, "It's hard to talk to him because you feel he is competent in every field. I never spoke with a person who is competent in everything."

By 1961, the thirty-year-old Gorbachev had become First Secretary of the regional Komsomol. He married, and as his wife, Raisa, received her PhD in sociology he earned a second degree, this one in agricultural production. Other promotions followed. Step by step, level by level, year after year, he continued rising. Given a task, he accomplished it without arousing jealousy or creating enemies. He had seemingly mastered the delicate art of accumulating power without alienating those left behind him, an essential political skill. In 1970, the party "elected" him one of the 1,517 deputies to the Supreme Soviet, representing his home region of Stavropol Krai.

It's difficult to pinpoint any specific incidents that caused Gorbachev to begin questioning the Russian Communist system. Certainly, he never forgot the imprisonment and torture his uncles had endured under Stalin. As a member of the Supreme Soviet, he was permitted to travel outside Russia, and while visiting several Western European nations he was struck by the fact that Europeans could freely and openly state their opinions and criticize their governments without any fear of reprisal. Later, he wrote of being surprised that "Often they disagreed among themselves about these matters, whereas we had to demonstrate complete unity of opinion on all questions . . . except for private conversations at kitchen tables."

Those trips, he admitted, "shook our a priori belief in the

superiority of socialist over bourgeois democracy . . . People lived better there. Why did our people live worse than in other developed countries? I could never get that question out of my mind."

Among those party officials whose attention he attracted was Yuri Andropov, the head of the State Security Agency, the feared KGB. The two men had met in 1968, when Andropov vacationed at a resort in Stavropol. They eventually grew close enough to allow Gorbachev to confide some of his doubts about the system—and its future—to Andropov. With Andropov's support, in 1980 he became, at forty-nine years old, the youngest of the roughly fifteen to twenty (the actual number was not publicized) full members of the politburo.

Upon Brezhnev's death in 1982, Andropov became First Secretary—and Gorbachev was his closest ally. It was obvious Andropov was grooming him to be his successor. At times, Gorbachev even chaired meetings of the politburo. But when Andropov died two years later, the hardliners were not ready for significant change. Instead, they elected Chernenko, the last of the "old guard" of stern, staid, aged Soviet politicians, men who carried with them the lessons of Stalin.

Gorbachev was the leader of a new generation, the Cold War veterans. His horizons were expanding. When he visited Britain, he met with Margaret Thatcher, who said, "I like Mr. Gorbachev. We can do business together." In Italy he ate at popular restaurants and savored the cuisine. In France, he and Raisa showed appreciation for culture and fashion. When Chernenko died in 1985, Gorbachev had successfully positioned himself as the natural successor.

At the meeting to elect the new secretary-general, the new leader of the Communist Party and the USSR, Foreign Minister Andrei Gromyko supported his nomination. "What features come to mind first when one evaluates the candidacy of Mikhail Sergeyevich? First of all, it is his boundless energy . . . Second is his attitude toward the people . . . he always holds the interests of the party, the interests of society and the interests of the people above all." But at a later point he reassured them, "Comrades, this man has a nice smile, but he has iron teeth."

It was a momentous vote. Officially, the politburo announced that Gorbachev had been unanimously elected the new leader of the Soviet Union. Unofficially, at least some of the older men were uncomfortable with that choice. But there were few viable alternatives.

Although he had been a voting member for five years, Gorbachev was significantly younger than many of them. He was the first Soviet leader to have been born after Lenin's 1917 revolution. Andropov and Chernenko had been sure things; the men who had elected them knew what they were getting. Gorbachev? He was from a different generation. Ironically, he was the product of the system these men had created. He tried to reassure them, telling the Central Committee, "We will do everything . . . to expand cooperation with the socialist states, to enhance the role and influence of socialism in world affairs."

America's response was cautious. "Urbane, polished, sophisticated, possessing an almost Western consciousness of image," reported *The Washington Post*, "but still a Russian mystery man on ideology."

Senator Richard Luger spoke for Congress when he said he expected "no immediate change in Soviet policies. It may take months, even years before we see any basic change in Soviet direction."

The world was changing rapidly when Gorbachev took control. In the West, the internet had become available to the public, and individuals and businesses were buying computers and printers. Clunky, expensive mobile phones had been introduced in the 1980s and soon streamlined versions would make it possible to speak with anyone, almost anywhere, at any time. Those tools and other technological advances greatly increased economic productivity wherever they were available. But for a closed society like the Soviet Union, technology was a danger.

For decades, the state had successfully controlled access to information. The problem the government faced was that the same tools necessary to compete economically with the West could be used for other purposes. A computer printer was a printing press, making it easier to distribute anti-Soviet "propaganda." Mobile phones could not easily be monitored by the government. Even the rudimentary internet, just beginning to emerge, made contact between people easier and opened a small window into life in the West. But without them the Soviet economy, already stagnant and still dependent on rudimentary machines, pens, and adding machines, risked falling even further behind in the Cold War.

Above all, Gorbachev was a realist. Weeks after taking office, he met with a group of young politburo members and industry leaders. As one of them remembered, "He talked to us about the real situation and appealed to us to speak openly and honestly. He told us things about our country I could not believe . . . We were used to being told we were first in everything."

It was a complex dilemma. The Soviet people knew only what the government wanted them to know. Television, radio, and the print media were censored and communicated government-approved propaganda. The Russian people had become used to shortages and empty shelves in the stores; rationing and breadlines were common. They had never been exposed to the abundance in the West. Travel was restricted and there was a yearslong wait to buy a car, even if a person could afford it.

It was impossible to provide the technology needed to compete without opening society to a world of wonders.

Gorbachev did not set out to destroy the system. His commitment to preserving a socialist state based on Marxist-Leninist principles never wavered, but without significant reform, he believed, the economy—and with it the state—might very well collapse. The goal was to be able to compete with Europe and America in this technologically developing world. In an effort to do that he introduced the concepts of perestroika, restructuring, combined with glasnost, openness, but made it clear he had no intention of abandoning the socialist dream, telling delegates to the Central Committee from the fifteen republics, "Some of you look at the market as a lifesaver for your economies . . . comrades, you should not think about lifesavers but about the ship, and the ship is socialism."

But almost immediately, Gorbachev began plotting a new course for that ship of state. Over the next few years, he pried open the closed society, eliminating economic barriers, restoring important individual rights. Instead of censorship and surveillance, people were allowed, even encouraged, to speak and debate about topics once considered subversive, from the crimes of the Stalin era to the greatly inflated statistics about agricultural production. Prosecuting corrupt officials from the Brezhnev era sent a strong message about the justice system. He met with Pope John Paul II and allowed religious freedom to flourish. To stimulate the economy, among many other changes, foreign investments were encouraged, state-owned industries were permitted to form partnerships with Western companies, regulations prohibiting privately owned businesses were relaxed, and efforts were made to boost productivity by providing incentives and supporting an anti-alcohol campaign. He began the orderly withdrawal of Russian troops from the decade-long, costly ongoing war in Afghanistan, and ordered a unilateral cut in troops in Eastern Europe. He granted Soviet states increased autonomy and met several times with President Ronald Reagan and later President George H.W. Bush.

Rather than the repression that had been a hallmark of the Soviet Union, Gorbachev remained committed to his own vision of socialism. When Baltic countries demanded more independence, for example, he refused to use the army to squash dissent. When cracks appeared in the Berlin Wall, which separated East and West Germany, instead of sealing them, he allowed the wall to eventually be torn down. In June 1989, Poland elected a noncommunist legislature; in the past the Soviet government had used troops in Hungary, Czechoslovakia, and even Poland to protect party rule—this time Gorbachev did not respond. In October of that same year, he said the Soviet Union "has no moral or political right to interfere in the affairs of its East European neighbors."

Without support from the Kremlin, Communist governments fell country by country. During the next few months, Hungary declared itself a democracy, opened the border with Austria, and held free elections. In November, Czechoslovakia's government resigned and free elections took place a month later. That same month, the Berlin Wall was ripped down, and within weeks Germany was unified. Bulgaria's president resigned and democratic reforms were instituted. In December, Romanians violently overthrew their repressive Communist leaders, replacing them with a presidential republic.

The changes were extensive and astonishing. This was a

new USSR. Finally, though, he began making fundamental changes to the structure that had created and perpetuated the state, the Communist Party. Gorbachev began turning the idea of perestroika into political reality by proposing sweeping reforms. These amendments to the constitution included turning the president from a figurehead into a powerful executive and creating a new national assembly; a 2,250-member Congress of People's Deputies would replace the Supreme Soviet. The majority of deputies in this body would be freely elected by a secret multicandidate ballot, while some seats would be held by state-approved social organizations, like the Communist Party. This Congress would elect both the president and a smaller, more responsive and representative 542-member Supreme Soviet. Explaining the new system, Gorbachev told the existing parliament, "All of us are in a school of democracy, and we should be good pupils in that school."

Gorbachev's objective was to revitalize the USSR by giving its citizens a real voice in their own future—and the tool he would use to do it was free elections. Soviet citizens would be allowed to choose among candidates nominated by the party, unions, collective organizations, academies, and newly formed groups. The existing Supreme Soviet approved those amendments—voting itself out of existence after fifty-five years. That vote, Gorbachev said, was "a green light for radical changes to our political system," which heralded "a new period for the Soviet state, on the basis of democratization and self-government of the people." Many people considered this the symbolic end to the terrors of Stalinism.

Trying to suddenly impose a new, competitive electoral system over an entrenched, decades-old, rigid way of doing things resulted in semi-organized chaos. Widespread disbelief that this was really happening had to be overcome. Most people did not understand the procedures or the regulations of a structured election. The Communist Party itself fought back. It had spent seven decades building a monolithic structure and would not easily be pushed aside. Many local officials considered this an effort to destroy the party, and with it their own privileged positions.

As Gorbachev later described it, "It was a devilishly complicated political operation." The party had tremendous advantages; its well-organized local apparatus allowed it to exercise considerable control over the nominating process. By also essentially running the Electoral Commission, the party determined who would be on the ballot. As a result, a majority of the candidates in that first slate of elections were either members or affiliated Communists.

Somehow, though, numerous independent candidates earned a place on the ballot—and began actively campaigning. It had been almost seven decades since the Soviet people had been exposed to real political campaigns. Candidates printed and distributed literature, rallies were held, voters were allowed to question and criticize candidates, and debates were broadcast on radio and TV. The candidates—including those running as Communists—campaigned on issues that mattered: food supplies, building infrastructure, the environment, changing the legal system, and how the economy would be restructured. One Communist candidate said proudly, "I favor that my party be the ruling one," but he also supported the establishment of a free-market economy and a private sector.

In 1989, more than 170 million Soviet citizens went to the polls in the first competitive election in most of their lives. Voters marked their choice on a secret ballot listing several candidates. The impact resonated throughout the world. As American political columnist Chris Matthews wrote, "For good reason, we Americans view this week's election in the Soviet Union with . . . awe and skepticism . . . Sometimes we just want to stand back and applaud. To those of us who have lived our whole lives in the Cold War, after all, the sight of agitated Moscow 'voters' crowding into political meetings, with candidates yelling their differences at each other is nothing short of apocalyptic.

"This is the conversion of Russia we had long prayed for, the first fragile sparks of liberty."

The results were startling. Even against the party's efforts, 292 independents were elected; a minority of the 2,250 seats, but a loud minority that had the freedom to speak out. Among the winners was liberal Boris Yeltsin, a popular antiestablishment politician who in 1987 had become the first person to resign from the politburo, claiming Gorbachev's reforms were too moderate. Yeltsin, who once had been the Communist Party leader in Moscow, defeated a party loyalist for an at-large seat in the city, receiving 89.4 percent of the vote.

While numerous problems tainted the entire process, including a dearth of capable opposition candidates, rules governing the nomination process that strongly favored the Communist Party, voter suppression in some areas, and a somewhat complicated runoff system, Gorbachev was elated. "These elections were exceptional in all our history," he told the politburo. "This is a major step in realizing the political reforms and the subsequent democratization of our society . . . It would be difficult to assume that we would have everything the way we wanted on the first try."

The new Congress of People's Deputies met two months later. The entire session was broadcast on radio and TV. Millions of people watched or listened to every minute in awe; if they were not at home, they carried radios or gathered around TV sets in public places as deputies openly, sometimes loudly, and without fear of retribution, criticized the party and the system. This was a mammoth event; nothing like it had ever taken place in their lifetimes. The Congress reflected the wishes of the people, pledging to continue the march toward democratization and engage with foreign nations in constructive dialogue.

Election by election, first via the party and then via the people, Gorbachev was transforming the Soviet Union. It was an extremely intricate process that required massive acceptance, but a failing economy and the desire for change allowed it to happen. Several months later, the Congress met to elect a president with greatly expanded powers for a five-year term. Much like in the United States, the new president would be able to propose legislation, negotiate treaties, veto bills, appoint a cabinet, declare war, and in emergencies, impose rule—essentially wresting control from the Communist Party. Emboldened Soviet citizens wanted a direct election, but Gorbachev, caught between reformers who demanded rapid change and hardliners who resisted change, and supposedly fearing the potential chaos a contested campaign might cause, handed that responsibility to Congress. There was considerable speculation that his real reason was concern he might lose a public election. One American reporter wrote, "Some observers speculate that Gorbachev, whose popularity at home has declined, was afraid to face the voters directly—before his plan to improve the consumer goods crisis has shown results." Gorbachev did promise, however, that direct elections would take place in the future.

The results were far closer than anyone imagined. A two-thirds vote in Congress was required to elect the president.

Anything less than that would trigger the general election that Gorbachev wanted to avoid. He received the necessary two-thirds—but only by forty-six votes. After taking the oath of office, he said, "An end is being put to the party's . . . direct interference in the solution of specific state and economic issues," warning that the changes he intended to make "may initially be accompanied by painful problems and badly affect some interests."

While the Soviet people continued to be confronted by empty shelves and shortages, the West celebrated his achievements. "In the long chain of Russian and then Soviet leaders there has never been a leader like him," reported the *Chicago Tribune*. "Peter the Great opened the country to Western thought. Lenin brought revolution. Stalin brought repression. Brezhnev brought corruption. But Gorbachev has brought a transformation that five years ago would have seemed impossible."

While Gorbachev remained extremely unpopular in his country, with one poll reporting a dismal 20 percent approval rating, in late 1990 he was awarded the Nobel Peace Prize for ending the Cold War, pursuing arms reduction, and fostering a climate of freedom in Eastern Europe.

The quest for freedom that Gorbachev had unleashed grew far beyond his ability to contain it. Each of the fifteen republics responded differently, but all of them moved toward autonomy. In an effort to hold the country together, Gorbachev proposed a new federation in which the republics had considerably greater control over their own policies. In March 1991, the first national referendum in USSR history asked the astonishing question, "Do you consider necessary the preservation of the Union of Soviet Socialist Republics as a renewed federation of equal sovereign republics in which the rights and freedom of an individual of any ethnicity will be fully guaranteed?" Six of the republics refused to participate, but 80 percent of voters in the remaining nine overwhelmingly approved this new alignment.

At that same time the Republic of Russia voted to replace its existing government with a freely elected president, an election that was scheduled for the following June. Russia was by far the most important member of the USSR. More than half the federation's population lived there; three-fourths of its territory and most of its natural resources were Russian. The campaign was brief, surprisingly calm, and extremely popular. Several rallies attracted more than one hundred thousand people. In this direct election, the Russian people elected Boris Yeltsin, who had officially resigned from the Communist Party months earlier.

Having been freely elected by the people of the largest republic, Yeltsin instantly became a powerful rival to Gorbachev. Almost immediately, he began the process of dissolving the Soviet Union—believing the changes necessary to modernize the state required an independent Russia.

There was little Gorbachev could do to prevent it. A last-gasp coup attempt in August by hardliners and military leaders to overthrow Gorbachev, arrest Yeltsin, and restore the Communist Party fell apart in three days, instead further accelerating the end of the Soviet Union. In December, the Soviet Union was legally dissolved, replaced by a loose Commonwealth of Independent States. On December 25, Gorbachev officially resigned, turning over the nuclear launch codes and all his powers to Yeltsin. In his televised farewell address to the nation he said:

> I have firmly stood for independence, self-rule of nations, for the sovereignty of republics, but at the same time for the preservation of the . . . unity of the country.

> Events went a different way . . . This society acquired freedom . . . The totalitarian system which deprived the country of an opportunity to become successful and prosperous long ago has been eliminated. A breakthrough has been achieved on the way to democratic changes. Free elections, freedom of the press, religious freedoms, representative organs of power, a multiparty [system] became a reality, human rights are recognized as the supreme principle . . .
>
> We live in a new world. The Cold War has ended, the arms race has stopped, as has the insane militarization which mutilated our economy, public psyche and morals. The threat of a world war has been removed . . .

After his resignation, Gorbachev began writing and lecturing. In 1996, he ran against Yeltsin and several other candidates for the presidency. But Russians continued to blame him for the loss of the international power and prestige the USSR had once enjoyed, without substantially delivering the promised economic returns. The attempt to transition to at least a partial market-based economy had failed; shelves remained empty, and the GDP, a measure of the economy, remained stagnant. In the election, he received only miniscule support.

Gorbachev remained actively involved in both Russian and world politics, speaking out freely to criticize both Eastern and Western governments. Boris Yeltsin served as president of the Russian Federation until resigning on New Year's Eve, 1999. But after the initial economic failure, the political reforms instituted by the two men brought Russia into the modern world, setting the stage for the creation of a middle class, significant new construction throughout the country, and at least limited personal freedoms.

In the presidential election of 2000, voters elected former KGB head Vladimir Putin. In the years since then, Putin has attempted to reestablish Russia's dominance in the former Soviet republics and curtailed many of the individual rights achieved under Gorbachev and protected by Yeltsin. In 2014, he annexed Ukraine's Crimean Peninsula, claiming it as part of the Russian Federation, and in 2022 launched a full-scale invasion of that country.

The realignment wrought by Gorbachev and Yeltsin—and now challenged by Putin—continues to ripple throughout the world. The Russian Communist Party remains active but serves mostly as opposition to Putin's ruling United Russia Party. An estimated nine-hundred thousand Russians who tasted freedom under Gorbachev and Yeltsin have left the country since the outbreak of the Ukrainian War, although accurate numbers are impossible to obtain. A substantial number of them are educated young men, fleeing potential military service.

The Union of Soviet Socialist Republics that existed when Gorbachev was elected by the Communist Party long ago has disappeared, replaced by a system and country in flux. But it appears that Churchill was prescient when he said almost nine decades ago, it remains "a riddle wrapped in a mystery inside an enigma."

FIFTEEN

May 10, 1994: Nelson Mandela Is Elected President of South Africa

ON MAY 10, 1994, an estimated 1 billion people around the globe—out of a 5.6 billion world population—watched in awe as seventy-five-year-old Nelson Mandela raised his right hand and became South Africa's first Black president, ending more than three hundred years of institutionalized racism in Southern Africa. "Democracy is based on the majority principle," Mandela said, heralding a new government structure that ensured "a legal framework that will assist . . . the awesome task of reconstruction and development of our battered society."

As Barack Obama so famously said, "Elections have consequences."

Mandela's election was the culmination of an extraordinary story of personal heroism, a display of fortitude and courage that enabled him to become an enduring symbol of the worldwide quest for freedom.

Beginning with the founding of a Dutch East India trading post, the Cape Colony, in 1652, Indigenous Black people at the bottom of the African continent had been subjugated to continuous and often brutal discrimination. In those early years, local tribes were displaced, while enslaved people were imported from elsewhere in the sprawling Dutch Empire. Through the centuries, additional restrictions passed by Dutch then British settlers stripped Black residents of fundamental rights. Although Great Britain outlawed slavery in the 1830s, legislation simply changed the status of local enslaved people to indentured laborers.

British expansion into the region caused Dutch settlers, mostly farmers known as Boers, to establish two large independent republics in addition to several smaller settlements. After the discovery of major gold deposits on Boer lands in 1886, miners raced to Africa, leading to the founding of the city of Johannesburg. In 1899, rising tensions—and the inevitable lure of massive gold riches—erupted into a bloody guerilla war between the Dutch settlers and the British Empire. During the three-year-long Boer War, twenty-two thousand British soldiers and fourteen thousand Boer troops were killed, while as many as twenty-six thousand Boer women, children, and men not qualified for military service died from disease in concentration camps. Black men and women were held in separate camps, in which somewhere between fourteen thousand and twenty thousand people died.

The peace treaty signed in 1902 granted England total control over the region, while explicitly giving all political and legislative power to white officials. The roots had been planted for the racist government and social structure that would emerge and grow. In May 1910, the two Boer republics and two British colonies formed a new state, the Union of South Africa. The constitution established a strong central government, largely influenced by Great Britain. "No nation ever started with better law, a fairer constitution, a more roseate future than South Africa," wrote the *Ottawa Journal.*

Except for the vast majority of residents, the approximately four million Black people living there.

Other than a few literate Black landowners in Cape Province, Blacks were not permitted to vote or run for office. That "fairer constitution" included restrictions on land ownership, which eventually became the 1913 Natives Land Act. This legislation confined Black "citizens" to designated urban areas and eventually prohibited them from buying land, creating a legally segregated nation. That racial separation extended to all areas of life, placing the type of jobs Black men and women could hold, membership in unions, and access to education under government control.

To stop Black South Africans from moving into the major cities, in 1923 the government passed the Urban Areas Act, which allowed working people—servants and other low-wage workers—to live in the cities, but forced others into so-called "townships," densely populated areas on the periphery of urban areas. One of the largest townships was Soweto, which was created in the 1930s to be a home for people working in Johannesburg. An acronym meaning South West Townships, Soweto eventually became the largest Black city in South Africa, its population growing to about one million people, many of whom lived in dire poverty.

The racial policies of the government were casually accepted by other nations. No foreign governments objected. While outright slavery had been abolished in most countries, racial segregation was common throughout the world. Laws and customs had been put in place to guarantee second- or even third-class citizenship for Blacks—even while they provided the low-cost labor needed to keep economies humming. In the United States, for example, the races remained separated through the legally accepted doctrine of "separate but equal" facilities, which enforced strictly separate conditions in most aspects of society—but were hardly equal. What made the bigotry practiced in South Africa, as well as other nations on the African continent, different from the rest of the world—in America or England, for example—was that the African countries had majority Black populations, controlled by minority white governments. That system could only be maintained by making certain that Black populations were not allowed to vote, have representation, or participate in the decision-making process.

In South Africa, the fight for those rights began in 1912. In response to the new constitution, Black and Colored people—as those of mixed races were known—formed the South African Native National Congress to advocate for voting rights in the more liberal area of Cape Province. A decade later, the organization was renamed the African National Congress, the ANC, which eventually would lead the decades-long fight against racist conditions.

Initially, the ANC was a nonviolent organization, committed to mobilizing political pressure to force change. But years later, when it became obvious that those tactics were having absolutely no effect, the party would adopt a different and far more dangerous strategy.

What was to become an historic international movement began when a group of educated young Black men formed the ANC Youth League on Easter Sunday, 1944. Among those leaders were

Walter Sisulu, Oliver Tambo, and Rolihlahla Mandela, or Nelson Mandela, the Christian name he had been given in primary school. Mandela was a twenty-six-year-old messenger, clerk, and student at a law firm. As he later wrote in his memoir *Long Walk to Freedom*, there was not one single moment, no specific event, that caused him to dedicate his life to fighting for freedom, but rather it was "a steady accumulation of a thousand slights, a thousand indignities . . . produced in me an anger, a rebelliousness, a desire to fight the system that imprisoned my people . . . I simply found myself doing so, and could not do otherwise."

Mandela had already established a reputation as a man unafraid to stand firm against authority. Four years earlier, he had been expelled from the University of Fort Hare for participating in a protest and boycott against the policies of the Student Representative Council. Although he was offered the chance to return to school if he accepted certain conditions, he resigned from the university. Instead, he continued his education through correspondence courses.

In response to the still small but growing threat to white rule the ANC presented, in 1948 white South Africans elected the repressive National Party, a party whose leaders had sympathized with Nazi Germany in World War II. This election, *The Guardian* warned, "would be a disaster." The National Party had campaigned to stop the *swart gevaar,* the "Black danger," and as soon as they gained power they introduced a brutal policy, *apartheid*, a word meaning "apartness" or separateness in the Afrikaans language. It came to describe the array of repressive, racist policies instituted by the National Party government.

Under apartheid, every aspect of Black life was regulated. Literally millions of Black South Africans were forcibly removed from their homes into segregated areas called Bantustans, or "tribal homelands." Mixed marriages and even sexual relationships between races were outlawed. Access to public facilities, among them buses, restaurants, movie theaters, beaches, even park benches, was restricted. In fact, in an effort to prevent access to information that might encourage resistance, television was not available in South Africa until 1976, and even then, programming was controlled by the government. The only channel broadcast programs in English and Afrikaans, rather than regional Black languages. For the first few years, Black citizens had only limited access to TV.

As these laws were passed and enforced, the ANC emerged as the voice of the oppressed. It remained committed to nonviolence, not necessarily as a strategy as much as a recognition of reality. As Mandela noted, at least initially the party continued to embrace nonviolence because the government would not hesitate to crush agitators.

Instead, he helped launch the Defiance Campaign, the first organized resistance to apartheid. Run jointly by the ANC and the South African Indian Congress, it began in 1952 when Mandela, the National Volunteer-in-Chief of the campaign, and fifty-one other Black and Indian South Africans defiantly marched into a restricted area without permits. In other cities, protestors walked into railroad stations and post offices through the "Europeans Only" entrance, sat on white benches, or violated other apartheid restrictions. The campaign spread slowly throughout the country—but it spread. For many people, this marked the first time they risked standing up for their rights. Thousands of people were arrested, and although most sentences were minor, some young defendants were whipped. Mandela was arrested, and as a leader of the incipient rebellion, he was sentenced to nine months of hard labor, although his sentence was suspended.

Although Mandela had not graduated from law school, he had earned a law degree by working at a law firm and passing all the required examinations. The same year as the protest, he and Oliver Tambo opened the first Black law firm in South Africa.

Three years later, an alliance of organizations representing oppressed South Africans, including the ANC, officially adopted The Freedom Charter; this was a statement of aspirations calling for complete freedom and equality for all South Africans—and envisioning the seemingly impossible—an end to apartheid. In response, the government charged 156 people who had created the charter, including Mandela, with "high treason and a countrywide conspiracy to use violence to overthrow the present government and replace it with a communist state." Treason was a death penalty crime.

The government was becoming increasingly wary; its efforts to crack down on dissidents were slowly backfiring. The various anti-government groups inside the country were growing and, for the first time, the international community began paying attention to conditions inside South Africa.

Eventually only thirty people were tried, and all of them were acquitted. The prosecution failed to produce any evidence that the ANC had attempted to violently overthrow the government. Mandela emerged from the prosecution as a leader of the freedom movement—and a distinct danger to the government.

By the time the trial ended, conditions in the country had changed drastically. In 1958 the National Party was pursuing a policy referred to benignly as "separate development." But it was far more ominous. Black people living in the Bantustans would lose their South African citizenship, instead becoming citizens of autonomous homelands; they would be permitted to work in South Africa but would not be entitled to any of the benefits of citizenship. They were to be legally exiled from their country.

Perhaps even more importantly, while the trial was still in progress, police opened fire on peaceful protestors in Sharpeville Township, killing at least 69 people and wounding another 180. Nonviolence was no longer an option.

Responding to Sharpeville, the government declared a state of emergency. The ANC and other freedom-seeking organizations were banned. Eighteen thousand people were arrested. While some leaders escaped to other countries, where they began raising international awareness, Mandela went underground. "I became a creature of the night," Mandela recalled, moving secretly around the country, often in disguise, holding clandestine meetings and planning sessions. A warrant was issued for his arrest, and government forces began searching for him. Newspapers began running articles claiming he had appeared in a certain town or been seen in another. Police set up roadblocks and pursued tips, but Mandela so successfully evaded capture that the newspapers began referring to him as the "Black Pimpernel," an admiring reference to the elusive French Revolutionary literary character The Scarlet Pimpernel.

By 1960, other nations began to find ways to support this struggle for freedom. That year ANC leader Chief Albert John Mvumbi Luthuli was awarded the Nobel Peace Prize. In other places throughout the world, including the United States, embryonic equality movements were gaining traction with varying degrees of success. But not in South Africa, which moved aggressively to prevent change. In an October 1960 referendum, white South Africans voted to transform the government from a constitutional monarchy, with the British Queen as official head of state, to a republic, and on May 31, 1961, the new Republic of South Africa was established. Although the government wanted to remain in the British Commonwealth, its application was turned down because of its apartheid policies.

This was among the early rebukes from the international community, but the government ignored it, refusing to even meet with ANC representatives. Left with no options for peaceful change, the ANC abandoned its commitment to nonviolence. A clandestine organization, *Umkhonto we Sizwe*, the "Spear of the Nation"—with Mandela, still evading capture, as its co-founder—was created to wage guerrilla war. His objective was not to spark a race war, he said, but rather to empower opposition and exact an economic toll by scaring away potential foreign investors.

Their first attacks targeted apartheid infrastructure, power stations, and government offices, carefully avoiding civilian casualties. The bombings stunned the nation; Black South Africans warily supported this new strategy, while the government began a massive effort to arrest the leaders.

Seeking to raise support, Mandela slipped out of the country and went to Tanganyika, a newly independent country governed by elected Black leaders, to speak at a freedom conference. For the first time in his life, he later wrote, he knew what it felt like to be a free man.

On August 5, 1962, as South Africa's rugby team defeated the British Isles 8–3, Nelson Mandela was captured while driving to Johannesburg. He had been betrayed by a new member of the resistance. In June 1964, *London Daily Mirror* reported that after an eight-month trial, "South Africa's 'Black Pimpernel' Nelson Mandela was found guilty of [221 acts] of sabotage and trying to overthrow the government by force. Manacled Mandela, arch enemy of racial segregation, was taken from court . . . he raised his hands high and shouted, 'Africa!'"

The penalty was life imprisonment or death by hanging. Before being sentenced, Mandela had made an impassioned four-and-a-half-hour speech, during which he said, "I have cherished the ideal of a democratic and free society in which all persons live together in harmony and with equal opportunities . . . but if need be, it is an ideal for which I am prepared to die."

Along with seven other ANC leaders, he was sentenced to life in prison. But rather than ending the freedom movement, the trial attracted more international attention to the struggle—and made Nelson Mandela a symbol of freedom.

Coincidentally, as Mandela was being sentenced, half a world away Martin Luther King Jr. was arrested in St. Augustine, Florida, for attempting to integrate a restaurant.

Mandela was sent to the notorious maximum-security prison on Robben Island. His cell was about the length of his body; when he lay down his feet touched one wall and his head touched the opposite wall. His days were spent at hard labor, crushing stones with a sledgehammer, and while his ability to communicate with the world beyond the prison was limited, his fight strongly influenced young Black South Africans. The prison itself became known as "Mandela University" because of the lectures about the fight for freedom he and other ANC leaders preached to other prisoners.

Although he was isolated, his influence continued growing outside the stark walls. As England's *Birmingham Post* noted several years later, "Despite being cut off from the mainstream of black politics in South Africa—his writings may not be published in [that] country, he has no access to news media and his reading is censored—Mr. Mandela remains the symbol of black nationalism for most blacks. Two years ago an opinion poll found he topped the list of candidates to become the first prime minister of a black-ruled South Africa."

The continued incarceration of Mandela and all the ANC prisoners became the rallying point every successful movement requires. The international community had begun taking steps to force South Africa to abandon apartheid, an effort that eventually would affect every aspect of South African society. Economic, academic, cultural, and social boycotts were imposed. Various unions around the world called for strikes against the nation. The International Olympic Committee barred the country from the 1964 games, and although it was reinstated in 1968 after agreeing to send a multiracial team, pressure from other nations forced the committee to rescind the invitation. In 1970, the IOC officially expelled South Africa.

The United Nations called apartheid a violation of its charter, in 1973 declaring it a "crime against humanity," and officially supported the boycotts—although for several decades, neither the United States nor the United Kingdom was willing to curtail firms doing business in that country. In 1974, South Africa was suspended from UN membership, prohibited from taking part in discussions or voting.

The government fought to maintain control. In 1976, ten thousand students in Soweto marched to protest a policy mandating that classes be taught in Afrikaans rather than local languages. Police once again fired on the demonstrators, killing almost two hundred people and wounding more than a thousand.

In an attempt to defuse the situation, Prime Minister John

Vorster secretly offered to free Mandela—*if* he agreed to live in the newly created "state" of the Transkei homeland and acknowledge its independence. He refused. This was, Mandela later revealed, only the first of numerous offers to release him—*if* he accepted certain conditions.

The worldwide "Free Mandela" movement began in earnest in 1980. A British anti-apartheid campaign sponsored rallies, boycotts, and named streets and buildings in his honor. Two thousand mayors of cities around the world issued a petition demanding his release. In 1988, the "Nelson Mandela: Freedom at 70" concert held at Wembley Stadium, featuring stars like Sting, Stevie Wonder, and Whitney Houston, was broadcast to sixty-three countries and seen by an estimated six hundred million people.

The next day South African Archbishop Desmond Tutu, who had been awarded the 1984 Nobel Peace Prize for leading the nonviolent effort to end apartheid, told an estimated 250,000 people at a rally in London's Hyde Park, "In 25 years in jail, Mandela has not spoken to the public, yet many people not born have been inspired by him." Soviet leader Mikhail Gorbachev added his country's support, telling Mandela, "It distresses one to realize you mark the birthday in a prison dungeon into which you were thrown by racists more than a quarter century ago."

Incredibly, after decades without a single appearance, without making a single public speech, Nelson Mandela was far more powerful than he had been at the height of his activism as a free man. American columnist Mary McGrory noted, "His reputation grew independently of all the machinery of modern day publicity. He lived by word of mouth among an adoring public . . ."

The South African government responded cautiously. In 1982, supposedly to prevent Mandela from influencing younger prisoners, but more likely to facilitate negotiations, after eighteen years on Robben Island he was moved to a more accessible prison. Three years later, President P.W. Botha made what has been referred to as "The Rubicon Speech." He would release Mandela and other political prisoners, he told a worldwide audience estimated at two hundred million people, if they pledged to renounce violence for political gain. But, he vowed, he would not support Black participation in the government, nor Black majority rule.

Mandela's daughter, Zindzi, read a statement rejecting the offer, which her father had dictated to her mother, Winnie. "I cannot sell my birthright," he responded to Botha, "nor am I prepared to sell the birthright of my people, to be free." He had turned to violence, he continued, only after other forms of peaceful resistance had been essentially outlawed, vowing to remain in prison until apartheid was ended and all South Africans had a voice in choosing their government.

Within months, Botha declared another state of emergency to fight the growing insurgency; he suspended constitutional rights and gave the police greater powers to act against potential threats in Black areas. It was a desperate, not quite last-ditch effort to stem the flow of history.

By 1989, the combination of international sanctions, which had severely impacted the economy, and internal unrest made it clear the racist government could not survive. In September, Parliament elected Frederik W. de Klerk as the nation's new president. The freedom movement initially dismissed him; there was nothing in his political past to suggest he would embrace reform. But on occasion men rise beyond their reputations and dare to take steps into an uncertain future. Most people expected de Klerk to try to continue Botha's policies; instead, he stunned Parliament by pledging to seek "a new South Africa," in which the Black majority "becomes part of the decision-making process."

De Klerk had taken his first step into an uncertain future. Far-right conservatives called his remarks "a knife thrust in the back" of the security forces and denounced him for "unconditional surrender." But their efforts to stop him failed. In February 1990, de Klerk told Parliament, "The season of violence is over. The time for reconstruction and reconciliation has arrived . . . The justification for violence which has always advanced, no longer exists." He lifted the ban on the ANC and thirty-three other previously banned political organizations, then announced that, after twenty-eight years, "The government has taken a firm decision to release Nelson Mandela unconditionally."

Days later, Nelson Mandela walked out of prison. He was greeted by exuberant crowds. A man who had existed only as a legend, a symbol, was suddenly flesh and blood, standing in front of millions of people. But the euphoria of the moment was soon tempered by reality. There was no plan in place for moving forward. The roughly twenty-eight million Black South Africans demanded equality and equal access to every aspect of the country, while five million whites wanted desperately to hold on to their power. As a reporter in South Africa wrote, "Black and white leaders say a major era in the country's history is coming to an end with the impending demise of white-minority rule. But the future is foreboding, they warn, with many obstacles and the threat of conflict ahead."

A fuse had been lit. It was up to Mandela and de Klerk to prevent a civil war.

The ANC and the National Party began negotiating, trying to carve a peaceful path through decades of distrust that could satisfy—if not please—both sides. An organization called the Convention for a Democratic South Africa was set up to create a new constitution. It was a long, complex effort, and at times talks collapsed. "Our country is on the brink of disaster," Mandela wrote to de Klerk in 1992, following an outbreak of violence that resulted in forty-five deaths.

Numerous obstacles had to be overcome in a process taking place amid considerable violence. In addition to many white leaders reluctant to cede power, some leaders of Black homelands fought against any agreement that would deprive them of their positions. Negotiations proceeded for more than three years through a seemingly endless series of starts and stops. Minor points became major hurdles. The outcome was always in doubt.

At times, Mandela and de Klerk struggled to maintain a working relationship. Finally, as Mandela later remembered, de Klerk decided to take a breathtaking gamble. He would hold a nationwide referendum allowing white South Africans to vote on the future of the country. Would they support the extraordinary reforms he was proposing, fundamental changes in the historic racial makeup of the country—which would necessitate negotiating with the ANC? He staked his career on it, warning that if this referendum was defeated he would resign.

Conversely, de Klerk recognized Mandela's essential role as the only leader capable of reaching some type of peaceful settlement. "My worst nightmare," he said, "is to wake up one morning and he is not there."

Freedom was on the ballot. It was a difficult situation for Mandela; Black South Africans were still excluded from voting in this national election, ignoring his fundamental demand—but without white support, there could not be a peaceful resolution. The election was a fundamental choice about the future of South Africa: ballots or bullets?

There was only one question on that ballot: "Do you support continuation of the reform process which the state president began on Feb 2, 1990, and which is aimed at a new constitution through negotiation?"

The results were overwhelming, far greater than had been predicted. According to the AP, "President F.W. de Klerk today won a mandate to end apartheid and share power with the black majority . . . an unprecedented declaration for peace and compromise by whites in a nation branded for decades as an intractable stronghold of racism." A massive 68.7 percent of the almost four million voters gave de Klerk the mandate he needed to continue negotiations. De Klerk told all South Africans, "Today we have closed the book on apartheid."

To honor their work in dismantling apartheid, Nelson Mandela and Frederik de Klerk were jointly awarded the 1993 Nobel Peace Prize. In his acceptance speech, Mandela paid tribute to de Klerk, acknowledging, "He had the courage to admit a terrible wrong had been done."

"Five years ago," de Klerk said in his own speech, "people would have seriously questioned the sanity of anyone who would have predicted that Mr. Mandela and I would be joint recipients of the 1993 Nobel Peace Prize . . . We are political opponents. We disagree strongly on key issues . . . It was not easy for [our] supporters to relinquish the ideals they had cherished for many decades . . . and because we did it, there is hope."

As difficult negotiations continued, Mandela and de Klerk signed the Record of Understanding, which led to an agreement to create a democratic government of national unity, a structure in which the various parties would have representation in the new assembly based on the number of votes they received. That meant the National Party would continue to be part of the new government—although it would not have any veto power. The compromise became known as "The Grand Bargain." Finally, the date for South Africa's first truly national election was set for April 27, 1994. On that day, voters would elect a four-hundred-member national assembly, which would then elect a president and write the country's new constitution.

Toronto's *Globe and Mail* summed up what was at stake in the election for South Africa's almost five million white citizens:

> The historic election marks the end of an era of dominance that began 340 years ago with the arrival of settlers from Holland, Germany and France. For [almost] 30 million blacks, as well as one million ethnic Indians and 3.4 million mixed-race "coloureds," it marks the formal conclusion of generations of white oppression and the beginning of an era in which they will be masters of their own house . . .

With this election, the story continued, the black homelands that were the "ultimate expression of apartheid" as well as the four white-ruled provinces would fade into history, to be replaced by a semi-federal state consisting of nine provinces, each of them electing their own legislature.

The government faced a massive task. The machinery necessary to conduct a nationwide election did not exist. It was estimated that almost twenty-two million South Africans would be eligible to vote—and sixteen million of them had never previously voted. Somehow, the government had to set up thousands of polling sites; figure out how to register sixteen million new voters—many of them illiterate and not knowledgeable about the voting process; create a security apparatus to protect voters against threats and intimidation while also preventing voting fraud; train poll workers how to conduct the election; and provide all the materials necessary, from pencils to ballot boxes. And they had to do it in four months.

In the entire history of elections, beginning with the Greeks and Romans, there was nothing to compare with the challenge that faced them.

A commission was established to conduct the election. To make a seemingly impossible situation even more difficult, the new organization was not permitted to use any information or materials created by the previous, all-white administration. As one member of the new group explained, "We were not allowed to use a pencil that came out of [the prior commission]. Not their systems, not their stationery, not their equipment, not their physical locations, nothing. So you had four months within which to set up this entirely from scratch."

It required a herculean effort. And more. As Mandela and de Klerk began campaigning, the committee began creating an electoral infrastructure. Almost every task created unanticipated problems, and the solutions often created a whole set of new and even more difficult problems. They began by setting up polling stations, trying to place a polling station within walking distance of every South African. But the commission had no way of determining how many people lived in any area outside the white cities. The townships and some rural areas had never been mapped. To identify population centers, they consulted sales data from South African breweries, assuming that people bought beer near their homes, so distribution figures would give them at least a rough idea where people lived. To provide actual places to vote outside the cities, more than twelve hundred rudimentary stalls—basically an enclosed awning made by covering aluminum poles with shade cloth—were constructed. Hundreds of small tailors in Cape Town spent weeks sewing curtains.

Registering millions of first-time voters, a great number of whom did not have any identity documents, was an equally monumental task. All South Africans eighteen years of age or older were eligible to vote. In addition to valid travel passes and identity books, fourteen hundred temporary registration centers eventually issued 3.5 million voters' cards. To ensure the widest possible participation, stations were set up in prisons, slums, squatters' camps, and hostels. During the voting, it was left to poll workers to determine eligibility, and generally anyone who wanted to vote was allowed to vote.

Nineteen different political parties nominated candidates. The ANC ran on a platform that included building a million new homes; providing electricity, running water, and flush toilets to millions of people; ending segregation in schools; and building an inclusive economy that would create a vast number of new jobs. Although he was not named on the ballot, a vote for the ANC was a vote to make Nelson Mandela president. The National Party promised to "defend individual freedoms, improve education, outlaw workplace discrimination, protect minority rights and stand up for a free market economy." An NP victory would allow de Klerk to remain in office.

Voters were given two ballots: one for the National Assembly, the second for their provincial legislature. They voted for parties rather than any individual. The turnout was massive, so much greater than anticipated that millions of additional ballots had to be quickly printed. Originally, the election was scheduled to take place over three days; the polls had been opened a day early to allow the elderly, handicapped, and the election staff to vote, but the desire to vote, to take part in the political process, was so extraordinary that hundreds of thousands of people lined up at polling stations that day and were permitted to vote. It was just a hint of what was about to come.

During regularly scheduled hours, millions of people waited patiently in lines in some places more than a mile long to vote. The turnout was so enormous that poll hours had to be extended, and when even that proved insufficient, they were allowed to remain open for an additional day. And what astonished observers was that in many places Blacks and whites waited in line together.

To prevent people from casting multiple votes, their fingers were marked with ink visible only under ultraviolet light. This invisible ink had been produced in the United States. When the supply ran out, officials were told to use water instead—but keep secret the fact that it was actually not secret ink. When some ultraviolet lights broke, they were told to pretend they were working.

Ballot boxes overflowed, leaving no place to store completed ballots. After space ran out in one rural polling station, an officer there simply stuffed them into an old pair of trousers.

The commission set up seventy locations to count the votes. It wasn't nearly enough. One counting station received three million ballots without the accompanying paperwork necessary to determine their source. "Nobody had signed them in," a member of the commission later explained. "We decided to count them. Otherwise, we would have had three million people who had stood for hours in the sun being disenfranchised because our process was defective . . . We would have had to have a new national election."

The results of the election were not surprising. There was never a doubt that Mandela's ANC would win a significant majority. As de Klerk recalled, "I remember having a debate with him before the election, and I was winning the debate hands down on points, but toward the end, he suddenly reached out and took my hand and said, 'We might be opponents, but in the end, we stand together,' and by that, he won the debate."

What mattered more than a precise count was the reality that a free and fair election in which all South Africans had been able to participate had taken place. The commission eventually reported counting 19,726,579 ballots. The ANC won handily with 62 percent of the vote, giving it a strong majority in the assembly—guaranteeing Mandela's election. Although there were numerous problems and many shortcuts were taken, little fraud was reported and observers from the UN, the European Union, and the Organization of African Unity certified the results, announcing, "The outcome of the elections reflects the will of the people of South Africa."

On May 11, 1994, political leaders from around the world—ranging from America's First Lady Hillary Clinton to Cuban Premier Fidel Castro—gathered to celebrate Nelson Mandela's inauguration. In his address that day Mandela promised, "Out of the experience of an extraordinary human disaster that lasted too long, must be born a society of which all men will be proud . . . The time for the healing of wounds has come . . . The sun shall never set on so glorious a human achievement."

South Africa's new constitution legally abolished racial segregation and guaranteed equal rights and liberties. While there has been significant change in the years since, the remnants of apartheid have continued to cast a long, dark shadow over the nation. Economic and social inequities remain, and South

Africa still is impacted by decaying infrastructure, poverty, unemployment, and high crime rates. But Mandela's election to the presidency after almost three decades in prison remains a legendary symbol of perseverance, commitment, justice, and decency throughout the world.

The reforms Mandela and the ANC fought for have endured. Regular, free elections have been held every five years since 1994. South African athletic teams have been welcomed back into international competition; the country even hosted the 2010 World Cup. Economic growth has been uneven, but multinational financial companies continue to invest, and the country remains the only permanent member of the G20, the organization of the world's leading economies, from the African continent. South Africa's constitutional parliamentary democracy, with national, provincial, and local governments sharing power and a system of checks and balances, has established stability and predictability that promise continued reform and future growth.

President Mandela served one term in office. Before he died in 2013, he and de Klerk had become good friends, frequently visiting each other's homes. Throughout the remaining years of his life, Nelson Mandela became a global advocate for human rights, utilizing his reputation to benefit people around the world.

Acknowledgments

SELECTING THOSE ELECTIONS THAT literally have resonated through history was no easy task. We knew we were creating a debate. We encouraged that. To determine which elections to include, we spoke with numerous people. Inevitably, after a thoughtful pause to consider their answers, they responded with several suggestions. Some of them followed up later to amend their choices. Each one of those people has our appreciation for their time and efforts.

We also are indebted to our publisher John Glynn and editor Mia Council, whose endless enthusiasm and tireless work to transform a concept into this book were extremely gratifying. We also want to express our thanks to Peter Joseph, who was there at the beginning. The publication process can often be difficult, but we have been fortunate to have Laura Gianino and Leah Morse heading publicity efforts, Abigail Sokolsky in marketing, and senior production editor Stephanie Van de Vooren.

While opinions are debatable, facts are not. And we would like to thank Emily Michel for her extraordinary work in keeping us on the correct path.

Dana Bash would like to thank her agent, Carole Cooper, who first introduced her to the magnificent David Fisher; and Pilar Queen, her tireless book agent.

Dana is also of course beyond grateful to her family: her son, Jonah; her partner, Spencer; as well as her parents, whose limitless support is extraordinary.

David Fisher would like to thank his sons, Taylor Jesse and Beau Stevens—and Beau's beautiful fiancée, Dr. Jeanne Lee—for their unfailing support. And, as always, nothing gets done without the assistance of his wife, Laura, who is always there, always, with the right words when they are needed and an endless reservoir of good cheer and love.

Bibliography

In addition to the resources enumerated here, in our research we made extensive use of contemporaneous newspaper coverage. In particular, the internet sites Newspapers.com and Timesmachine.com provided daily coverage of events as they unfolded, giving us direct access to the last 160 years of world history.

Anderson, Totton J. and Eugene C. Lee. "The 1966 Election in California," *The Western Political Quarterly* 20, no. 2, part 2 (June 1967): pp. 535–554. https://doi.org/10.2307/446081.

Bradford, William. "Of Plymouth Plantation." Excerpted from *Historical Classical Readings*. Effingham, Maynard & Co., 1890, (no copyright claim).

Brovkin, Vladimir N. "The Making of Elections to the Congress of People's Deputies (CPD) in March 1989," *The Russian Review* 49, no. 4 (October 1990): pp. 417–442.

Butler, Benjamin. *Autobiography and Personal Reminiscences*. A.M. Thayer & Co. Boston, MA, 1982. Reprinted by Amazon.com.

De Groot, Gerald J. A. "Goddamned Electable Person: The 1966 Gubernatorial Campaign of Ronald Reagan," *History* 82, no. 267 (July 1997): pp. 429–448.

Donald, David Herbert. *Lincoln*. Touchstone Press/Simon & Schuster, New York, NY, 1995.

Duff, A. *Lincoln Prairie Lawyer.* Rinehart & Company, NY, 1960.

Ecelbarger, Gary. *The Great Comeback: How Abraham Lincoln Beat the Odds to Win the 1860 Republican Nomination.* Thomas Dunne Books/St. Martin's Press, New York, NY, 2008.

Fraser, Rebecca. *The Mayflower: The Families, the Voyage and the Founding of America.* St. Martin's Press, New York, NY, 2017.

Friedan, Betty. "How Mrs. Gandhi Shattered 'The Feminine Mystique,'" *Ladies Home Journal*, May 1966.

Ferling, John. *Adams vs. Jefferson.* Oxford University Press, New York, NY, 2004.

Gelzer, Matthias. *Caesar: Politician and Statesman.* Translated by Peter Needham. Harvard University Press, Cambridge, MA, 1968.

Getty, J. Arch. "State and Society under Stalin: Constitution and Elections in the 1930s," *Slavic Review* 50, no. 1 (Spring, 1991): pp. 18–35.

Goldsworthy, Adrian. *Augustus: First Emperor of Rome.* Yale University Press, New Haven, CT, 2014.

Gray, Fred D. and Dan Abrams. *Alabama v. King.* Hanover Square Press, NY, 2023.

Gray, Fred D. *Bus Ride to Justice.* New South Books, Montgomery, AL, 1995.

Headlam, James Wycliffe. *Election by Lot at Athens.* Prince Consort Dissertation, Cambridge University Press, Cambridge, England, 1891. Reprint Forgotten Books London, United Kingdom, 2012.

Hebblethwaite, Peter. *Pope John XXIII: Shepherd of the Modern World.* Doubleday & Company, Garden City, NY, 1985.

Hill, Joshua. "Free Elections and the First Republic: Parties and the Press, 1911–1913." In *Voting as a Rite: A History of Elections in Modern China*, 1st ed., 417: pp. 106–36. Harvard University Asia Center, 2019. https://doi.org/10.2307/j.ctvrs90d2.9.

Hourly History. *Ronald Reagan A Life from Beginning to End*. GVL Express, Goleta, CA, 2017.

Jones, Dan. *Magna Carta*. Head of Zeus/Clerkenwell Green, London, England, 2014.

Langdon, George D. Jr. "The Franchise and Political Democracy in Plymouth Colony," *The William and Mary Quarterly* 20, no. 4 (October 1963): pp. 513–526. https://doi.org/10.2307/1923528.

Mallock, Daniel L. *Agony and Eloquence: John Adams, Thomas Jefferson and a World of Revolution*. Skyhorse Publishing, New York, NY, 2016.

Mandela, Nelson. *Long Walk to Freedom*. Back Bay Books/Little, Brown and Company, NY, 1994.

Mawson, Amy. "Organizing the First Post-Apartheid Election: South Africa." Case study Princeton University, 1994. Mawson drafted this case study on the basis of interviews conducted in Pretoria and Johannesburg, South Africa, in February 2010.

Moe, Richard. *Roosevelt's Second Act: The Election of 1949 and the Politics of War*. Oxford University Press, New York, NY, 2013.

Pasley, Jeffrey L. *The First Presidential Contest: 1796 and the Founding of American Democracy*. University Press of Kansas, Lawrence, KS, 2013.

Peretz, Don. "Israel's 1969 Election Issues: The Visible and the Invisible," *Middle East Journal* 24, no. 1 (Winter, 1970): pp. 31–46. https://www.jstor.org/stable/4324551.

Reagan, Ronald. *An American Life*. Threshold Editions/Simon & Schuster, New York, NY, 1990.

Staveley, E.S. *Greek and Roman Voting and Elections*. Cornell University Press, NY, 1972.

Stratton, Eugene Aubrey. *Plymouth Colony: Its History and People 1620–1691*. Ancestry Publishing, Provo, UT, 1986.

Sun Yat Sen. *Kidnapped in London, Being the Story of my Capture By, Detention At and Release From the Chinese Legation.* J.W, Arrowsmith, London, 1897.

West, Ed. *1215 and All That: Magna Carta and King John.* Skyhorse Publishing, New York, NY, 2017.

Wood, Gordon S. *Friends Divided: John Adams and Thomas Jefferson.* Penguin Books/Random House, New York, NY, 2017.